Joseph Smith's Gold Plates

A model of the gold plates created by Gordon Andrus for "The Heavens Are Opened" exhibit in the Church History Museum in 2014. Courtesy the Church History Museum and Gordon Andrus.

Joseph Smith's Gold Plates

A Cultural History

RICHARD LYMAN BUSHMAN

OXFORD
UNIVERSITY PRESS

OXFORD
UNIVERSITY PRESS

Oxford University Press is a department of the University of Oxford. It furthers
the University's objective of excellence in research, scholarship, and education
by publishing worldwide. Oxford is a registered trade mark of Oxford University
Press in the UK and certain other countries.

Published in the United States of America by Oxford University Press
198 Madison Avenue, New York, NY 10016, United States of America.

© Oxford University Press 2023

CIP data is on file at the Library of Congress

ISBN 978-0-19-767652-3

DOI: 10.1093/oso/9780197676523.001.0001

Printed by Sheridan Books, Inc., United States of America

For
Petra Javadi-Evans
and
Jed Woodworth

Contents

Preface   ix
Acknowledgments   xiii

1. The Gold Plates Imaginary   1

2. Translator: Joseph Smith, 1823–1829   8

3. Making Scripture: The Book of Mormon, 1830   27

4. Presence: Family and Friends, 1827–1830   39

5. Rationalism: Apologists, Critics, and Imitators, 1832–1860   59

6. Fascination: Fiction, Lore, and Psychology, 1860–1910   81

7. Art: 1833–2023   98

8. Instruction: 1893–2023   119

9. Scientific Approaches: 1900–2023   135

10. Global Perspectives   157

Appendix A. The Composition of the Plates   171
Appendix B. The Translation Debates   175
Source Abbreviations   183
Notes   185
Index   239

Preface

Growing up Latter-day Saint, I learned about Joseph Smith's gold plates very early in life. We heard stories of Smith retrieving the plates from the Hill Cumorah under the direction of an angel, and then "translating" the strange characters engraved on their surfaces into the Book of Mormon. Besides the stories, we saw pictures of the plates based on the descriptions of those who said they had seen them. The plates, we were told, were a stack of thin metal sheets about six inches wide, eight inches long, piled six or so inches high, bound together by three large rings, and covered with ancient writing. I believed in the gold plates as Christians believe in the Resurrection and Jews in the parting of the Red Sea. They were part of history.

As I grew older, I learned that most people were skeptical, especially since Smith refused to show the plates to inquirers, and instead of keeping them, said that he returned them to the angel a little less than two years after he supposedly got them. Like most Mormons, I argued that the statements of the eleven men who were shown the plates as witnesses were sufficient to prove their reality. Critics responded that the report of a few of Joseph Smith's friends and family members was scarcely enough to support such a fantastic proposition as Smith's possession of gold plates.

A logical path for a Latter-day Saint growing up in the modern world, especially one who became a historian, would be to grow out of my childhood beliefs. The plates would be spiritualized and their meaning made allegorical. But my life did not follow that course. The plates have continued to have a hold on me, and the same is true for other Mormons. Polls show that more than three-quarters of American Mormons believe that "the Book of Mormon is a literal, historical account," a likely indicator of belief in the plates.[1] This makes a big difference in one's outlook on the world. With the plates comes an angel and divine intervention in ordinary human lives. The plates imply a world where God is an active agent in human affairs in opposition to the skepticism that has eroded religion for the past two hundred years.

Mormon belief in turn has made a difference in the history of the plates. Mormon conviction has given them a weight they would not otherwise have. In June, nine months before the Book of Mormon was published, the newspapers began reporting on the discovery of a "*Golden Bible*." Within a few years more than a hundred articles on Mormonism had appeared in American newspapers, most of them highlighting the plates.[2] Editors would not have taken note if no one believed in them, and the same holds true today. The plates turn up in novels, dramas, and TV shows. They make a star appearance in Tony Kushner's 1993 Pulitzer Prize–winning drama *Angels in America.* Latter-day Saints depict them in models, videos, and paintings. This literature would have been much shorter and thinner had Latter-day Saints lost faith in the plates.

Widespread belief does not mean, however, that the plates were easy to comprehend. Thin sheets of gold, engraved with Egyptian characters, containing a lengthy record of an ancient people—imagined or real, there were no precedents. Smith's writings make clear that even he was confused at first. He doubted his own vision, thinking of the plates as treasure rather than a book. Nothing in his culture or in the Bible prepared him to understand a historical record, written in an obscure language in ancient times and buried in the ground. Added to this, he was required to translate the plates, a feat far beyond his capacities and totally without precedent in his experience. It appears to have taken years for Smith and his family to grasp all that was involved.

Outside of Joseph Smith's small circle, the plates raised other questions. Almost immediately they were caught up in a major cultural conflict. Joseph Smith's early critics thought that the plates, and Mormonism in its entirety, reversed the progress of civilization. In September 1829, before the Book of Mormon was published, the Palmyra *Reflector* noted that "The 'Gold Bible' is fast gaining *credit*; the *rapid spread* of Islamism was no *touch* to it." The editor linked the little-known Joseph Smith and his tiny handful of impoverished followers to Mohammad, the archetypical false prophet, and to Islam, the premier fanatical religion. The plates received attention because they were the latest evidence of a ruinous human weakness for "superstitious error and imposition."[3] "Every impostor since the creation, has owed his success to the ignorance of the people, and the propensity inherent in their natures, to follow every thing absurd or ridiculous."[4]

Latter-day Saints, of course, had to respond. From the early years, apologists assembled evidence to defend the plates—their existence and their worth—and the debate has continued ever since. Over the years, controversy has gradually softened. In the late nineteenth century, the plates began to seem more amusing than ominous. They were a prop in a fascinating if ludicrous tale, not the work of a villain who must be exposed. Mark Twain said he was quite ready to believe in gold plates on the basis of the witnesses' statement that an angel was there even though he did not "know the name of the angel, or his nationality either."[5] Beginning in the early twentieth century, scholars brought psychology to bear. They characterized Smith not as a charlatan but as a deluded misfit who invented the plates out of psychological need. Most recently, outside scholars have accepted Joseph Smith's sincerity without questioning his sanity. Even though they still pursue naturalistic explanations, they view the plates as a creation of a sincere religious mind. I write in the spirit of this conciliatory moment. My aim in tracking these disputes is not to adjudicate the question of the plates' reality but to understand the outlook of the observers. How have people of all persuasions accounted for the plates?

Besides being the subject of debate, the plates have been used for many purposes. Newspaper editors, treasure-seekers, critics, novelists, artists, scholars, missionaries, and Church teachers have told the plates' story. These accounts have been written from many perspectives, some believing, some not, but implicit always is the desire to explain what the plates are about. Where do they fit in the world? They have been seen as buried treasure, as the scheme of a confidence man, as a gift from heaven, as an amusing tale. The plates have been imitated by a prophet who aspired to succeed Joseph Smith, diagnosed as a delusion, made into poetry, blended with the Bible, turned into a toy for children, and analyzed scientifically. The history of the plates' fortunes through two centuries is the subject of this book.

In spite of efforts on all sides, after two hundred years the mystery of the gold plates remains. The source of the idea, other than being the gift of an angel, has never been identified. At the end, I provide another context for understanding the plates. Rather than looking for precedents, the last chapter ranges through history in search of similarly charged religious objects. I consider pseudepigrapha, holy writing attributed to ancient writers; relics that gained their power to heal from their association with holy persons from the past; the stone tablets of Moses on which the finger of the Lord inscribed the Ten Commandments; and terma, holy writings that were buried by Buddhist gurus for later teachers to uncover and teach from. None of these categories is a perfect match, but they point to realms of the religious imagination where the gold plates might find a home.

The plates entered Joseph Smith's life as a peculiar mixture of the heavenly and the earthly. On the one hand, they were a gift from heaven. Smith said that he learned of them from an angel and translated them "by the gift and power of God." On the other, the plates were thoroughly earthly, buried in a stone box on the side of a hill. They had size, color, and weight; Smith said that he sprained his thumb carrying them home. The combination made the plates a hybrid, both material and spiritual, standing at the line between the human and the divine. In the pages to come, I follow this strangely configured material/spiritual object through the evolving cultural landscape of the past two hundred years.

Acknowledgments

When I first conceived of this study around 2011, I pointedly mentioned my plans whenever I had the opportunity. Usually, announcements of that kind lead to trouble. Research agendas have a way of shifting as the years go by. But in this case, I took the risk in hopes I could enlist the help of people familiar with the sources. I knew that references to gold plates or metal plates were scattered everywhere in Latter-day Saint sources and even more widely throughout the world. Because of their investment in Joseph Smith's gold plates, Latter-day Saints have often made note of plates whenever they have run across them in Korea or Spain or wherever. I hoped to draw upon the work of friends and fellow scholars to collect these references. The strategy worked. I am grateful to many people for keeping my project in mind. I am grateful for all who sent in clues but name just two. My cousin Joanne Bushman Doxey sent me the lengthy files she had accumulated during long hours working on parallels to the plates that she came across in Spain. Christopher Smith, an ace archival researcher, found references in many strange corners and generously passed them along to me.

Christopher has also dug out the story of twentieth-century plates discovered, or claimed to be discovered, by Jesus Dávila Orozco in Mexico and Earl John Brewer in southern Utah. That chapter of the plates' history is a natural extension of the material in this book and will soon appear, I am confident, in scholarly journals. I called on Elisa Pulido to research the uses of the plates in art and popular culture. She solicited the help of Laura Howe, curator of global art at the Church History Museum, who produced a detailed list of references that were invaluable in the writing of this work. Elisa also drafted a chapter on popular culture that formed the basis of two of my chapters. Craig Rossell's unpublished study of Mormon cave lore got me into that material very efficiently.

I frequently rely on Andrew Kimball for comments on my writing. He has read all the chapters of this book and offered his usual astute observations. I asked John Peters for his reaction to a key chapter, which he generously gave. Richard Brown offered useful comments on the Preface. I am grateful to all the others who have contributed comments or information since I sent out the call a decade ago.

At the end, a number of people came to my rescue in obtaining suitable art work: Katie Payne, Amiel Cocco, John Hajicek, Gordon and Maryanne Andrus, Laura Howe, Carrie Snow, Ben Whisenant, Christine Cox, Tiffany Wixom, Richard Oman, and Anthony Sweat. I was in a rush and they went out of their way to help.

Theo Calderara at Oxford University Press read the entire manuscript for tone and style and straightened out some of the most difficult passages. He selected the two outsider readers for the proposal both of whom had many useful observations. Theo has overseen development of the manuscript from the beginning.

Claudia Bushman, as usual, picked out stylistic errors and offered her judgment on what was working and what not. It helps a lot that she is always interested in what I am working on and always has an opinion.

In one of the most generous acts of scholarly friendship I know of, Petra Javadi-Evans and Jed Woodworth offered to check the footnotes. That onerous task is of vital importance in assuring scholarly accuracy, and they carried the work far beyond merely checking for errors in quotations. They tested every assertion in the text against the evidence in the sources and called me to account when I had gone beyond the mark or twisted the evidence to suit my purposes. They suggested improved wording and recommended new lines of research. They enriched the notes with relevant citations. The dedication to the two of them falls far short of the thanks they are due.

1

The Gold Plates Imaginary

Joseph Smith tells us that he first saw the gold plates on September 22, 1823, when he was seventeen years old. The night before, a brilliantly lit being had appeared in the Smith family's crowded cabin in Manchester, New York, told him about the plates, and showed him where they were buried. The next day Smith walked to a hill a little over two miles from his house to the place he had seen in his vision. He scraped away the grass and earth from a large, rounded rock, pried up a stone lid, and saw the plates sitting on pillars of cement in a stone box. He bent over and tried to lift the plates from the box but could not. Frightened and anxious, he cried out to know why. The being from the night before appeared again and told him that it was because he wanted the plates to get rich. He must repent and wait.[1]

Four years later, on September 22, 1827, Smith went to the hill with his wife of eight months, Emma Hale Smith. This time, he was able to retrieve the plates and eventually got them home.[2] Once they were in his possession, he took pains to guard them like a treasure, keeping them out of sight, hiding them in boxes, stashing them under floorboards, wrapping them in cloth, and putting them under the bed covers.[3] A strange translating instrument had been stored with the plates, a device Joseph initially called spectacles and later Urim and Thummim.[4] It consisted of a breastplate fitted with a support for two crystals through which a translation of the engravings on the plates could be seen. The spectacles pointed to the purpose of the plates.[5] They were not a treasure of the kind the Smiths and their neighbors had sought for many years in nocturnal expeditions.[6] The plates contained a text that had to be translated. In early July 1829, Smith finished the translation and returned the plates to the angel. He never again claimed to possess them. In March 1830, he published his translation as the Book of Mormon.[7]

Imagining the Plates

The first newspaper report appeared in June 1829, nine months before the book was published, and others followed through the summer.[8] Smith's friend Martin Harris told publishers and bankers about the plates when he asked for help with publication.[9] Doubtless, news of the plates spread through local gossip and rumor. Gradually an image formed in the public mind. Insiders must have described the plates' appearance, and as time went by, more and more details were added. In 1840 in one of the first published histories, Orson Pratt, a Church leader, was able to give a vivid description. "These records were engraved on plates, which had the appearance of gold. Each plate was not far from seven by eight inches in width and length, being not quite as thick as common tin. They were filled on both sides with engravings, in Egyptian characters, and bound together in a volume, as the leaves of a book, and fastened at one edge with three rings running through the whole. This volume was something near six inches in thickness, a part of which was sealed. The characters or letters upon the unsealed part were small, and beautifully engraved. The whole book exhibited many marks of antiquity in its construction, as well as much skill in the art of engraving."[10] That was how the plates looked in the mind's eye. With all this detail, the plates were easily envisioned and not easily forgotten.

What were people to make of the plates? In their first public notice in the June 1829 *Wayne Sentinel*, the editor announced that the book "is generally known and spoken of as the '*Golden Bible*.'"[11] The term gained no currency among believers, but among outsiders, the characterization stuck. The first book about Mormonism, Eber D. Howe's derogatory *Mormonism Unvailed* (1834), put the words "Golden Bible" in large bold type on the title page.[12] The label was the first public attempt to understand the plates. The name was evocative and at the same time tongue-in-cheek, emphasizing how intriguing but also how outlandish the plates were. In its juxtaposition of "golden" and "bible," the name was also an implicit characterization. The combination seems to put the plates at odds with themselves: gold so material, the bible so religious. Gold stood for greed, wordliness, and self-aggrandizement. The Bible was God's word and implied devotion and faith.[13] The label was fraught with tension and contradiction.

The word "golden" in "Golden Bible" was not entirely fixed in its meaning. Through history, gold had played many roles. Traditionally it was the color of God. Jehovah commanded Moses to cover the ark for carrying the stone tablets with gold, along with the cherubim, all the furniture, and every surface. Gold was also the color of honor, as in the Libra d'Oro (Golden Book), containing the names of the Venetian aristocracy. Closer to home in 1830s America, gold coins stood for monetary stability as contrasted to the paper currency issued by banks. The Coinage Act of 1834 specified 232 grains of pure gold for each American Eagle coin valued at ten US dollars. Gold was hard money, the anchor of the monetary system.[14]

But in Smith's immediate circle of treasure-seeking associates, gold stood for greed. At first, even Smith was tempted to think of the plates as a source of immediate wealth. On his first visit to the hill where they were hidden, he had to be admonished by the angel to stop thinking of the plates' monetary value.[15] In Smith's day, gold was a way to achieve wealth with little work. The money-diggers he associated with hoped to find a trove that would bring them immediate riches. The California Gold Rush held the same promise. It attracted people like Lewis Bidamon, the second husband of Joseph Smith's wife Emma. Bidamon, a clever operator but only moderately successful, left Emma and her children in 1849 in hopes of making a strike in California where thousands of eager prospectors were heading. Panning for gold was hard work and not usually successful, but it offered the possibility of quick wealth, with life on easy street to follow. Bidamon was no more successful than most of the Forty-Niners, but his decision to go revealed the allure of gold as a path to instant riches—a sort of lottery ticket.[16] The Golden Bible played to the American urge to strike it rich.

That version of gold stood at odds with the Bible as the word of God. The term "Golden Bible" evoked a polarized national culture formed around the quest for wealth at one pole and the worship of God at the other. Perhaps unconsciously, whoever invented the term revealed what he thought an angel would say if he spoke to the American nation: the nation was divided against itself in its deepest impulses, one noble, the other crass. In fact, that was pretty much what the angel did say. The strain between "gold" and "bible" was embedded in the text of the Book of Mormon. The great flaw in the Nephite nation was that they loved wealth more than God. They forgot Him whenever their industry brought prosperity, hardening their hearts against heaven and turning their backs on the poor. They chose gold over the Bible and in the end suffered destruction because of their pride and selfishness.[17]

Heaven and Earth

The name "Golden Bible" embodied one polarity; Joseph Smith's story of the plates' recovery, translation, and return evoked another. As his account made clear, the plates were both of the earth and of heaven. They were mundane, material, historical, on the one hand, and divine, mysterious, holy, on the other. They moved back and forth across the line that divided the natural and the supernatural. That hybrid nature made them useful for exploring the boundary between the ordinary world of the natural and the mysterious world of the invisible and supernatural.

In Joseph Smith's account of getting the plates, a glorious angel appears out of heaven and tells him about their location. He wears robes of "exquisite whiteness" and stands in the air, his feet not touching the ground. When he leaves, the angel ascends through "a conduit open right up into heaven."[18] But this luminous being does not bring the plates with him as he presumably would if the plates had been stored in heaven. Instead, Smith has to walk to the hill, scrape away the dirt, use a lever to elevate the stone, and exert himself to lift the plates out of the box where they had lain for centuries. When he finally gets the plates, he has to lug them home—dislocating his thumb when an assailant attacks him—and find a box to store them.[19] Their materiality is emphasized in nearly every detail of the story. The object he carried home was both holy and ethereal and earthly and material.

The plates' double nature was evident for the twenty-two months Joseph possessed them. On the one hand, they were troublesome to care for. He had to hide them in various places: a wooden box, under the floorboards, in flax in the loft, in a barrel of beans, in the woods, under the bed covers, wrapped in a linen cloth.[20] The accounts of translation always noted where the plates were hidden. On the other hand, they were at the center of the mysterious process of translation by which an inspired text flowed from Smith's mouth as scripture. All the while, they had to be kept hidden, forbidden to look at. Like the face of God, one could not look at the plates for fear of being destroyed.[21]

When a few of Smith's friends and family were allowed to view the plates, their testimonies again broke down into heavenly and mundane versions. Three of them said that "An Angel of God came down from heaven" to lay the plates before them, and the voice of God proclaimed that they "have been translated by the gift and power of God." The remaining eight experienced nothing like the first three. There was no heavenly presence, no angel, no voice from heaven. The eight witnesses said only that they had "seen and hefted" the plates. The angel turned the pages of the plates for the three witnesses; the eight turned the pages for themselves.[22]

Some Latter-day Saints lament that the plates did not remain in Smith's possession as proof he was not making everything up. But that would have broken the spell. The tension between earthly and heavenly would have ended. The plates would have fallen into the hands of archeologists, historians, and metallurgists and become solely an earthly artifact. In returning to the angel who had guarded them, the plates retained their hybrid nature, material and spiritual, their mystery preserved.

Searching for the Sublime

The heaven-earth polarity made the plates of particular interest to people entering into modernity. The early nineteenth century was a time when doubt began creeping in around the edges of religious thought. Many of the people who became leaders in this era began with a period of skepticism: Charles Finney, William Miller, James Strang, Orestes Brownson—and Joseph Smith. Some, like Abraham Lincoln, never recovered. Others remained curious and uncertain. Still others like Smith and Miller became religious leaders.[23] With the fundaments of religious belief eroding, any sign of the marvelous was intriguing. Nathaniel Hawthorne, Charles Brockden Brown, and Edgar Allan Poe played upon these uncertainties.[24] Marvels were not mere curiosities; they were tantalizing possibilities. To people experiencing the disenchantment of the world, tales of the supernatural restored mystery.

The immensely popular painters of the Hudson River School looked for the sublime in nature. Was God in that dark cloud overhanging the complacent peace of Thomas Cole's farmscape (see Figure 1.1)? Was He hidden in the heights of Frederic Church's soaring, terrible mountain peaks? Skeptics like the atheist Robert Owen were drawn to spiritualism because the séance enabled him to hear whispers from another sphere.[25] Even Moby Dick, the sublime, supernatural beast that enthralled Ahab and terrified his crew, showed the face of divinity in its massive white skull. Herman Melville evoked a horrifying supernatural in the form of a monster with preternatural power.[26]

Gold plates were less terrifying than a white whale, but there was something sublime about them, something fearful and divine. They offered access to God as the whale portended a terrifying, hostile supernatural. Because the plates were invested with divine power, Smith's friends feared to look upon them. Martin Harris yearned to know if Smith had the plates but dared not

Figure 1.1. Thomas Cole, *View from Mount Holyoke, Northampton, Massachusetts, after a Thunderstorm—The Oxbow.* 1836. Oil on canvas, 51½" × 76" (130.8 cm × 193 cm). Gift of Mrs. Russell Sage, 1908 (08.228). The Metropolitan Museum of Art/New York.
Tortured tree and dark clouds hang ominously over a peaceful landscape.

lift the cloth when the plates sat on his knee.[27] They were both familiar and frightening. That was their fascination. An object Harris could touch and see promised access to the powers of heaven. He could catch a glimpse of the divine while still planted on the earth. As a device for reaching toward God, the plates link Joseph Smith to Herman Melville, Thomas Cole, and Frederic Church, artists of the sublime.

For Joseph Smith himself, the plates' double nature was more troublesome, especially the earthly part. Had he only claimed to see God in the woods, Smith would have been lumped with all the others who claimed to see heavenly beings throughout history.[28] If he had published the Book of Mormon as a text received by inspiration, he would have been one more poet and visionary like William Blake who wrote under divine influence. It was not the claims to divine revelation that led to trouble. It was the claim to possess earthly plates dug from a hill and kept in a wooden box. Visions were possible; gold plates found in a hill were not. From an outsider's perspective, the plates had to have been contrived to deceive people. They turned Smith into a charlatan.

After their recovery in 1827, the plates sent Joseph Smith down his own path, setting him apart from the other prophetic voices of his time. Ann Lee, Nat Turner, Orestes Brownson, Charles Finney, and Ralph Emerson called on the nation through sermons, orations, essays, and revelations. Not so for Smith. His first task was to deal with the language inscribed on the plates, one that so far as he could tell was unintelligible even to learned men. The plates required him to perform a task beyond his capacities and one he could scarcely imagine for himself. No one to his knowledge had ever begun a prophetic career as a translator, but that was what the plates required of Joseph Smith.

2

Translator

Joseph Smith, 1823–1829

Soon after Joseph Smith organized the Church of Christ on April 6, 1830, a revelation titled "Articles and Covenants" briefly summed up his history over the past ten years. The revelation focused on two events: first, "it was truly manifested unto this first elder that he had received a remission of his sins." This referred to what was later called the First Vision, which came when he was fourteen and concerned for the state of his soul. In the second, after he was "entangled again in the vanities of the world" and repented, "God visited him by an holy angel" who "gave unto him power, by the means of which was before prepared that he should translate a book."[1] The second was the visit of Moroni, which led to the translation of the Book of Mormon.

The forgiveness of sins promised in the first event lay at the heart of the revival culture of upstate New York in the 1820s, and heavenly visitations like Joseph Smith's encounter with God were not uncommon.[2] The First Vision fits comfortably into Joseph Smith's time and place.[3] The second event, the gift of translation, was something else entirely. In Smith's time, only students headed to college learned to translate and then primarily Latin. When he and Martin Harris looked for help with translation of the plates, Harris went to New York City to consult professors who taught in universities. Translators of strange languages were not to be found in Palmyra and certainly not among poor farmers. As Smith protested when he felt the pressure to translate the Book of Mormon himself, "[I] cannot for I am not learned."[4] Moreover, there were no precedents. No prophetic figures in Smith's environment or in the course of religious history as he knew it were translators.

Toward Translation

Puzzling as it is, Smith eventually gave way to this impossible demand. In the spring of 1828 at age twenty-two, he dictated 116 pages of text, and in the spring of 1829 in the space of three months, he dictated the entire Book of Mormon.[5] Day after day, his assistants took down text believing that he translated "by the gift and power of God."[6] Later in life, he undertook to "translate" the Bible and Egyptian scrolls that he believed contained the writings of Abraham. It was an audacious and outlandish presumption to "translate" any of these texts, making it hard to understand how Smith made this spectacular leap.

It is a difficult story to piece together from the sources. Statements from Smith's neighbors were clearly meant to discredit him, and Smith's accounts of his own experiences are filled with angels and gold plates. How can a credible narrative be contrived from the hostile reports of the neighbors and the miracle-filled accounts from Smith himself? Getting at some sense of objective, historical "truth" is essentially impossible. But what we can do is examine the subjective experiences of Smith and those close to him—friend and foe—and explain what happened as it appeared to them.

Smith's progression from unpretentious farmer to aspiring translator appears to have come in stages. Smith reported that the angel who visited him when he was seventeen told him that "there was plates of gold upon which there was engravings which was engraven by Maroni & his fathers the servants of the living God in ancient days and deposited by th[e] commandments of God and kept by the power thereof and that I should go and get them."[7] He may not have understood all that at first, and nothing, according to his reports, was said about him doing the translating. But at some point during the four-year period between the angel's visitation and his retrieval of the plates, he began to grasp that the plates contained a written record in a strange language, making clear the need for translation. The translating instrument, later called the Urim and Thummim, that was said to accompany the plates reinforced the point. By their very nature, the plates and the instrument pointed him toward his impossible task.

Nothing about Smith's experience was easy for him to understand, making it hard for him to grasp what was expected, but plates full of an ancient text and an instrument sometimes called "interpreters" implied translation.[8] Possessing or even thinking about the plates pushed Smith in that direction. The interaction of minds with objects in cases like this has been conceptualized by Sonia Hazard, a scholar of religion who has argued that material objects—even if imagined—can profoundly shape religious experience. In an essay on "The Material Turn in the Study of Religion," Hazard writes: "It helps us see how religions are buzzing imbroglios populated by things, human and nonhuman, like Bibles, golden plates, transatlantic tele-graph cables, radio waves, pheromones, and strands of DNA." Humans and things, she believes, combine into "assemblages" where the collection to-gether takes directions any part alone would not have followed. Humans are not entirely in control. The presence of the things makes a decisive differ-ence.[9] Without plates, covered with writing, Joseph Smith would never have thought of himself as a translator. With them, the transition from dirt farmer and treasure seeker to translator of ancient writings seemed like a necessity. After reporting to a friend that he had recovered the plates from Cumorah, Smith blurted out, "I want them translated."[10]

Treasure Lore

Because the task seemed so extraordinary, it may have taken longer than is commonly believed for Smith to have recognized his responsibility. There was no known precedent for a history on gold plates buried in the ground. His first vision had many parallels in Christian history and many examples from his own culture; the charge to recover the plates had none at all. With nothing to compare, how was he to comprehend what was required of him? Smith had to make two great leaps: first, to believe that an ancient history written on gold plates was buried in a nearby hill, and, second, that he was to translate the characters on those plates.

Smith said the angel came to his room three times the night of September 21–22, 1823, repeating the command to retrieve the plates each time. But there are signs that three times was not enough to convince him the visit was real. Smith did not immediately go to the hill the next morning as the angel had commanded, nor did he say anything about the vision to his family. As Smith and his mother told the story, it took another appearance of the angel before he told his father about the vision. Only when Joseph Sr. urged him to follow instructions did Joseph Jr. go to the hill.[11] When he arrived at the site of the stone box, he wavered again. He wrote in 1832 that "I immediately went to the place and found where the plates was deposited as the angel of the Lord had commanded me and straightway made three attempts to get them." When his attempts failed, he began to doubt. As he wrote in the first record made of the experience, "Being excedingly frightened I supposed it had been a dreem of Vision."[12] Perhaps, he began to think, the angel was not real. The experience the night before must have been a dream.

The plates could not settle into his mind because he lacked a frame for such an outlandish idea. No matter how many times the story of the plates was repeated, it made no sense. Part of the problem was that Smith had a framework where the plates did fit, though not a religious one. The gold plates seemed like buried treasure, something familiar to the Smiths and their neighbors.[13] The plates had the appearance of gold and were buried in the ground. The similarities meant Smith had to fight off his natural inclination to see them as treasure before he could see the plates as a record calling for translation.

For a number of years, Joseph Smith Sr. had been involved in treasure expeditions with his neighbors. William Stafford said he went out with Joseph Sr. to hunt for kegs of gold and silver. Martin Harris named Alvah Beman, Samuel Lawrence, and George Proper as members of the company. "They dug for money in Palmyra, Manchester, also in Pennsylvania, and other places."[14] Joseph Sr. often involved Joseph Jr., who was known for his ability to find lost objects with a seer stone, a useful skill in locating treasure. When the Smiths told their treasure-seeking associates about the plates, they had no trouble believing. Gold plates fit right into their view of the world.[15]

The treasure-seekers' frame for understanding the plates was described by Abner Cole, a local lawyer and editor of the Palmyra *Reflector*.[16] When the Book of Mormon was first published, Cole had more to say about the gold plates than anyone outside the Smith family and their friends. Cole explained the plates by attributing them to the Smiths' involvement in money-digging. In six issues from January through March 1831, Cole laid out the frame of mind that made it possible for treasure-seekers to believe in the plates.[17] He had a supposed correspondent, "PLAIN TRUTH," refer to the "money digging mania," which he said pervaded the region. In Ontario County, New York, where the Smiths were living, "the *mania* of money digging soon began rapidly to diffuse itself through many parts of this country; men and women without distinction of age or sex became marvellous wise in the occult sciences." Visions and dreams disclosed "deep in the bowels of the earth, rich and shining treasures."[18]

Cole perceived a recurring story line at the heart of the treasure-seeking ventures. "The vulgar, yet popular belief" was that "these treasures were held in charge by some *evil* spirit." What drove the story were the seekers' efforts to elude the barriers put up by this spirit. "Divers devices and implements were invented." "Mineral rods and balls" were "supposed to be infallible guides to these sources of wealth." They were managed by "some *wizzard* or *witch*" with the particular skills required to locate the treasure. Doubtless thinking of Joseph Smith's use of a seer stone to find lost objects, Cole noted that "'*Peep stones*' or pebbles, taken promiscuously from the brook or field, were placed in a hat or other situation excluded from the light." The adept one, gazing in the stones, would declare "they saw all the wonders of nature, including of course, ample stores of silver and gold." The leader would then put their followers to work digging for the treasure.[19]

That was the story line underlying the quests: a treasure guarded by a spirit, a band of seekers led by one adept in magic, a struggle to outwit, satisfy, or overpower the guardian spirit, hard digging by a band of followers.[20] Cole blended this widespread understanding of treasure-seeking culture with the facts about the gold plates.[21] Smith was made into the adept who discovered the location and Moroni into the spirit who guarded the treasure, exhibiting the usual wily ways. "Jo" made "league with the *spirit*, who afterwards turned out to be an angel."[22] Dealing with the spirit/angel tested Smith when he first went to the hill for the plates. "This rogue of a spirit who had bafled all the united efforts of the money diggers, (although they had tried many devices to gain his favor . . .) intended it would seem to play our prophet a similar trick on this occasion; for no sooner had he delivered the book according to promise, than he made a most desperate attempt, to regain its possession." In Cole's telling, Joseph held on to the plates, and returned with them to his father's house.[23]

Cole's comparison of the Smiths' angel with the money-diggers' guardian spirit made sense at the time. Both guarded a treasure and prevented the seekers from obtaining their goal.[24] Cole was less successful in explaining the book and the need for translation. Treasure-seeking lore did not include buried histories. In an attempt to account for the ultimate outcome of the Smiths' searches, Cole imagined Luman Walters, a well-known adept, parading "an old copy of Cicero's Orations, in the latin language, out of which he read long and loud to his credulous hearers, uttering at the same time an unintelligible jargon, which he would afterwards pretend to interpret, and explain, as a record of the former inhabitants of America."[25] These seem to have been Cole's contrivances, mixed in to round out his account. None of the Palmyra residents who later were asked to record their memories of the Smiths made any mention of Walters or Cicero's Orations.

Treasure-Seekers

One test of Cole's hypothesis was the reaction of the treasure-seekers. Their beliefs about guardian spirits and treasure enabled them to believe Smith's tale of angels and gold plates without hesitation. Instead of scoffing at the stories of the plates, they wanted their fair share. Probably they thought of themselves as being in business with the Smiths. When Joseph Sr. and Jr. joined Josiah Stowell in the hunt for Spanish treasure in Harmony, the diggers signed "Articles of Agreement" to establish in advance how to divide their finds and who was to bear the expense.[26] They thought of themselves as a business, just as searchers for sunken Spanish galleons do today. The Smiths' "Gold Bible Company" in Palmyra was more loosely organized than the Harmony searchers.[27] No one mentioned articles of agreement, but likely they agreed beforehand to divide their find should they be so lucky, and that was the source of the trouble for the Smiths. David Whitmer said that "before I knew anything about Joseph Smith I had heard about him and the plates from persons who declared they knew he had them and swore they would get them from him, and that he had promised them an interest in them when he should get them."[28]

One of the money-digging associates, Samuel Lawrence, seemed to feel he had a particular claim. Joseph Knight, Joseph's friend and employer in Colesville, remembered that Lawrence had been to the hill where the plates were buried and was interested in obtaining the treasure for himself. Knight said that Lawrence was a local seer, perhaps a rival to Joseph. According to Willard Chase, Joseph thought Lawrence was the man he was to bring to the hill in compliance with the angel's directions.[29] Knight remembered that the day before Joseph obtained the plates on September 22, 1827, he worried enough about Lawrence to send his father to the neighbor's house to scout out any plans to obtain the record himself. According to Knight, "Joseph was some affraid of him [Samuel Lawrence] that he mite be a trouble to him. He therefore sint his father up to Sams as he Called him near night to see if there was any signs of his going away that night. He told his father to stay till near Dark and if he saw any signs of his going you till him if I find him there I will thrash the stumps with him." Nothing was stirring at the Lawrence house, and Joseph went with Emma to the hill on September 22 without running into trouble.[30]

The trouble came later when the money-diggers thought Joseph had the plates. Martin Harris said "the money-diggers claimed that they had as much right to the plates as Joseph had, as they were in company together. They claimed that Joseph had been traitor, and had appropriated to himself that which belonged to them."[31] Driven by their grievance, the money-diggers invaded the Smiths' property in search of the plates. Joseph's mother Lucy Smith said Willard Chase gathered ten or twelve men to help him. "What was still more ridiculous, they had sent 60 or 70 miles for a certain conjuror, to come and divine the place where they [the plates] were secreted." To protect them, Lucy said, the Smiths removed a hearthstone, dug a hole, deposited the plates and the breastplate, and replaced the stone.[32]

Eventually the money-diggers gave up their hunt for the plates but not because of unbelief. They accepted the plates' existence as readily as anyone in the Smith family. Their understanding of the world had a place for gold plates, the very one Cole described. They had, however, no place for a sacred book. After their initial frenzied efforts to get their share of the great find yielded nothing, they dropped out of the picture and disappeared into the landscape of midnight quests and magical lore.

The Smith Family

Cole thought of himself as a critic with a mission to discredit Joseph Smith's Golden Bible. But the gulf between Smith's account of an angel with a sacred record and Cole's account of a guardian spirit and a treasure may not be as wide as Latter-day Saints have believed. The outward details of Joseph's angel story conformed so closely to the standard treasure-seeking plot that one must ask if the Smiths themselves might at first have understood Joseph Jr.'s report much as Cole did. They too needed a framework for understanding the plates. A heavenly angel charging Joseph Jr. with uncovering and translating a history of an ancient people would have been incomprehensible. The natural way for them to understand a gold book buried in the earth was as treasure.

It seems to have taken time for Joseph Jr. to discard his old way of thinking and grasp the meaning of an angelic visitation. He admitted that as he approached Cumorah in September 1823, he could not help thinking of treasure. In his 1832 account, he said that during his walk, he "had been tempted of the advisary and saught the Plates to obtain riches."[33] That implies that the angel's presence in his room the night before had not erased treasure-seeking from his mind. He still thought it possible that he was being led to a cache of gold. Oliver Cowdery's 1834 history, which Smith read and approved, went on for pages about his struggle to beat back the desire for wealth. As he approached the hill, Cowdery said, Smith would think of "the heavenly messenger; but again a thought would start across the mind on the prospects of obtaining so desirable a treasure." Cowdery said that it seemed like "two invisible powers were operating upon his mind during his walk." One urged the "certainty of wealth and ease," while the other, "the great object . . . named by the angel." At the hill, according to Cowdery, the angel left Smith's mind and the desire for gain took over completely. "Only a fixed determination to obtain now urged him forward." When he pried up the stone cover and looked on the "sacred treasure," he was exultant. "He supposed his success certain." Before taking the plates, he looked inside the box for something more to "add to his store of wealth." Then suddenly he was stopped in his efforts. When he tried to lift out the plates, he received a shock from "an invisible power." Trying again, he was shocked even more severely.

Puzzled by his failure, his mind did not go back to the angel's instructions. Instead, he turned to treasure-seeking lore for an explanation. "He had heard of the power, of enchantment," Cowdery reported, "and a thousand like stories, which held the hidden treasures of the earth." Trying a third time, Joseph failed again. Finally, the angel appeared and reminded Smith of "the wonderful things connected with this record." "They are not deposited here for the sake of accumulating gain and wealth," but "because of the knowledge which they contain." They had "no worth among the children of men, only for their knowledge."[34] As Cowdery told the story, it took time for Smith to learn that lesson.

Brigham Young later hinted that the angel was patient in setting Joseph straight. Treasure and historical record were allowed to mingle for a time. In the rough stenographer's notes for an 1868 address, Young is reported as saying that the Lord "called upon his servant Joseph told him what to do in the first place revealed to him that there was a treasure in the earth that is there was some golden plates did not tell him what they were at the first beyond is a treasure it is my will for you to possess it." Young knew this might surprise his listeners. "It may be a strange idea to say that Joseph Smith did not know what it was a treasure to make his Father's house [ready/rich?] he did not conceive the great things for the Lord could not reveal it to him but he led him along day after day week after week year after year until he delivered unto his hands the plates this Book of Mormon translated."[35] Young implied that only gradually did the Smiths realize that the Book of Mormon, not some form of gold, was the promised treasure.[36]

Treasure-seeking both prepared the Smiths to recover the gold plates and confused them. The Smiths were ready to accept a precious gold object buried in the earth, but the treasure version of the story coincided so closely with the gold record version that it took time to grasp the plates' true purpose. For a while, treasure and book, guardian spirit and angel were jumbled together.[37] Especially in the mind of Joseph Smith Sr., the purpose of the plates was not entirely clear for years. Joseph Sr.'s testimony at his son's trial for glass-looking in 1826 in South Bainbridge, New York, offers a glimpse of family thinking in the interim period. He and Joseph Jr. had come south the previous fall to help Josiah Stowell search for Spanish gold near Harmony, Pennsylvania. Stowell wanted Joseph's help because of his gift for seeing. The search had yielded nothing, but Stowell's nephew felt that the Smiths were taking advantage of his uncle and charged Joseph Jr. with being a disorderly person practicing "glass-looking," an illegal activity in New York because it was believed to be a device for cheating people.[38] When Joseph Sr. was called to testify at the 1826 trial, he expressed his regret that "this wonderful power which God had so miraculously given" his son "should be used only in search of filthy lucre, or its equivalent in earthly treasures." He told the court that he "trusted that the Son of Righteousness would some day illumine the heart of the boy, and enable him to see His will concerning him."[39] The words suggest that years after Joseph Jr.'s first visit to the hill, Joseph Sr. was still thinking of treasure and struggling to clarify what his son's mission actually was.

A year later, the picture was beginning to clear up. Willard Chase, one of the Smiths' money-digging friends, was close enough to the family to hear the story of the plates from Joseph Sr. in June 1827. In Chase's retelling, Joseph Sr.'s stories were laden with treasure-seeking lore about Joseph having to take certain persons with him on his visits to the hill and an encounter with a toad that turned into a man. Chase also remembered that Joseph Sr. opened his narrative by saying "that some years ago, a spirit had appeared to Joseph his son, in a vision, and informed him that in a certain place there was a record on plates of gold." Whatever Joseph Sr. thought in 1823 about the treasure in the hill, by 1827 he called it a record. Throughout his recounting of Joseph Sr.'s story, Chase spoke of a "book" in the hill. Apparently by summer 1827, the key issue of treasure versus historical account had been settled in Joseph Sr.'s mind.[40]

Chase said that sometime before September 1827 when the plates were recovered Joseph had taken Samuel Lawrence to the site on the hill where the plates were buried. Lawrence urged Joseph to look in his stone for anything buried with the plates. Lawrence "told him to look again, and see if there was not a large pair of specks with the plates; he looked and soon saw a pair of spectacles, the same with which Joseph says he translated the Book of Mormon."[41] Joseph may have learned of the interpreters before but did he comprehend them? The Chase statement confirms that well before the plates were obtained, the Smiths envisioned an unusual instrument to be used for translation. That meant the main elements of the story—record and interpreters—were in place at least by summer 1827 and probably much earlier. The Smiths not only had heard the words from an angel, the family had made them part of their thinking.

The remnants of the magic culture still hanging over the plates did not hinder belief in Joseph as a prophet after the Book of Mormon was published. Friends like Josiah Stowell, who had employed Joseph to search for treasure, and Joseph Knight, who knew of these pursuits, sensed no conflict between the folk magic culture and the angelic visitor. In 1843 when Stowell was seventy-three and living in Elmira, New York, he wrote Joseph to say that "he never staggard at the foundation the work for he knew to mutch concerning it." He remembered being "the firs[t] person that took the Plates out of your hands the morning you brough[t] them in." The Joseph seeking treasure with a seer stone blended imperceptibly with the Joseph translating the plates with Nephite interpreters.[42]

Stowell's friend Joseph Knight owned a farm and gristmill in Colesville, New York, a few miles south of Stowell's farm in South Bainbridge. After the failed treasure-seeking venture in Harmony, Smith had worked for both men before marrying Emma Hale whom he met while boarding with the Hale family in Harmony.[43] Knight planned a business trip to Rochester in September 1827 and then stayed on at the Smiths until after September 22. He and Stowell likely knew that September 22 was the appointed date and came to Manchester to be on hand. Both were there that morning when Joseph and Emma came back from the hill.[44]

The two of them had gone for the plates not long after midnight on September 22 and were not back until morning. According to Knight, Joseph said nothing about the plates when he came into the house. After breakfast, "Joseph Cald me into the other Room and he set his foot on the Bed and leaned his head on his hand and says, 'Well I am Dissopinted.' 'Well,' say I,

'I am sorrey.' 'Well,' says he, 'I am grateley Dissopinted; it is ten times Better then I expected.' Then he went on to tell the length and width and thickness of the plates, and said he, 'they appear to be Gold.' "[45] Knight's is the climactic account of the plates as they figured in the minds of Joseph Smith and his circle up through September 1827. By then the plates had taken on a visual and tactile form.

Translation

Recognizing that the treasure was a book not just a pile of gold was a breakthrough. At least by June 1827 when Joseph Smith Sr. told Willard Chase about Joseph Jr.'s revelation, that key idea had taken hold even with the father. The quest for "filthy lucre," as Joseph Sr. put it at the 1826 trial, had been laid aside, and the recovery of a book had become the point. Going a step further, what did it take to realize that the book required translation? The realization that engravings covered the plates and that interpreting stones to aid translation came with the plates would point Joseph in that direction.

When did interpreters and engravings register? Joseph's 1838 history brought the interpreters into the picture on the first visit to the hill in 1823. "I looked in and there indeed did I behold the plates, the Urim and Thummin and the Breastplate as stated by the messenger." Joseph's 1832 account said much less. In this earlier version, Joseph went to the place "where the plates was deposited" but said nothing about a breast plates or stones. The interpreters were not mentioned until Joseph related the Martin Harris story of seeking a translation from Charles Anthon. Then Joseph wrote that "the Lord had prepared spectacles for to read the Book."[46] Other retellings were similarly silent on interpreters. Oliver Cowdery's 1834–1836 history of the event spoke only of Joseph beholding a "sacred treasure" when he went to the hill in 1823.[47] Nothing about spectacles or Urim and Thummim. The interpreter stones are given a glancing reference in Joseph Sr.'s long accounting to Willard Chase in 1827 but only tangentially. Joseph Sr. said that when Samuel Lawrence and Joseph Jr. visited the hill together, Lawrence asked Joseph if he had ever "discovered anything with the plates." Lawrence urged Joseph to look in his stone again for something more. According to Chase, Joseph "looked and soon saw a pair of spectacles, the same with which Joseph says he translated the Book of Mormon."[48] Joseph Sr.'s 1827 story introduced the stones but at Lawrence's initiative not Joseph's, as if Joseph had little interest in the stones at that point.

Joseph's interest in translating instruments rose quickly after recovering the plates in September 1827. According to Knight, the interpreters that came with the plates fascinated him. After relating Joseph's description of the plates, Knight observed that "he seamed to think more of the glasses or the urim and thummem then [than] he Did of the Plates, for, says he, 'I can see any thing; they are Marvelus.' "[49] Joseph valued the interpreters, as they were called in the Book of Mormon, but it is not certain that he understood them.[50] His comment about the spectacles seems slightly off the point. While enthusiastic, he prized them because they enabled him to "see," not to translate. He thought of them as a high-powered version of the seer stone he had been using for the past four years, not as a means for turning reformed Egyptian into English.[51]

Slim as the evidence is, what does exist suggests that until September 1827 there was no real interest in the Urim and Thummim, slight acknowledgment of the ancient language written on the plates, and no realization of the need to translate the characters. Joseph's exclamation "I want them translated" seems to have arisen after he got the plates in his hands in September 1827. Earlier, he and his family had come to realize they were pursuing a book not a horde of gold, but it was not entirely clear that it needed to be translated. Not until Joseph had the plates in his hands and saw the ancient characters engraved on their surfaces did he understand what was required. The gold plates drove him to translation.

Perhaps the most puzzling period in the history of Joseph Smith and the plates is the months that followed the retrieval from the hill. How did untrained, inexperienced Joseph Smith come to believe he should translate the plates—or even attempt to write the history that was supposedly on them?[52] The sources disagree on the moment when Joseph Smith began to translate. The exclamation "I want them translated" implied someone other than himself would do the job. In September 1827, he had yet to realize the task was his. One view is that he began experimenting with the interpreters through the fall and early winter of 1827–1828 and translated a few characters that he copied off for Martin Harris to take to scholars in New York City in February 1828.[53] A letter from one of the professors, Charles Anthon of Columbia, seemed to indicate Joseph had already begun to translate before Harris's visit. Anthon recounted his meeting with Martin Harris in a letter to Eber D. Howe, the Ohio printer who in 1834 published a volume titled *Mormonism Unvailed* meant to discredit Mormonism. Anthon said Harris told him that Smith possessed an "enormous pair of '*gold spectacles*'" and "whoever examined the plates through the spectacles, was enabled not only to *read* them, but fully to *understand* their meaning." Smith "looked through one of the glasses, decyphered the characters in the book, and, having committed some of them to paper, handed copies from behind the curtain, to those who stood on the outside." Anthon's account is a little puzzling because Anthon said that another New York City scholar, Samuel Mitchill, had asked Anthon "to decypher, if possible, a paper, which the farmer would hand me."[54] Had the characters been translated before they were presented to Anthon and Mitchill or not? Sustaining this version of the story, Joseph's 1838 history said that before Harris left for New York, Joseph "copied a considerable number of them and by means of the Urim and Thummin I translated some of them."[55] In the same vein, Harris said Anthon attested that characters he was shown were "true characters and that the translation of such of them as had been translated was also correct."[56] All that implies Joseph had learned to translate before Harris visited Anthon. Harris's story of Anthon attesting to the translation, however, is a bit shaky since Anthon was not in a position to verify a translation from Egyptian, the purported language on the gold plates. Champollion's Egyptian Grammar was not to be published until 1836, and Anthon made no pretenses to understanding Egyptian.

Family and friends tell a different story. They say that Smith had no idea of how to translate until after Harris saw Anthon. Despite having the stones and breastplate, Joseph did not attempt to translate. Lucy Smith said they first looked to learned men for help. "It soon became necessary to take some measures to accomplish the translation of the record into English but he was instructed to take off a fac simile of the charecters composing the alphabet which were called reformed egyptian Alphabetically and send them to all the learned men that he could find and ask them for the translation of the same. Joseph was very solicitous about the work but as yet no means had come into his hands of accomplishing it."[57] (See Figure 2.1.)

Smith seems not to have realized that he had the means in his hands already. He was an apprentice prophet, modest about his own talents, and unsure about how to proceed. Like Lucy, Joseph Knight thought the reason for Martin Harris's visit to Charles Anthon and Samuel Mitchill in February 1828 was to get help with the translation. "He now Began to be anxious to git them translated. He therefore with his wife Drew of[f] the Caricters exactley like the ancient and sent Martin Harris to see if he Could git them Translated. He went to Albany and to Philadelpha and to new york and he found men that Could Translate some of the Carictors in all those places."[58] Before the

Figure 2.1. The Anthon Transcript showing characters said to have been copied from the gold plate for inspection by scholars, including Charles Anthon of Columbia.

translation began, Smith had no idea that the characters on the plates were an exotic combination of Hebrew and Egyptian. The angel had told him the plates contained a history of the ancient inhabitants of this continent, making an Indian language their likely tongue. Mitchill seemed like the right person to consult because of his recognized expertise in American Indian languages.[59]

How soon after that Smith came to think of himself as a translator remains unclear.[60] In his 1832 history, Joseph linked the breakthrough to Martin Harris's visit to Anthon. Joseph said of Harris that "the Lord had shown him that he must go to new York City with some of the characters so we proceeded to coppy some of them and he took his Journy to the Eastern Cittys and to the Learned saying read this I pray thee and the learned said I cannot but if he would bring the blates [plates] they would read it but the Lord had forbid it and he returned to me and gave them to me to translate and I said cannot for I am not learned but the Lord had prepared spectacles for to read the Book therefore I commenced translating the characters."[61]

Joseph had taken the pen from the hand of Frederick Williams in 1832 to write those sentences, as if they meant a lot to him. He paraphrased the words of Anthon as he heard them from Harris to conform to a passage in Isaiah 29 about a book being delivered to a learned person "saying, Read this,

I pray thee: and he saith, I cannot; for it is sealed: And the book is delivered to him that is not learned, saying, Read this, I pray thee: and he saith, I am not learned."[62] The combination of the learned Anthon's refusal to translate and the similarity to the Isaiah passage seem to have been the key to Joseph's discovery of his role. At last he had a framework for understanding his mission. In Joseph's Bible-based world, believing "the Propicy [prophecy] of Isiaah was fulfilled" was enough to inspire the unlearned Smith to try translating himself.[63] He came to believe that his unlikely role as translator had been foreseen as if he were foreordained to the task.

These were critical months in the development of Joseph Smith as a prophet. The late fall of 1827 and the winter of 1828 was the time when he found his prophetic voice. By June 1828 he had dictated 116 pages of the Book of Mormon. In July he recorded a revelation that began: "The works & designs & the Purposes of God cannot be frustrated neither can they come to ground for God doth not wa[l]k in crooked Paths." The words came from Joseph's mouth but in the voice of God: "I the Lord am God I have given these things unto him [Joseph]."[64] He had learned to speak for God, all the while dictating the text of the Book of Mormon at a rapid pace. Those gifts came after the gold plates began to work their influence on him, compelling him by their nature to translate. His exuberant "I want them translated," as he told Joseph Knight about the plates, had become a flood of scripture flowing from his mind at an amazing rate.

Methods

Smith began his work in the spring of 1828.[65] Earlier, he may have translated a little with Emma writing his dictation, but he took up the task in earnest in April with Martin Harris. Using the Urim and Thummim with Joseph behind a blanket, they translated through June 1828, the first of two extended spurts of activity while Joseph had the plates. Their work was interrupted when Martin begged to carry the 116-page manuscript home to his wife Lucy and lost it. Martin suffered for his error but so did Joseph. According to Smith's 1832 history, "I also was chastened for my transgression for asking the Lord the third time wherefore the Plates was taken from me by the power of God and I was not able to obtain them for a season."[66]

For an indeterminate period after June 1828, the plates and the interpreters were gone and translation was suspended. Soon after returning to Emma in

Harmony in the summer of 1828, Joseph says an angel appeared to him while he was out walking "and handed to me the Urim and Thummin," which had been taken away with the plates. Through the instrument, he received a revelation rebuking him for his foolishness in relinquishing the manuscript to Harris, but he did not "go immediately to translating," probably because he did not have the plates.[67] The sources are unclear on when the plates were returned. Lucy quotes her son as saying that "on the 22d of September, I had the joy and satisfaction of again receiving the Urim and Thummim; and have commenced translating again, and Emma writes for me." The two of them worked on the text until the spring of 1829 when, as Smith noted in his 1832 history, the "Lord appeared unto a young man by the name of Oliver Cowd[e]ry and shewed unto him the plates in a vision and also the truth of the work."[68]

Cowdery arrived on April 5, 1829, and the second long period of translation began. They worked together from April 7 through to completion of the manuscript probably by early July 1829.[69] In early June, the little band moved from Harmony, Pennsylvania, where they had worn out their welcome with Emma's parents, to the house of Oliver's friends in Fayette, New York, the Peter Whitmer family.[70] There the work went on to completion. On June 11, Smith obtained a copyright for the manuscript, submitting the complete title page where, to conform to federal law, he was listed as "author and proprietor" rather than translator.[71] After finishing the translation, the effort to secure a printer began in earnest. Presumably the plates' mysterious departure occurred soon after. By his own account, Smith had the plates in his possession no more than twenty-two months and likely less depending how long his probation for losing the manuscript lasted.

If you looked in on the translation sessions while Smith had the plates, what would you have seen? The sources offer two pictures. One has Joseph Smith looking at the plates through the translating instrument—the breastplate and crystals, which for want of a better term he called spectacles. Since he had been forbidden to let anyone see either the plates or the spectacles, a blanket separated him from the recorder. Joseph dictated from behind the curtain, and the scribe took down his words.

Traditionally, Latter-day Saints had believed this to be the method of translation from beginning to end, but in recent years many historians have come to believe in a second procedure. In this reconstruction, Joseph looked at a seer stone in a hat to exclude light and dictated while the plates themselves lay covered on a table. Since the plates were hidden and the spectacles had been replaced by a seer stone, no blanket was necessary. Nothing sacred was in sight, allowing the scribe to sit at the same table to record Smith's dictation. A number of Joseph Smith's contemporaries, including his wife who was with him during the entire translation period, described translation this way. "In writing for J[oseph]. S[mith]. I frequently wrote day after day, often sitting at the table close by him, he sitting with his face buried in his hat, with the stone in it and dictating hour after hour, with nothing between us." "The plates often lay on the table without any attempt at concealment, wrapped in a small linen table cloth, which I had given him to fold them in."[72]

Many historians today believe scene one depicted the way Martin Harris took the dictation of the 116 pages in the spring of 1828, and scene two was the way Oliver Cowdery worked with Joseph in the spring of 1829. One usage in the records, however, complicates this growing consensus. The most common name for the translating instrument in accounts of the early years was "Urim and Thummim," a term borrowed from the Bible. In Exodus, the Urim and Thummim were stones placed in the "breastplate of Judgment" worn by Aaron over his heart for aid in delivering judgments.[73] During Joseph Smith's lifetime and long after, Mormons attached the term to the object that in the Book of Mormon was called "interpreters" and Joseph Smith called "spectacles." King Mosiah, in the Book of Mormon, had an instrument "wherewith that he can look, and translate all records that are of ancient date . . . and the things are called interpreters; and no man can look in them, except he be commanded."[74] The biblical Urim and Thummim and Mosiah's wondrous interpreters were not a perfect match in appearance or function but the interpreters seemed worthy of the biblical label. That causes problems for those who believe Joseph Smith used a stone for the bulk of the translation. Why did so many observers, including Joseph Knight, call the translating instrument the Urim and Thummim? Did a stone found in a well by Willard Chase qualify for the biblical name?[75]

The term "Urim and Thummim" did not come into common use among Latter-day Saints until 1834, when Oliver Cowdery employed it in a series of letters to the Latter Day Saints' Messenger and Advocate rehearsing Joseph Smith's early history.[76] Cowdery's letters may have been partly a response to the devastating effect of Eber D. Howe's Mormonism Unvailed published that same year. The affidavits from the Smith family's neighbors that Howe purchased from Philastus Hurlbut blackened the family's name. The Smiths were charged with being lazy, dishonest, and untrustworthy and with wasting their time on money-digging rather than working their farm.[77] Lucy Smith still felt the sting of the accusations when she dictated her autobiography in 1844. When she began to tell of visions, she had to insist that readers not think that "we stopt our labor and went at trying to win the faculty of Abrac drawing Magic circles or sooth saying to the neglect of all kinds of buisness." Joseph himself fended off the "very prevalent story of my having been a money digger" by admitting in his 1838 history that he had dug for Josiah Stowell until he persuaded "the old gentleman" to give up the fruitless quest as if that were his only involvement.[78]

One reason for Cowdery's use of the term "Urim and Thummim" in his *Messenger and Advocate* letters was to downplay the money-digging episodes in Smith family history, which in respectable society were cause for shame. He explained that Joseph "translated with the Urim and Thummim, or, as the Nephites should have said, 'Interpreters,' the history, or reccord, called 'the book of Mormon.'" Cowdery wrote, to those who believed "amid the frowns of biggots and the callumny of hypocrites."[79] Howe's work obviously stung. The term "Urim and Thummim" associated Joseph's translation with the Bible rather than the money-digging culture of the seer stone. The label dignified a process that Howe disparaged.

The usage became the standard from then on. Smith's 1838 historical narrative described his recovery of the plates in September 1827 using the term: "At length the time arrived for obtaining the plates, the Urim and Thummin and the breastplate."[80] The 1838 narrative added that he also translated the characters given to Martin Harris for Charles Anthon using the Urim and Thummim. To be perfectly consistent, editors of the 1835 edition of the Doctrine and Covenant introduced the term into a revelation published previously in the Book of Commandments. The early version of the revelation given in the spring of 1829 chastised Joseph for giving Martin Harris "many writings, which you had power to translate."[81] The 1835 edition of the Doctrine and Covenants expanded the language to say "power given unto you to translate, by the means of the Urim and Thummim."[82] By 1835 the editors wanted to associate translation with the Bible rather than the seer stone and treasure-seeking. "Urim and Thummim" elevated the work. Later the term was added to two headings of revelations in the Doctrine and Covenants, where it was not found prior to 1834.[83]

Revising his past was only suitable for a person whose life had been transformed over the past decade. What Joseph Smith had become simply did not fit with what he had been. Joseph Smith in 1834 was worlds away from the seventeen-year-old who in 1823 had struggled to understand the gold plates. For three or four years after the angel's first visit, Smith could scarcely perceive his destiny. To recover a gold book of ancient records was far-fetched enough; to become a translator of an ancient record was unimaginable. The idea of a record engraved on gold plates came first. By 1826, Joseph and his family had rescued that idea from the confusion caused by buried treasure in the magic culture. But not until he had the plates in September 1827 did Smith realize that the book required translation, and only after experimentations of various kinds over the next six months did he fully grasp that he was to be the translator. When he composed his history in 1838, he realized that the angel and the record had been there all along. The confusion with a guardian spirit and treasure was due to his ignorance. The story he was to live by was of an angel leading him toward his role as translator.

Once into the role, he took to it. As he sat with his scribes, the words flowed from his mouth. His tongue loosened by translation, he soon spoke as a revelator. In the summer of 1828, he spoke for God for the first time. From that time on, the revelations kept coming until the end of his life. Translation was more difficult, but he avidly embraced that too. He and Sidney Rigdon sat together day after day "translating" the Bible, and in 1835 he undertook to translate Egyptian scrolls that he believed contained a history by ancient Abraham. No other prophetic career was quite like it. How he lit upon it is difficult to explain. That the gold plates moved him toward it seems likely. Their nature, as Smith understood it, demanded translation. The engravings of ancient characters on their surfaces and the presence of a mysterious instrument to aid in the work called out for translation, and the intrepid Smith answered the call.

3

Making Scripture

The Book of Mormon, 1830

Knowledge of the gold plates came to Joseph Smith gradually between 1823 and 1827. By September 1827 when he said he recovered them from the hill, he could describe their physical appearance—their color, shape, and weight. He knew they contained an ancient record that had to be translated. But what was that record about? His 1838 history said he was told it held an account of "the former inhabitants of this continent and the source from whence they sprang." In 1832, he remembered hearing of "plates of gold upon which there was engravings which was engraven by Maroni & his fathers the servants of the living God in ancient days."[1] These were at best vague hints. The nature of the text became evident only as he translated.

Given Joseph Smith's background, the text could have taken many directions. It could have conveyed ancient lore from the Smith family's money-digging practices: formulas for eluding the guardian spirits or incantations for finding treasure. Perhaps the plates would lay out rules for virtuous living as did the Gaihwiyo, the "Good Word" of the indigenous prophet Handsome Lake, who lived into Joseph Smith's lifetime and whose disciples came to Smith's hometown of Palmyra in the 1820s and may have met him.[2] The text might have retold early American history in faux biblical language like the accounts sometimes appearing in newspapers in Joseph Smith's time.[3]

All of these were possible. Instead, the gold plates told the story of a small party of Israelites who left Jerusalem just prior to the Babylonian captivity to seek a new promised land. They carried Hebrew scriptures with them, were visited by Christ, and perished when they sank into iniquity in the fifth century CE.[4] The plot, the style, the message were all biblical. As the editor of the *Wayne Sentinel* reported in 1829, the book was a "Golden Bible."

Book Making

Among the features yet to be determined was how the plates figured in the Book of Mormon. The Smiths had trouble enough understanding that the plates were a record; their role within the book was yet to emerge. They were first mentioned on the title page: "An Account Written by the Hand of Mormon, upon Plates Taken from the Plates of Nephi."[5] This first announcement signaled that the plates were to be prominent in the story. Texts do not ordinarily inform readers that they were written on parchment or printed on paper or cut in stone. The Bible, on which the Book of Mormon is clearly modeled, says almost nothing about the medium on which it was inscribed or its sources. The Ten Commandments were written on tablets of stone.[6] The word "parchments" occurs once in the Bible, at 2 Timothy 4:13. References to "roll," implying parchment or papyrus scrolls, occur more frequently. "Take thee a roll of a book, and write therein all the words that I have spoken unto thee," the Lord tells Jeremiah.[7] Slight references like these are the only hints about the materiality of the original source. Bible dictionaries could only speculate on the medium for writing scripture. *A Dictionary of the Holy Bible*, a book found in Joseph Smith's Nauvoo library, spoke of the materials in terms found in many other reference books: "Men used anciently to write upon tables of stone, lead, copper, wood, wax, bark, or leaves of trees."[8] No one knew for sure how the Bible was recorded. The Book of Mormon lets you know immediately that it was written on plates.

Nephi speaks of his record in the first chapter of the book. "Yea, I make a record in the language of my father," he writes. "I make an abridgment of the record of my father, upon plates which I have made with mine own hands." He tells us when he made his plates and when he was commanded to make another set. Later, the record tells us when the plates are getting full.[9] In the ten centuries of Nephite history recorded in the Book of Mormon, the plates pass from one record-keeper to another more than twenty times, and each handoff from one writer to the next is carefully recorded.[10] "And now my son Helaman, I command you that ye take the records which have been entrusted with me," Alma tells his son.[11] The plates, as an object, appear repeatedly down to the final pages where Moroni bids farewell to his readers and seals them up.[12] Plates are mentioned over a hundred times.

According to the Book of Mormon, the plates Joseph Smith received from the angel were only a fraction of all the plates passed down from generation to generation. Besides the two sets of plates Nephi made, Zeniff, the leader of a colonizing expedition, made plates to record his story. Mormon made plates for the history he made of his own times. Long before the Nephite migration to the New World, Ether, the last prophet of a previous civilization, kept a record on plates of gold.[13] These named plates seemed to have been a small portion of the cache of records that accumulated over the course of Nephite history. Mormon injects an editorial note in his abridgment about his discovery of Nephi's second set of plates. "I searched among the records which had been delivered into my hands, and I found these plates."[14] He inherited so many plates, he at first missed a set that later proved to be of immense value. Add to all these the brass plates taken by Nephi from Laban's treasury in Jerusalem, and the Book of Mormon is overflowing with plates. The reason for the words on the title page "taken from the plates of Nephi" was to tell readers which of all the sources at his disposal Mormon had relied upon most.

Scattered among references to the plates are clues about how the record was kept. Readers are told the names of the authors, their roles in society, and what they chose to record. The engravers of the plates were not plain men with a message or lone prophets emerging from the wilderness. The record was kept by society's cultural elite. Writing was the responsibility of kings and generals, church leaders, and heads of clans. The first Nephi was the son of the family's patriarch and was eventually elected king.[15] For a long stretch, the records were kept by monarchs, and then passed to chief judges and high priests. Alma, who was the high priest but not the ruler, tried to transfer the plates to Nephihah, the chief judge, and only when refused did he confer them on his son Helaman.[16] Mormon was the general of the Nephite army and his son Moroni a commander of ten thousand troops.[17] The plate-keepers who did not occupy high office were familiar with the nation's political and military chieftains.[18] The story line in the book never strays far from the court and the centers of power.

The language of the plates was not accessible to everyone. The brass plates were written in Egyptian. Lehi could read them, "for he having been taught in the language of the Egyptians, therefore he could read these engravings, and teach them to his children, that thereby they could teach them to their children, and so fulfilling the commandments of God."[19] From then on, the plates of Nephi were written in the language of Lehi, which consisted of "the learning of the Jews and the language of the Egyptians."[20] Keepers of the plates had to be inducted into this learning before they could assume their duties. The sons of King Benjamin had to be "taught in all the language of his fathers, that thereby they might become men of understanding; and that they might know concerning the prophecies, which had been spoken by the mouths of their fathers."[21] By Mormon's day, a half millennium later, the plates were still written "in the characters, which are called . . . the re-formed Egyptian," which had been "handed down and altered by us, ac-cording to our manner of speech."[22] By that time, the plates' language was unrecognizable outside this small coterie: "none other people knoweth our language."[23] These bilingual elites not only spoke the ordinary language of the Nephites, but could read and write in "reformed Egyptian." Esoteric language erected a barrier around the plates that restricted plate-keeping to the learned.

All this information filled out the picture of how the book was made and by whom. Mormon, its principal author, left still more clues. Poring over the records of the years immediately preceding the visit of Christ, he found nothing worth recording on his own plates, so he simply wrote, "and thus had the twenty and second year passed away, and the twenty and third year also, and the twenty and fourth, and the twenty and fifth; and thus had twenty and five years passed away." He leaves a picture of himself as editor reading through the reformed Egyptian characters on the plates of Nephi, looking for signal events. Finding nothing worth adding to his record, he simply notes the passing of the years. But then he worries that he had ne-glected something of value: "And there had many things transpired which, in the eyes of some, would be great and marvellous; nevertheless, they cannot all be written in this book; yea, this book cannot contain even a hun-dredth part of what was done among so many people, in the space of twenty and five years." The passage lets it be known that Mormon struggled with decisions about what was relevant and what was not.[24] Then, having shown his hand in the editing process, Mormon introduced himself to his reader-ship: "Behold, I am called Mormon, being called after the land of Mormon, the land in which Alma did establish the church." He wanted his readers to know that he was a real person doing his best to write a history. "Therefore I do make my record from the accounts which hath been given by those which were before me."[25] Mormon writes with disarming frankness. His comments show his willingness to explain how he worked. Mentions of the plates throughout the text reflected a general transparency about the book's making.[26]

The Documentary Hypothesis

The Book of Mormon's candor about its own making is at odds with the prevailing sense of how scriptures came to be. Most Christians in 1830 thought that the Bible, which the Book of Mormon devotedly emulates, had been composed by pure inspiration. They assumed that words came to prophets in the manner described by the ancient Jewish philosopher Philo, who believed that prophets "proffer nothing of their own, but matter altogether foreign to themselves, and communicated to them internally by the operation of God. So long as the state of a prophet be rapture, he knows nothing of himself."[27] Scripture was purely God's word, unsullied by human thought. The Book of Mormon was compiled in another way. Mormon selected and blended materials from various plates, making editorial decisions all along the line. Scripture emerged from his work as an editor, extracting the history from his sources, much like other historians.[28]

This unconventional view had relevance in 1830. This was a time when the problems of constructing the Bible were of growing interest to Christian scholars.[29] In the century preceding the publication of the Book of Mormon, scrutiny of the Bible had made the text seem more like a history than the privileged word of God. This movement toward the historicization of biblical texts came primarily from Germany where scholars were emphasizing the human influences on the production of the scriptures. They argued that to understand the composition of biblical texts readers had to grasp the historical conditions under which they emerged, in the process humanizing scripture-making.[30] American scholars were bringing back this new biblical scholarship just as Joseph Smith was translating the gold plates.

In some instances, this turn toward history had startling consequences. As scholars considered biblical texts as products of their times and places, they began to wonder who had written them. How did they come to be? It was less disruptive to direct this line of reasoning at classical text: were Homeric epics written by one man, a person named Homer, or were they a composite production, perhaps by a group of authors or bards?[31] Querying the authorship of classical texts, however, led inexorably to questions about Isaiah and the Pentateuch.[32] Were they truly what they claimed to be, the inspired writings of the prophet whose name they bore, or were they composite works shaped by nameless editors too?

Scholars who investigated such questions soon found themselves in contested territory. Tampering with holy writ aroused the fears of the

orthodox who, as one scholar put it, were accustomed to "the merely theological use of the Scriptures of the Old Testament." The scriptures "were
searched only for religious ideas, and men remained blind to their other
contents."[33] The consideration of the Bible's place in history disturbed the
traditional reading.

The German biblical scholar Johann David Michaelis (1717–1791) began
as a defender of the standard view of biblical infallibility, but later underwent
a "mental crisis" and came to see that the texts had been altered over time. By
adopting a historical perspective, he identified distinctive qualities in each of
the New Testament books, undermining the basic assumption that the Bible
was a unified, inspired whole.[34]

Subsequent scholars such as Johann Gottfried Eichhorn (1752–1827),
a student and admirer of Michaelis, saw individual texts as blends of previous texts.[35] In his *Einleitung in das Alte Testament* (Introduction to the
Old Testament), published in 1780–1783, Eichhorn proposed that the
books of the Old Testament, as a modern historian writes, did not come
to us "as one piece from the hand of their authors. Sometimes the authors
themselves, later disciples or collectors put fragmented parts together."
Eichhorn thought that this should not be too difficult to accept. "Supposing
the Mosaical books in their present disposition not to be the work of Moses,
still they are composed of Mosaical materials, merely put into form by a
later hand."[36] Eichhorn felt he was defending the Bible against its despisers,
but others found him dangerously subversive in "trifling with the most sacred subjects." Conservatives later saw these years as "the period at which
the great revolution in the opinions and mode of study of the theologians"
occurred.[37]

American scholars who studied in Germany or read the scholarship were
impressed with the new learning but realized that American audiences
could not bear the disturbing implications.[38] Most of the American clergy
based their thinking on the traditional Protestant doctrine of biblical infallibility, which insisted that the books of the Bible were the impeccable word
of God. Historicizing them threw their veracity into question and eroded the
foundations of Christian belief.[39]

Anxiety about fallible human influence on scripture-making was absent from the Book of Mormon. A book whose origins were enshrouded
in miraculous events was surprisingly at ease with historical influences
on the actual production of scripture. Although Joseph Smith had no
known connections with German biblical scholarship, his translation

depicted scripture as emerging from specific historical circumstances and consisting of texts stitched together by a later editor much as the German scholars envisioned the origins of the Bible. While the text of the Book of Mormon insists on its privileges as inspired writing, readers of the Book of Mormon are permitted to view the very human process by which the text came into existence.[40] It was a conglomeration of texts just as the new critics claimed the Bible was. Mormon, the general editor, took pains to explain exactly where the various elements of his book came from, making clear that the Book of Mormon consisted of the writings of various prophets and leaders going back through time and recorded on various plates.[41] The book does not even shy away from the possibility of human errors creeping into the text.[42] The Book of Mormon's title page warns that "if there be fault, it be the mistake of men," pretty much summing up the Unitarian view of holy writ.[43]

The Book of Mormon and the higher criticism both returned scripture to history. The essence of the German critical approach was to imagine biblical authors as writers grounded in concrete cultural and historical circumstances. Eighteenth- and nineteenth-century Bible critics read the book as they would any historical document, discerning the influences of its times on its production. Book of Mormon writers followed the same pattern. In the book's pages, the scriptures are a human production: minds writing under heavenly influence but in particular historical circumstances, diligently inscribing events and inspiration on plates made by human hands.

Alike as humanistic scholarship and the Book of Mormon were, however, the two actually pointed in opposite directions. If the thrust of German scholarship was to turn holy scriptures into human history, the Book of Mormon did the reverse: it turned history into holy writ. The biblical critics said little about how texts edited, blended, and revised by human editors rose to be treated as the word of God. The Book of Mormon offers itself as an example of that elevation. It reveals how a record kept as a history was in time transmuted into scripture.

History as Scripture

The difference begins in the two books themselves. Nothing in the Bible quite matches the compulsion to keep records that is found in the Book of

Mormon.[44] The first sentence in Nephi's account on the opening page of the Book of Mormon announces that "I make a record of my proceedings in my days." He soon lets it be known that his father, Lehi, was also keeping an account of his visions, dreams, and prophecies.[45] This was the beginning of a practice that lasted for a thousand years down to the apocalyptic destruction of the Nephite people.[46]

These record-keepers understood historical writings to be of singular importance. Soon after the family's departure, Lehi sends his sons back to Jerusalem to recover the record kept by their distant kinsman Laban, who possessed plates containing the writings of previous prophets.[47] To obtain the brass plates, Nephi and his brothers sacrificed all of their father's considerable property, and Nephi ultimately killed Laban.[48] Though questioning his right to take Laban's life, Nephi reasoned that his people could not keep God's commandments unless they had the law, and he knew that "the law was engraven upon the plates of brass."[49] To close the argument, the Spirit of God spoke to him, explaining that it was "better that one man should perish, than that a nation should dwindle and perish in unbelief." A book with the power to preserve a nation justified murder.[50]

The Mulekites, another group of migrants from Jerusalem in Nephi's day, brought no records and paid the price. When the two groups met a few centuries after their arrivals, Mulekite culture had decayed. "Their language had become corrupted; and they had brought no records with them and they denied the being of their Creator; and Mosiah, nor the people of Mosiah, could not understand them."[51] Without records, the whole culture deteriorated. A subsequent monarch, King Benjamin, taught his sons to read the Egyptian on the brass plates in the belief that without those writings their forefathers "would have dwindled in unbelief." How could faith be sustained without a sacred history? How else to "understand of his mysteries, and have his commandments always before our eyes"?[52]

In the authors' eyes, the writings on the plates of Nephi would change the course of history. Other books, coming from other peoples, served a similar purpose. So heavily is this point underscored that one might say that the Book of Mormon is a book about the importance of books.[53] Where record-keeping went wrong, true religion lost its way. In his vision of the corruption of the Bible, Nephi foresaw it coming forth initially as a true revelation: "Thou hast beheld that the Book proceeded forth from the mouth of a Jew; and when it proceeded forth from the mouth of a Jew, it contained the plainness of the Gospel of the Lord, of whom the twelve apostles bear record;

and they bear record according to the truth which is in the Lamb of God."[54] But when these writings fell into the hands of subsequent editors, significant parts were removed. A great and awful church took control of the texts and defaced them: "They have taken away from the Gospel of the Lamb, many parts which are plain and most precious; and also, many Covenants of the Lord have they taken away; and all this have they done, that they might pervert the right ways of the Lord; that they might blind the eyes and harden the hearts of the children of men."[55] From a book of truth, the Bible became a marred, partial account. The omission of the plain and precious truths caused its readers to lose their way: "Because of these things which are taken away out of the Gospel of the Lamb, an exceeding great many do stumble, yea, insomuch that Satan hath great power over them."[56] Malevolent editing yielded a flawed holy book and a faulty religion. Behind it all, Nephi saw the hand of Satan, thwarting God's purposes. The devil's method was to corrupt the holy books.

The attention paid to plates suggests their high purpose. The Book of Mormon presents itself as part of a massive project of creating scripture. Those who believed the Bible was sufficient were radically wrong. "A Bible, a Bible," some Gentiles would say, "We have got a Bible, and there cannot be any more Bible." Their mistake was to forget the Bible was the product of a people, the Jews. "Thou fool, that shall say, A Bible, we have got a Bible, and we need no more Bible. Have ye obtained a Bible, save it were by the Jews?"[57] Nephi's point was that the Jews were not the only people to write holy words. Record-keeping was a global phenomenon practiced by many peoples. "Know ye not that there are more nations than one," asks the Lord through Nephi. "I bring forth my word . . . upon all the nations of the earth." Every people was capable of producing a bible, the tribes of Israel scattered about the earth and many others. "All men, both in the east, and in the west, and in the north, and in the south . . . shall write the words which I speak unto them." Eventually all these words would blend. "The Jews shall have the words of the Nephites, and the Nephites shall have the words of the Jews; and the Nephites and the Jews shall have the words of the lost tribes of Israel." The people shall be gathered in one; and "my word also shall be gathered in one."[58] The whole world would come together in a great congress of records, all of them bibles, God's word.[59]

These mighty purposes raised historical records to a lofty place; Nephi came close to considering the records of all world's peoples to be scripture.[60] That eased the process of elevating Nephi's and Mormon's writings to that level. Initially the Nephite prophets' writings were not honored by the label "scripture." In Nephi's time, Laban's brass plates were the scriptures. Just prior to writing extensive passages from Isaiah into his own record, Nephi reflected, "I write the things of my soul, and many of the Scriptures which are engraven upon the plates of brass," as if they were different kinds of records. Jacob read to his people from Isaiah, and Nephi copied long excerpts into his record. People looking to understand doctrine and sacred history searched the brass plates.

Sometimes Nephi's small plates were not treated by their own makers as a holy record. They contained prophecies and revelations from the founding prophets, but later a confessedly wicked man made an entry. Another said he knew of no revelations to record and so wrote nothing, and still others dutifully made entries with no pretense to inspiration.[61] These figures had little sense of keeping a sacred record to be honored as scripture. They wrote to fulfill a record-keeping obligation imposed by their predecessors.

But by Benjamin's time (about 130 BCE), the brass plates and the plates of Nephi came to be held in equal regard. Benjamin taught his sons in "the language of his fathers" that they might "know concerning the prophecies, which had been spoken by the mouths of their fathers." Those prophecies included the records "engraven on the plates of brass" but also "the plates of Nephi, which contain the records and the sayings of our fathers, from the time they left Jerusalem, until now." Both records deserved close study. "Search them diligently, that ye may profit thereby." Around 90 BCE, Ammon, a Nephite missionary, expounded "all the records and Scriptures, from the time that Lehi left Jerusalem, down to the present time," as if the plates were both record and scripture. During His time with the Nephites, Christ "expounded all the Scriptures in one, which they had written," seemingly categorizing Nephite writings with other scriptures.[62] The Book of Mormon viewed itself as one historical record among many, but it was the repository of revelations and stories of God's ongoing struggle with his people. By the time of Christ's visit, the plates of Nephi had become a sacred record.[63]

Sacred Plates

Along with this change in status, the plates themselves took on a new character. In the Book of Mormon, they were not described as gold. Nephi, the lead character in the Book of Mormon's opening pages, told of making "plates of ore," without specifying what kind. The only gold plates in the Book of Mormon were the ones on which the Jaredites, a still older civilization than the Nephites, were said to have inscribed their history.[64] The treasure part of Joseph Smith's gold plates, the part that tempted Smith when he first went to the hill and attracted the local treasure-seekers, was missing from Nephi's plates.

Neither were the plates thought of as a hallowed object. In Smith's time, no one was allowed to look upon the plates without divine permission. Martin Harris worried that looking on them was like looking on the face of God. In the Book of Mormon, no such restrictions applied. They were kept safe but not shut away. Nephi's plates were akin to the brass plates which were held in the treasury open to Laban's servants.[65] Nephi showed no hesitation in picking up the brass plates and carrying them off. His own plates, though considered sacred, were similarly accessible. They had no mysterious, magical origin; he made them with his own hands. In time, the plates were stored among the treasures of the king, classed with the precious objects hallowed by their connection to the first migration: the sword of Laban, the brass plates, and the Liahona.[66] The connection honored the plates, but nothing was said about shielding them from human gaze.

That changed when Smith retrieved the plates from the hill. Martin Harris feared he would be struck down if he saw them. In his mind, the plates were like the Ark of the Covenant which could not be touched, or the face of God which could not be looked at.[67] Smith covered the plates when they sat on the table during translation or concealed them in a box when carrying them about. To see the plates was a high privilege granted only to a few. Emma, Joseph's wife and assistant in translating, never saw them. She was content to thumb their edges under the linen cloth she had provided as a cover.[68] The plates had become a holy object in keeping with their nature as scripture. When Joseph Smith came to describing the Book of Mormon in the Articles of Faith, it was natural for him to say the Bible was the word of God, and "we also believe the Book of Mormon to be the word of God."[69]

During the year and a half while Joseph Smith was translating the Book of Mormon, the functions of the gold plates had assumed a higher form. From being a precious object mysteriously recovered from a hill, the plates had become another Bible. They were portrayed as the fruit of an ongoing record-keeping program stretching over hundreds of years and involving many generations of prophets. The text assumed from the outset that a record would be kept; the leading figures in the history constructed plates as if by second nature. Then without ever saying they were making scripture, over time their records rose to scriptural status. In a period when the question of how scriptures were made occupied biblical scholars in both Europe and the United States, Joseph Smith's Book of Mormon offered an example of how it was done.

4

Presence

Family and Friends, 1827–1830

What happens when someone talks to Our Lady on a hillside, or hears an angel commanding her to go to war, or brings home gold plates found in a buried stone box? In an essay on the impact of religious experience on human relationships, the historian Robert Orsi calls happenings like the Virgin's appearance to the young Bernadette at Lourdes "abundant events." "The abundant event," Orsi writes, "is not exhausted at its source. Presence radiates out from the event along a network of routes, a kind of capillary of presence, filling water, relics, images, things, and memories. 'Routes' are not to be understood here simply as pathways of commerce or as networks of church affiliation and connection. The routes are formed and shaped by the abundant event: they develop through successive transactions among people wanting to share their experience of presence, and in this way the routes themselves become media of abundance."[1]

By "presence" Orsi means divine presence. Sometimes when God is experienced in the world, the event overflows with energy. News radiates outward, creating passages for its own communication, just as floodwaters create channels for themselves. "Capillary" is a good word for describing the spread of news about Joseph Smith's "marvilous experience" with the angel Moroni.[2] It traveled via formal proselyting, newspaper reports, rumor, gossip, and through family relationships and friendships. Reports of the Golden Bible and its fabulous back story rapidly filtered out into the nation.

Abundant events, Orsi continues, always occur within dense networks of already established relationships. "One of the first things to say about an abundant event," Orsi suggests, "is that it serves as a focusing lens for the intricacies of relationships in a particular area at a particular time."[3] The event insinuates itself into human connections, giving them new forms. Where it struck home, knowledge of the plates brought people together in new ways. Everything was seen in relationship to the event. Although kept out of sight, hidden in a sack or a box, seen by no one but Smith himself, the gold plates for a time consumed the Smith family. Everything turned on protecting and translating the treasured record. The plates acted like a dense star, warping the lives of people who came within range of their gravitational pull.

No matter that most of those affected never saw the plates and those who did looked only for a few minutes. No one saw Mary at Lourdes save for Bernadette; Our Lady of Guadalupe came only to a Mexican peasant and his uncle. Twelve people saw the plates, more than usual for abundant events, but they already had an impact in the months while they remained concealed. Struck by their experiences, people recorded their dealings with the plates in autobiographical writings, correspondence, and, most frequently, interviews. Joseph Smith, his mother, his family, his scribes, and nearly everyone close to the Smiths in those years talked or wrote. After the plates were gone, the curious came back year after year to hear more from those who had initially encountered them.

The Asael Smith Family

Soon after translation got underway in 1828, stories of the plates followed one of the most accessible capillaries: Smith family kinship ties in northern New York. The first known mention of the gold plates in writing occurred in the fall of 1828 in letters to Asael Smith, Joseph Smith Jr.'s grandfather.[4] Joseph Smith Sr. had not seen his father for twelve years. By the 1820s, Asael and his sons had moved from Vermont to St. Lawrence County in northern New York State to acquire land for the next generation.[5] Also on the move, Joseph Smith Sr. took a different course. He migrated to Palmyra, New York, near the route of the Erie Canal, putting hundreds of miles between the two branches of the family. In the early nineteenth century, a separation like that was often permanent.[6] When Joseph Sr. later visited his parents Asael and Mary Duty Smith, they were overjoyed to see their son, "for he had been absent from them so long, that they had been fearful of never beholding his face again in the flesh."[7]

The Book of Mormon brought the family back into contact. The Palmyra Smiths first wrote not long after Martin Harris lost the first batch of manuscript pages, and Joseph Jr. was starting from scratch again.[8] Although far from complete, the translation of the plates was news the Smiths wanted to share. Their letters are lost, but a reply from Joseph Sr.'s brother Jesse dated June 17, 1829, refers to letters from Joseph Smith Sr. and two sons Hyrum and Joseph Jr. Jesse quotes Joseph Jr. as saying that "the Angel of the Lord has revealed to him the hidden treasures of wisdom & knowledge, even divine revelation, which has lain in the bowels of the earth for thousands of years." Jesse also refers to spectacles and hieroglyphics as if one of the letters had talked about translation.[9] The family apparently was told the whole story.

The St. Lawrence Smiths were skeptical at first, but most of them took an interest. Jesse was the exception. In the letter to Hyrum, he foresaw "everlasting fire" for "such as make lead books, and declare to the world that they are of the most fine gold." Jesse did everything in his power to protect Asael from young Joseph's wicked scheme. "Had he been forty years younger, he would have discov[er]ed barefaced falsehood in every line of your statement." Unfortunately for Jesse, another of Asael's boys had gone along. It was "your good, pious & methodistical uncle Asahel," who had "induced his father to give credit to your tale of nonsense."[10] The plates divided the family from the moment the news arrived.

Unfazed by Jesse's hostility, Joseph Smith Sr. visited the St. Lawrence County Smiths soon after the Church was organized in April 1830. When Joseph turned the conversation to his son's translation, Jesse warned them, "If you say another word about that Book of Mormon, you shall not stay a minute longer in my house; and if I cannot get you out any other way, I will hew you down with my broad axe."[11] Grandfather Asael, on the other hand, welcomed the news. According to his son John's reminiscences, he said "he had always expected, that something would appear to make known the true gospel."[12] Joseph Jr. later said his grandfather Asael Smith "long ago predicted that there would be a prophet raised up in his family, and my Grand Mother was fully satisfied that it was fulfilled in me." Remembering the 1830 visit, Joseph Jr. claimed that Asael, "having received the Book of Mormon . . . read it nearly through, and he declared that I was the very prophet that he had long known, would come in his family."[13] Perhaps because the book fulfilled his father's prophecy, Jesse's attempts to prevent Joseph Sr. from speaking a word about the Book of Mormon were of no avail. The brothers let Joseph Sr. have his say, and a copy of the book was left with John. Except for Jesse, all of Joseph Smith Sr.'s brothers—John, Asahel, and Silas—eventually believed the story and were baptized. Near the end of her life, the grandmother Mary Duty Smith joined the Latter-day Saints in Kirtland, Ohio.[14]

Joseph Sr.'s visit was a turning point in Asael Smith's family history. After many years of separation, the family was reunited. Jesse was the only one to resist the family's destiny as Asael foresaw it. Somewhat sadly at the end of the 1829 letter to Hyrum, Jesse sent his "compliments to your Father and Mother." He reproved them for not writing more often. "The time has been when they were glad to see me, but I am suspicious that the length of time since we last parted, has in some measure obliterated me from their memory," adding piteously, "so that they would not now be pleased to recieve a visit from me." He wanted their favor and friendship, and yet there was now a gulf between them.[15] While the plates story brought Joseph Sr. and his brothers together, Jesse the unbeliever was omitted from the family's destined role. When the other Smiths moved to Kirtland, he stayed behind.[16] The gold plates reconfigured the "intricacies of relationships," as Orsi called them, with Jesse replacing Joseph Sr. as the outlier.

Joseph Smith Jr.

Joseph Smith Jr. was more affected by the gold plates than anyone. They required that he become something impossible, a translator. They also placed a heavy emotional burden on him as he guarded them and tried to finish the work. He wrote two accounts of recovering the plates, one in the summer of 1832 when he attempted to start a history and the other in the spring of 1838 when the First Presidency of the Church set out again to start a record. The two covered roughly the same time period, but in quite different fashion. The 1838 history was a polished account of an innocent young man who encountered divinity and sought to follow his inspiration despite strong opposition. It bears the marks of a skillful writer who knew how to control a narrative. The 1832 account was much shorter and more free-flowing. It appears to be spontaneous and unedited. Parts of it were written by Joseph Smith in his own hand; the rest appears to have been dictated to his scribe Frederick G. Williams. The text is poorly punctuated; the sentences flow into one another without pause. The account comes across as a stream of consciousness, the telling of one event triggering a retelling of the next. The 1832 story makes it possible to speculate on how events were linked in Smith's mind—what, in his memory, was attached to what. The account is expressive and uncalculated, propelled by a rush of feeling. Smith's letters to his wife and the few journal entries in his own hand show this same spontaneity. They leave the impression of a man with strong feelings who freely expressed them when he spoke or wrote for himself.

What did Joseph Smith feel as visions and revelations came to him in the decade after 1820? In the first place, he felt the story was his, almost his alone. He opened the 1832 account with the declaration: "A History of the life of Joseph Smith Jr. an account of his marvilous experience and of all the mighty acts which he doeth in the name of Jesus Ch[r]ist."[17] Others came into the picture with his marriage to Emma and the entrance of Martin Harris as financial backer, but other than these, Joseph's early account spoke of the recovery of the plates as a solo performance. "When I was seventeen years of age I called again upon the Lord and he shewed unto me a heavenly vision for behold an angel of the Lord came and stood before me and it was by night and he called me by name and he said the Lord had forgiven me my sins and he revealed unto me that in the Town of Manchester Ontario County N.Y. there was plates of gold upon which there was engravings which was engraven by Maroni & his fathers the servants of the living God in ancient days and deposited by th[e] commandments of God and kept by the power thereof and that I should go and get them." Joseph said the angel appeared to him three times that night and again the following day, but said nothing in his 1832 telling about his father or any of his family.[18] He saw himself as a reluctant visionary on a lonely quest.

The prevailing emotion throughout his 1832 account is anguish. There were occasional high moments, but most of the time he was anxious. He remembered the years leading up to Moroni's visit as painful. "I fell into transgressions and sinned in many things which brought a wound upon my soul and there were many things which transpired that cannot be writen and my Fathers family have suffered many persicutions and afflictions." He personally suffered from a "wound upon my soul" inflicted by his transgression, and the family was in anguish too, suffering from afflictions too painful to mention. The Lord's forgiveness from the angel brought some relief but not for long. The vision of the Lord three years earlier had been a cause for happiness. "My soul was filled with love and for many days I could rejoice with great Joy and the Lord was with me." The trip to the hill to see the plates brought no such joy. When he was unable to get the plates from the stone box, he became "excedingly frightened" and "cried unto the Lord in the agony of my soul." The angel showed no mercy but rebuked him for having "saught the Plates to obtain riches and kept not the commandme[n]t that I should have an eye single to the Glory of God therefore I was chastened." Joseph felt no relief, only rebuke.[19]

Conditions did not improve much after he began to translate. What stuck in his mind was the loss of the 116-page manuscript when Martin Harris begged to show it to his friends. Joseph felt the burden of responsibility for this error. "Martin was Chastened for his transgression and I also was chastened for my transgression for asking the Lord the third time." The plates were taken and he received them again but only "afte[r] much humility and affliction of Soul." Oliver Cowdery's willingness to translate brought some relief. Joseph learned of Cowdery's vision of what the Lord planned to do "through me his unworthy Servant." The 1832 account ended with Cowdery's arrival in the spring of 1829. In his final words, Joseph summed up the situation when they began translating again. "We had become reduced in property and my wives father was about to turn me out of doores & I had not where to go and I cried unto the Lord that he would provide for me."[20]

Although a more disciplined narrative, the 1838 history expressed the same apprehensions in more measured language. It added the angel's admonition in 1827 to protect the plates. He was told that "I should be responsible for them. That if I should let them go carelessly or through any neglect of mine I should be cut off, but that if I would use all my endeavours to preserve them untill he (the messenger) should call for them, they should be protected."[21] Joseph showed no delight in at last obtaining the plates. They were mostly trouble. "No sooner was it known that I had them than the most strenious exertions were used to get them from me. Every stratagem that could be invented was resorted to for that purpose. The persecution became more bitter and severe than before, and multitudes were on the alert continualy to get them from me if possible."[22] For Joseph himself, the plates were the embodiment of a demanding and troubling call that he did not especially desire, an onerous duty more than a magnificent gift.

Lucy Mack Smith

Lucy Mack Smith, Joseph's mother, remembered the story of the plates' recovery quite differently. In her telling, the family was involved from the beginning, making them a chosen circle with a grand mission to fulfill. Lucy has the angel admonishing Joseph for holding back from his family after the night of instruction in 1823, an episode her son did not mention in 1832. When Moroni appeared by an apple tree in Lucy's account, he asked, "Why did you not tell your father, what I commanded you to tell him?" When

Joseph said he feared his father would doubt him, the angel replied, "He will believe every word." Lucy's angel insists on the family being included. Joseph Sr. immediately begins to counsel his son, charging him "not to fail of attending strictly to the instructions which he had received from the angel."[23]

Lucy dictated her reminiscences in the winter of 1844–1845 when the memory of the spilt blood of Hyrum and Joseph was still fresh in her mind. Her position in the Latter-day Saint movement had been weakened by the death of both sons plus Samuel who might have been a candidate for the presidency of the Church had he not perished in July 1844 a month after his two brothers. Her daughter-in-law Emma was alienated from Brigham Young the new leader, and Lucy's one remaining son William's tenure as church patriarch had failed.[24] From being the mother of the living prophet, she was in 1844 an honored relic and little more. As Lucy began dictating her account, she had every reason to underscore her family's central role in the Restoration.

She loved the stories Joseph told the family. After his first visit to the hill, the Smiths gathered every evening to listen to him talk about the angel and the plates. "Joseph would occasionally give us some of the most amusing recitals that could be imagined: he would describe the ancient inhabitants of this continent; their dress, mode of travelling, and the animals upon which they rode; their cities, and their buildings, with every particular; he would describe their mode of warfare, as also their religious worship. This he would do with as much ease, seemingly, as if he had spent his whole life with them." These were happy times for Lucy. The image of the family circle stayed with her for two decades. "I presume we presented an aspect as singular, as any family that ever lived upon the face of the Earth: all seated in a circle, father, mother, sons, and daughters, and giving the most profound attention to a boy, eighteen years of age, who had never read the Bible through in his life."[25] She turned the gathering into a kind of performance, pleased with how the family would look as they sat listening to their gifted son convey privileged knowledge of a lost people.[26]

Later, after the plates had been obtained and translated, the manuscript prepared for the printer was concealed under Lucy's bed. As she lay there awaiting sleep, she said, "my Soul swelled with joy that could scarcly [be] heigtened except by the reflection that the record which had cost so much labor and suffering and anxiety [is] now in reality being beneath my own head." "This identicle work had not only been the object which we as a family had pursued so eagerly but that Prophets of ancient days and angels even the Gr[e]at God had his eye upon it, and said I to myself Shall I fear what man can do will not the angels watch over the precious relict of the worthy dead and the hope of the living and am I indeed the mother of a prophet of the God of Heaven." She had long suffered from an absence of a comforting faith. She had lost children, suffered privation, been subject to humiliation and poverty. "I did not receive a direct [answer] to my prayers for the space [of] 21 years." Finally it came. Lying on her bed over the completed manuscript, she spent the night "in an extacy of happiness." "Truly I can say that 'my soul did magnify and my spirit rejoiced in God my savior.'"[27]

Recovery of the Plates

Lucy wrote her account of the fateful night of September 21–22, 1827, when Joseph went to get the plates in slow motion, much as films slow down for dramatic effect. She remembered that around midnight on September 21, Joseph asked for a chest with a lock and key. A few minutes later as the appointed day began, Emma walked through the room in her bonnet and riding dress.[28] Lucy spent the night in "prayer and supplication to God, for the anxiety of my mind would not permit me to sleep." When she arose to prepare breakfast her "heart fluttered at every footstep." When Joseph Knight who was visiting announced that his horse and wagon were missing, Lucy—knowing Joseph and Emma had taken it—calmed him with a little excuse. When Joseph finally appeared, Lucy said, "I trembled so from fear lest all might be lost on account of some failure in keeping the commandments of God, that I was under the necessity of leaving the room to conceal my fealings." Joseph sensed her anguish and assured her "all is right—see here, I have got a key." Then he handed her an object covered with a silk handkerchief which she said "consisted of two smoothe three-cornered diamonds set in glasses, and the glasses were set in silver bows, which were connected with each other in much the same way, as old-fashioned spectacles."[29]

Joseph did not bring the plates home that morning. According to Lucy, he hid them in a decaying birch log. But their invisible presence still took over their lives. Everything turned on managing the plates. Where were they to be kept? How were they to be protected from the curious and the greedy? Lucy's story shifted from anxiety about obtaining the plates from the guardian angel to management of their safety. Joseph needed a box to hold them, and none was available in the house. When Lucy suggested they have one made, there was no money to pay. Joseph got a job repairing a well in the nearby town of Macedon to raise the funds, but then he was not around to look after the plates in their hiding place. When Joseph Sr. overheard the plans of a band of treasure-seekers to steal the plates, Joseph had to be sent for. Emma offered to ride to Macedon to fetch him and was provided with a stray horse the Smiths had found and marked with a hickory withe around its neck as required by law.[30]

Lucy said Joseph would know if the plates were in danger through a seer stone he always carried with him. As Emma approached the place where he was working, he had already climbed out of the well to meet her. Mrs. Wells, his employer, provided a horse, which Joseph mounted "in his linen frock, and, with his wife by his side, on his horse decorated as before with a hickory withe round his neck, he rode through the village of Palmyra."[31] The ride became a small performance as the young couple on a divine mission unknown to the villagers dashed through the town.

After arriving home, Joseph headed for the spot where he had left the plates, which was about three miles away. When he retrieved them from the log where they had been concealed, he wrapped them in a linen frock and headed home. Leaving the road, he struck out through the woods to avoid interference. But as he hopped over a fallen tree, a man sprang up and hit him with a gun. Joseph managed to knock his assailant down and run off through the woods. Twice more he was assailed, and in striking the third man dislocated his thumb. When he finally reached the Smith farm, he fell to the earth to recover his breath and then made his way to the house.[32]

After recovering, Joseph sent his brother Don Carlos to ask Hyrum for a chest.[33] In Lucy's telling, "when Carlos arrived at Hyrum's he found him at tea with two of his wife's sisters. Just as Hyrum was raising a cup to his mouth, Carlos touched his shoulder: without waiting to hear one word of the child, he dropped the cup, sprang from the table, caught the chest, and turned it upside down; and emptying its contents on the floor, left the house instantly, with the chest on his shoulder." The important thing in this scene was the two girls' reactions. "The young ladies were greatly astonished at his singular behavior, and declared to his wife . . . that he was certainly crazy."[34] Lucy's pleasure in retelling the incident came from the story going on below the surface. Hyrum knew that Joseph at last had the plates and rushed away to help care for the precious object. The two sisters, not being in on the secret, could only be astonished. They could not imagine the concealed drama playing out behind the scenes.

Joseph Smith Sr.

Joseph Smith Sr. never told his side of the story. We learn about him from Lucy and from his appearances now and again in other accounts. The gold plates were a turning point in his troubled life. They reversed his declining fortunes and led to prominence in the church his son founded. Joseph Sr. brought his family to Palmyra in 1816 after more than a decade of economic setbacks. He had lost the farm he received from his father, could not pay his debts as a storekeeper, and was forced to move when his crops failed in Vermont. After the move to Palmyra, he purchased a farm but lost it when he overextended himself to build a bigger house.[35] In 1827 when Joseph Jr. received the plates, Joseph Sr. was fifty-six, about to move in with his son Hyrum, with no land to dispense to his children. He was ashamed of his own weakness for drink. Perhaps worst of all, he had no religious home. When Lucy and a few of the children joined a Presbyterian congregation, he refused to attend, having lost faith in the minister. He was adrift and in his deeper self knew it. He dreamed of hesitating to enter a church building and when at last he approached the door, it was closed. He dreamed of harsh landscapes inhabited by beasts.[36] Perhaps he found in his money-digging ventures hope for both financial relief and contact with spiritual powers.

When Joseph Jr. hesitated to follow the angel's instructions for recovering the plates in September 1823, Joseph Sr. urged him to go to the hill immediately. In Lucy's telling, he was an enthusiastic backer, always urging his son to be more aggressive in going after the plates. His comment at Joseph Jr.'s 1826 trial for glass-looking showed his aspirations for his son. He lamented that "this wonderful power which God had so miraculously given him should be used only in search of filthy lucre, or its equivalent in earthly treasures."[37] There was both affection and ambition in his statement that he "trusted that the Son of Righteousness would some day illumine the heart of the boy, and enable him to see His will concerning him."[38] Perhaps there was hope and ambition for himself as well.

The feelings on both sides came to a head when Joseph Jr. watched his father's baptism. Joseph Knight remembered how Joseph Jr. "bast [burst?] out with greaf and Joy and seamed as tho the world Could not hold him. He went out into the Lot and appeard to want to git out of site of every Body and would sob and Crie and seamed to Be so full that he could not live." "He was the most wrot upon that I ever saw any man," Knight recalled. "His joy seemed to Be full."[39] The plates had brought father and son together and for Joseph Sr. opened a path back to faith.[40]

Emma Smith

Emma was another who was close to the plates but wrote nothing herself about her experience. Was there an awkward moment in their courtship when Joseph had to broach the subject? She seemed not to have hesitated about marrying the teller of the gold plates story. Lucy said they went to the hill together in the early morning hours of September 22 to recover the plates, and she was the messenger who told Joseph to come quickly when the treasure-seekers threatened to find them. She remained loyal to her husband until plural marriage threatened to drive them apart.[41]

Emma spoke most openly about the plates in an interview with her son Joseph Smith III in 1879, thirty-five years after her husband's death and almost fifty years after the translation was completed. In that time, she had separated from Brigham Young's church, remarried, and raised her children outside of the influence of Utah Mormons. In 1860, Joseph III took up the mantle of his father and accepted the leadership of a second body of Latter-day Saints who had coalesced in the Midwest in the decades after Young's exodus to Utah. Joseph III's church believed in the Book of Mormon as warmly as the Utah Mormons, and his purpose in interviewing his mother was to collect evidence to support their faith.

By 1879, the reigning explanation for the Book of Mormon held that Joseph Smith was incapable of composing the book himself. It was most likely a work of historical fiction by Solomon Spaulding, a Dartmouth graduate who supposedly had written a fantasy that resembled the Book of Mormon.[42] Critics hypothesized that the Spaulding manuscript fell into the hands of Sidney Rigdon, the most learned of Joseph Smith's early converts who, it was conjectured, injected religious language into Spaulding's romance and smuggled the text to Joseph Smith.[43] The questions of the hour when Emma talked to her son in 1879 were whether there was a concealed manuscript in Joseph Smith's hands as he translated in 1829 and whether Sidney Rigdon was in or near Palmyra before translation began.

Guided by Joseph III's questions, Emma spoke as defender of her husband. No, they had not been married by Sidney Rigdon in 1827. She did not meet Rigdon until late 1830, well after the book was published. No, Joseph Smith was not reading from a manuscript. "He had neither mss [manuscript] nor book to read from. If he had had anything of the Kind he could not have concealed it from me." She not only watched Joseph while she wrote for him, she was there when he dictated to Cowdery. "O[liver]. Cowdery and J[oseph]. S[mith]. wrote in the room where I was at work." It could hardly be otherwise in the small cabin the Smiths were using on her father's farm.[44]

To test her further, Joseph III asked "could not father have dictated the Book of Mormon to you, Oliver Cowdery and the others who wrote for him, after having first written it, or having read it out of some book?" Of course not, Emma came back, "Joseph Smith . . . could neither write nor dictate a coherent and well-worded letter, let alone dictating a book like the Book of Mormon." The Joseph Smith she knew was incapable of composing anything like the Book of Mormon. Moreover, he performed feats that went well beyond normal human capacities. "When acting as his scribe he would dictate to me hour after hour, and when returning after meals or after interruptions, he would at once begin where he had left off, without either seeing the mss [manuscript] or having any portion of it read to him. This was a usual thing for him to do. It would have been improbable that a learned man could do this, and for so ignorant and unlearned as he was it was simply impossible."[45]

Emma viewed herself as one who had never left the faith. "I know Mormonism to be the truth; and believe the Church to have been established by divine direction." She knew she had "been called apostate; but I have never apostatized, nor forsaken the faith I at first accepted." She felt she had good reasons for her belief. In the interview, she showed the rationalist bent of her mind. She said nothing about her love for her husband or her trust in his character. Hers was not a sentimental or spiritual faith. It was based on her observation of Joseph translating. Nothing she knew about him qualified him to dictate the book. "It is marvelous to me," she said, "as much so as to any one else."[46]

Containers

Emma, the Smith family, and close friends like Josiah Stowell and Joseph Knight seemed to have had no trouble believing in the plates that Joseph claimed to bring home from the Hill Cumorah in September 1827. Knight accepted Joseph's story of the plates and the spectacles at face value. Lucy was anxious to know if Joseph had them, but believed him when he said that they were hidden in a hollowed log.[47] Emma dashed through the town to get Joseph when the treasure-seekers threatened to find their hiding place. The immediate family was more concerned about where to conceal the plates than to establish the plates' reality. Great efforts were made to find a box to hold them since they had to be concealed from human gaze. From then on scrupulous attention was paid to where they were and what contained them. According to Willard Chase, Joseph had previously asked him to make a chest with a lock and offered to give him a share in the book, but Chase wanted to see the book first.[48] After Joseph got them home, Don Carlos sent word to Hyrum to bring his box. From then on, the plates occupied a number of boxes: a cherry box, a glass box, a box made by Benjamin Wasson, Emma's brother-in-law, a box made by Alvah Beman, Joseph's money-digging friend, and a red Morocco trunk.[49] Boxes protected the sacred object like a reliquary preserving the bones of a saint. When the treasure-seekers hunted for the plates, great effort was made to hide them—under a floorboard, in the flax in the loft, in a barrel, in the woods outside the Isaac Hale house in Harmony. The tale of Joseph and Emma moving back to her parents' house in Harmony made a big point of how the plates were carried out of town in a barrel one-third filled with beans and then topped off.[50] While the translation proceeded, Emma was aware of them sitting on the table covered in a cloth or lying under the bed.[51]

The family seemed not to have been troubled by the question of the plates' existence. The prohibition on seeing added to their fascination. They were a potent, precious object conveyed by a messenger from another time and too holy or dangerous to look at.[52] Their presence in the house was like a visit from a king. Everything turned on the location of his majesty. Where and what he was doing affected everyone. Even though the king never emerged from his room, it was all the more important to know the door behind which he sat.[53]

Martin and Lucy Harris

Not everyone was as sure as the family members about the plates' existence. Among those who wondered about the reality of the plates were Martin Harris and his wife, Lucy. Martin was the most skeptical of all the early believers. Though at the moment of resolution, husband and wife came down on opposite sides, for a time they both were uncertain. When most

Palmyrans scoffed as news of the gold plates spread in October of 1827, Martin reserved judgment. "How do you know that he has not got such gold plates?" he asked. Unsure of what to believe, he took the trouble to interrogate individual members of the Smith family trying to catch them in a contradiction. "I talked with them separately, to see if their stories agreed, and I found they did agree."[54] Their consistency added to the plausibility of the plates, but did not settle all doubts. For months, Martin looked for evidence to either dispel the illusion or to confirm the marvelous. His expedition to New York City sought a judgment from a learned man about the characters. Were they authentic or not? In hopes of confirming their existence, Harris pled to see the plates more passionately than anyone.

Lucy Harris was enthralled more briefly than her husband, but even more obsessively. Lucy Smith said Martin's wife began pressing money on Joseph in exchange for a view of the plates. On visiting Joseph Smith, Lucy Harris insisted that "she was determined to help him publish them," but was frustrated by his refusal to show them to her. After Joseph and Emma moved to Harmony, Lucy Harris made the long trip from Palmyra. In Lucy Smith's account: "On arriving there she informed Joseph, that her object in coming, was to see the plates; and she would never leave until she accomplished it. So, without delay she commenced ransacking every nook and corner about the house—chests, trunks, cupboards &c &c; on account of which, Joseph was under the necessity of removing, both the breastplate and record from the house and secreting them elsewhere. After making diligent search in the house, and not finding them, she concluded, that Joseph had burried them; and so the next day, she commenced searching out of doors; which she continued until 2. o'clock P. M."[55] Lucy Harris was no believer, but not a skeptic either. She could not decide. The plates might very well be concealed in a cupboard or buried in the ground near the house. She had to find out.

Both Lucy and Martin acted out a pattern of suspended disbelief found in stories of the fantastic as understood by the literary theorist Tzvetan Todorov. By the fantastic, Todorov did not mean fairy stories about imaginary creatures with magic powers. Stories of the fantastic begin in the world readers know and accept, the ordinary world we all live in. Then gradually the stories introduce happenings that could not occur in the ordinary world. In the story, these happenings are made entirely plausible. The possibility of a natural explanation for the fantastic events is reduced to nearly zero, so much so that the reader hesitates, unsure whether these happenings are real or imaginary.[56] In the moment of hesitation, the question remains up in the air. For a time, the reader wonders if unnatural or supernatural things do happen. This was the moment Lucy and Martin were caught in, an excruciating moment of hesitation.

Stories of the fantastic captivated nineteenth-century readers (and many to this day) because they flourished in an atmosphere where the existence of the supernatural was in question. The nineteenth century had seen the spread of doubts about the reality of the spiritual. There was as much religion as ever in the public realm, but alongside it lay skepticism and uncertainty. Stories that toyed with the supernatural, that dangled it before the public mind, that teased people with possibilities, fascinated readers who were themselves suspended between belief and disbelief.[57] Like the fantastic stories, the gold plates played upon these anxieties and uncertainties. The plates allowed people to enter for a moment into an enchanted world before returning to the mundane reality of modern existence.

Eventually, Lucy Harris lost confidence in the gold plates project, and Martin was unable to turn her around. He begged Joseph Smith to allow him to show her the early manuscript of the translation, but that only temporarily placated her. Eager to convince his friends as well as his wife, Harris exhibited the manuscript to others contrary to instructions from Smith, as if settling their doubts would help quiet his own. By then, Lucy Harris was adamant in her opposition to the plates. Lucy Smith thought Harris's wife stole the manuscript and plotted to discredit Joseph Smith by altering its words.[58] Eventually differences in belief broke up their marriage. Martin mortgaged his farm to fund the publication of the Book of Mormon and left Lucy behind when he migrated with the Mormons to Ohio. His was the saddest of the family reconfigurations wrought by the plates.[59]

Witnesses

Martin Harris, Oliver Cowdery, and David Whitmer were the first ones chosen to see the plates. Their testimony, printed in the back of the first edition of the Book of Mormon and reprinted in every edition since, was Smith's ultimate effort to satisfy questioners.[60] Until the three saw the plates, people had sensed them through touch and hearing.[61] They lifted the plates, felt their weight, and ran their fingers along the edges. William Smith "thum[b]ed them through the cloth and ascertained that they were thin sheets of some kind of metal." Martin Harris said he "hefted the plates many times" and once held them on his knee for an hour and a half. William Smith lifted them in a pillowcase. People heard the leaves "rustle" when thumbed and a "jink" when they were put in a box. Emma said the individual plates were "pliable like thick paper."[62] The accounts left little room to doubt that something heavy and plate-like existed in the boxes, the cloths, and the knapsacks they saw and felt. But the plates had not been seen. They remained the forbidden object that no one was to gaze upon.

A March 1829 revelation to Martin Harris recognized that Harris "hath desired A witness that my Servant Joseph hath got the things which he hath testified." The revelation showed some impatience: "O ye unbelieving ye stiffnecked Generation." Moreover, seeing the plates may be futile: "If they will not believe my words they would not believe my servants if it were possible he could show them all things."[63] But the revelation to Smith indulged Harris's plea, "for this Generation they shall have my word yea & the testimony of three of my Servants shall go forth with my word unto this Generation."[64]

Joseph said the four of them went into the woods near David Whitmer's house and prayed in turn. When nothing happened, they went around again. Martin Harris, the troublesome doubter, then said it must be his fault and left. The remaining three prayed again, as Joseph put it in his 1838 account, and this time a bright light appeared above them. "And behold, an angel stood before us; in his hands he held the plates which we had been praying for these to have a view of: he turned over the leaves one by one, so that we could see them, and discern the engravings thereon distinctly." David Whitmer was admonished to keep the commandments, "when immediately afterwards we heard a voice from out of the bright light above us, saying 'These plates have been revealed by the power of God, and they have been translated by the power of God; the translation of them which you have seen is correct, and I command you to bear record of what you now see and hear.'" Joseph left Cowdery and Whitmer at that point to search out Harris. As the two of them prayed together, Joseph saw the same vision and assumed Harris saw it too, for he cried out: "'Tis enough, 'tis enough; mine eyes have beheld, mine eyes have beheld."[65] Sight of the plates had been granted, and he was satisfied, or that is how Smith remembered it.

It is not known who drafted "The Testimony of Three Witnesses" published with the Book of Mormon in 1830. David Whitmer said all the witnesses signed their names.[66] The testimony gets to the heart of the matter immediately: we "have seen the plates." That answered the question in everyone's mind: were they real and did Joseph Smith have them? But the plates' reality becomes secondary as the testimony goes on. Little is made of the plates themselves. The testimony says nothing about their appearance or size; they are not even described as gold. The only feature mentioned is the "engravings which are upon the plates."[67]

Emphasis is not on the plates' existence but the mercy of God in showing them. The witnesses saw the plates, so the testimony says, "by the grace of God the Father, and our Lord Jesus Christ." It was the condescension of God that mattered. The witnesses knew that the plates had "been translated by the gift and power of God, for his voice hath declared it unto us." They had seen the engravings on the plates but even this was possible only because "they have been shewn unto us by the power of God, and not of man." The witnesses testify of divine power as much as the reality of the plates. "We declare with words of soberness, that an Angel of God came down from heaven, and he brought and laid before our eyes, that we beheld and saw the plates, and the engravings thereon." The testimony sought to answer the questions of rational observers, but it spoke more directly to religious concerns about finding God. The witnesses' great desire in bearing testimony was "to be obedient unto the commandments of God." They had begun by addressing questions from the Enlightenment; they ended by making a Christian pledge. "And we know that if we are faithful in Christ, we shall rid our garments of the blood of all men, and be found spotless before the judgement seat of Christ, and shall dwell with him eternally in the heavens."[68]

The testimony of the eight witnesses had a different character. Five of the eight witnesses were from the Whitmer family with whom Smith had completed the translation. The other three were two of Joseph's brothers and their father. Much less was said about this group. In his 1838 history, Joseph said only that after the three witnesses, "the following additional tes[t]imony was obtained." Lucy Smith expanded a little on her son's version. She said the Whitmers came over to Manchester soon after the angel showed the plates to the three witnesses. "Soon after they came, all of the male part of the company, together with my husband, Samuel [Smith], and Hyrum [Smith], retired to a place where the family were in the habit of offering up their secret devotions to God. They went to this place because it had been revealed to Joseph that the plates would be carried thither by one of the ancient Nephites: Here it was that those eight witnesses, whose names are recorded in the <u>Book</u> of <u>Mormon</u>, looked upon them and handled them." John Whitmer, one of the eight witnesses, placed the experience in Joseph's house and said the witnesses were divided into two groups. "At that time Joseph showed the plates to us, we were four persons, present in the room, and at another time he [Joseph] showed them to four persons more."[69]

The main source for what the eight men saw is the printed testimony itself. It makes no mention of an angel or a Nephite, only Joseph Smith, "the Author and Proprietor of this work."[70] The witnesses did not claim more than they knew. The plates "have the appearance of gold," the testimony said. "And as many of the leaves as the said Smith has translated, we did handle with our hands; and we also saw the engravings thereon, all of which has the appearance of ancient work." And that was it. The witnesses solemnly declared that "we have seen and hefted, and know of a surety, that the said Smith has got the plates," and then gave their names to the world in witness.[71] The testimony was plain, a little flat, without any religious embellishments. When John Whitmer was later asked if he saw the plates "covered with a cloth," he answered no. Joseph "handed them uncovered into our hands, and we turned the leaves sufficient to satisfy us."[72]

That was the kind of testimony rationalists could understand. It assimilated the plates into the ordinary world of material objects. No guardian spirits, no angels, no magical rituals. If accurate, the testimony of the eight witnesses satisfied the requirements of the rational enlightenment for sensory evidence. The problem was that too much rested on the testimonies. Belief in what they said implied acceptance of too many fabulous items: an angel appearing in Manchester, a simple young man conversing with the heavens, another Bible from ancient America. The problem was posed by Cornelius Blatchly, a onetime Quaker who wrote Martin Harris in 1829 only a few months after the witnesses said they saw the plates. Blatchly wanted to know more about this "wonderful record" but only if it could be "substantiated by indisputable evidences and witnesses." In November 1829, Oliver Cowdery wrote back on Martin's behalf. Knowing his account was fabulous, he insisted the witnesses could not have been mistaken in what they saw. "It was a clear, open beautiful day, far from any inhabitants, in a remote field, at the time we saw the record." It was "brought and laid before us, by an angel, arrayed in glorious light." Blatchly thanked Cowdery for his account but concluded that "so important a matter as a new bible" required "the most incontrovertible facts, circumstances and proofs." Oliver's account, in Blatchly's judgment, failed to meet that high standard.[73]

Mary Whitmer

John's mother, Mary Whitmer, another plain-spoken witness, said she saw the plates when she went to do the milking. In 1878, years after the event, her son said that his mother had grown weary with the work of housing and feeding the translating contingent. In June 1829, Joseph, Oliver, and Emma squeezed into an already crowded household. Emma must have been pressed into service, but the two men were of no help. They spent their days in an upstairs room recording the translation. Mary Whitmer had reason to complain of the added burden.

Mary's son David told Orson Pratt and Joseph F. Smith in 1878 that as his mother was going to milk the cows, an old man carrying a pack met her in the yard. He recognized that "you are tried because of the increase of your toil," and so "it is proper therefore that you should receive a witness that your faith may be strengthened." Then he took the plates out of the knapsack and showed them to her. Whitmer said that seeing the plates "nerved her up for her increased responsibilities." One of Mary's grandsons, John C. Whitmer, added that "this strange person turned the leaves of the book of plates over, leaf after leaf, and also showed her the engravings upon them." Then he vanished with the plates.

Mary Whitmer did not record the experience herself, but she told the story to her grandchildren "on several occasions." Her account was of a piece with other stories the Whitmers told. David Whitmer linked his mother's angel to the "very pleasant, nice-looking old man" he had seen on the road while bringing Joseph and Oliver to Fayette. His nephew John also described the visitor as "a stranger carrying something on his back that looked like a knapsack" and "spoke to her in a kind, friendly tone." Oliver Cowdery and Joseph Smith never mentioned this figure or told either of David Whitmer's stories in their histories. The old-man stories were part of Whitmer family lore, sustaining their belief that family members were important aides in the translation of the Book of Mormon. The Whitmers left the Church during the turmoil caused by the failure of the Kirtland bank. It may have given David Whitmer satisfaction to tell his stories to two apostles from the church that had dropped him. The witness stories were a reminder that the Whitmers had once been preeminent in the Mormon movement.[74]

Although many fell under the influence of the plates, they affected people quite differently. Joseph himself saw them as part of an anguished quest that he pursued largely on his own. Lucy welcomed the plates as a privilege bestowed on her family, distinguishing them from all others. Late in life, Emma found in Smith's miraculous translation of the plates confirmation of her faith in her husband. It had not been a mistake to give her life to this peculiar and powerful man. Joseph Smith Sr., according to his family, at last came to rest in the spiritual home provided by his son and the gold plates. Outside of the family, Martin and Lucy Harris hoped the plates would settle the questions about spiritual realities that troubled many in their generation. The Whitmers saw in the angelic visit to their mother further evidence of their importance in the early days of the Restoration. Friends and family absorbed the plates into their lives and memories in ways that satisfied personal needs. The plates were both a public presence and a private support.

Save for the Harrises, it did not matter that, until the end, no one saw the plates but Joseph Smith. The effort to recover the plates, to protect them, and to translate them was carried on with hardly any evidence of their reality. From the fall of 1827 through the summer of 1829, the people around Joseph Smith lived with this fabulous, invisible object, concealed in its containers, as if it were real. The plates' "Presence" seems to have enabled belief without proof. Family and friends accepted the plates as if the Enlightenment, with its demand for rational evidence, had never occurred.

The disregard for rational inquiry was not to last. The Smiths and their friends were surrounded by newspaper editors, liberal clergy, and lawyers who were steeped in Enlightenment values. The need for evidence in support of Christianity was widely felt by the Protestant clergy and eventually by Latter-day Saint apologists. Evidence never figured as the basis of belief; no one joined the Mormons because of the witnesses or any other material evidence. But as a matter of self-respect and public relations, Mormon writers began to marshal rational support wherever they could. It was not a matter of proof so much as a counter to the charges of being backward and superstitious. To present themselves as civilized and cultivated people, they had to have evidence.

5

Rationalism

Apologists, Critics, and Imitators, 1832–1860

By the end of the eighteenth century, rational skepticism had filtered into all levels of American society.[1] At the high end, the philosopher David Hume, the star of the Scottish Enlightenment, cast doubt on religious miracles and the very idea of a divine Creator.[2] At a more popular level, Thomas Paine's best-selling *The Age of Reason*, which derided Christian doctrine and biblical revelation, circulated widely.[3] Lucy Smith said that when her husband attended Methodist meetings contrary to the wishes of his father, Asael Smith came to the door and "threw Tom Pain's age of reason into the house and angrily bade him read that untill he believed it."[4] Believers knew that despite frequent revivals and an abundance of churches, the foundations of religious belief were being challenged by science and reason. While "infidels," as Deists and atheists were called, were ridiculed and denounced, they were also feared.[5]

Mormon Rationalism

Joseph Smith himself may have encountered skepticism at the Palmyra debating society he attended as a young man. Oliver Cowdery spoke of a time when Joseph wondered "if a Supreme being did exist."[6] Smith showed that he had had a brush with rational doubt when he invoked the argument from design, the standard theological response to skepticism, in his 1832 history. The sun, the moon, the stars, the earth, and man, he wrote, "walking forth upon the face of the earth in magesty . . . all these bear testimony and bespeak an omnipotant and omnipreasant power."[7] Such sentiments would be familiar to anyone who had encountered unbelief. In 1834, the men in Zion's Camp were surprised at how well Joseph grasped the case for skepticism. One Sunday when the marchers were trying to disguise their Mormon identity before a crowd of curious onlookers, Smith spoke for an hour pretending to be a "liberal free thinker." According to George A. Smith, "those present remarked he was one of the greatest reasoners they ever heard."[8]

The debates with skeptics gave Christian theology a rationalist cast.[9] The nineteenth century produced shelves of books on Christian evidences. All made the case for belief based on rational proof with titles such as *Lectures on the Evidences of the Christian Religion*, and *Essays on the Truth of the Christian Religion*.[10] Like all Christians, Mormons hungered for confirming evidence. Charles Thompson's *Evidences in Proof of the Book of Mormon, Being a Divinely Inspired Record* borrowed the methods of Christian apologists.[11] Mormons found in John Lloyd Stephens's 1841 account of his travels in Mexico and Central America—with drawings by Frederick Catherwood of eight cities—proof for the Book of Mormon. John E. Page wrote that the account "so completely proves the truth and divinety of the book of Mormon there is not a gentile dog left to stir a tongue in an attempt to put down the collateral testimony which those records afford me in proof of the Book of Mormon."[12] Here was hard evidence of the Book of Mormon's authenticity.

The witness statements printed in every copy of the Book of Mormon seemed to provide exactly the kind of evidence Mormons longed for. Eleven men attested they saw the plates and eight of them passed them around from hand to hand. Short of producing the plates themselves, what better evidence could be had? By the same token, discrediting their testimony would strike a fatal blow. In the midst of the defections in the spring of 1838, when the failure of the Kirtland Safety Society had embittered many former Mormons, Stephen Burnett thought he found just such a flaw. Burnett wrote to a friend, Lyman Johnson, that Martin Harris admitted in a public meeting that he "never saw the plates with his natural eyes only in vision or imagination." Harris said he viewed the plates as a visionary sees "a city through a mountain." Burnett understood the words to mean that Harris saw the plates only in his imagination. The admission, Burnett thought, destroyed everything. If the witnesses never saw the plates, "there can be nothing brought to prove that any such thing ever existed." "The last pedestal gave way, in my view our foundations was sapped & the entire superstructure fell a heap of ruins."[13]

Martin Harris was among the defectors in 1837 and 1838; he turned on Joseph Smith for the same reasons as Burnett—the failed bank and a loss of confidence in Joseph Smith. But strangely, his statement about seeing the plates in a vision was not meant to undermine the Book of Mormon. Burnett also heard Harris say that "he was sorry for any man who rejected the Book of Mormon for he knew it was true."[14] Harris was actually warning his fellow apostates they would suffer if in rejecting Smith they relinquished faith in the book. Harris's visionary description of the plates was not intended to undermine their reality. He spoke of not seeing the plates "with his natural eyes only in vision," because he believed that was the only way a mortal could view heavenly things. Pomeroy Tucker, the Palmyra printer who later wrote a book on Mormonism, remembered Harris speaking "a good deal of his characteristic jargon about 'seeing with the spiritual eye.'"[15]

In Harris's world, the plates were enchanted. He said he was "told by Joseph Smith that God would strike him dead if he attempted to look at them." When Charles Anthon asked him to bring the plates to New York, Harris told him that the "human gaze was not to be permitted to rest on them."[16] Harris's thinking was based on Bible passages suggesting that human eyes could not look upon God without preparation.[17] He did not dare to look into Smith's seer stones "because Moses said that 'no man could see God and live.'" Though intensely curious, Harris had not snuck a peek of the plates while helping Smith translate. He feared that he, an unworthy mortal, would suffer if he did. When Joseph offered to show Harris the plates in return for his help, Harris refused "unless the Lord should do it." He told Burnett's audience that the three witnesses had seen the plates "only in vision" because that was the only safe way.[18] He had no intention of undermining the reality of the plates or questioning the Book of Mormon.

The Witnesses as Evidence

Harris's effort to explain himself to the defectors had little effect on either critics or converts. No one seemed to be paying attention. Eyewitness testimonies were not as influential in the life of the church as might be expected in a world so preoccupied with evidence. In conversion stories, the witnesses played a minor part. John Corrill's account of his 1831 acceptance of Mormonism tells of his methodical weighing of all the facts in a measured effort to determine its truth. In describing the Book of Mormon, he noted only that "eleven persons besides Smith bore positive testimony of its truth. After getting acquainted with them, I was unable to impeach their testimony." Corrill was much more detailed in his evaluation of scriptural support for Mormon claims. He enlarged on the biblical evidence of lost books, the Book of Jasher and the Book of Nathan the Prophet, as parallels to the Book of Mormon. He spent a few weeks reading the Book of Mormon, "comparing it with the scriptures, and in reflecting and conversing with others upon the subject." He cited over twenty scriptures and filled six pages with scriptural analysis but wrote only three sentences on the witnesses.[19]

Early on, attempts to preach to outsiders made little use of the witnesses. Lucy Mack Smith's 1831 letter to her brother and sister-in-law, Solomon and Esther Hayward Mack, mentioned that the Book of Mormon was "engraven upon plates which have the appearance of gold." The description drew upon language from the testimony of the eight witnesses, but Lucy never mentioned them in the letter. Instead, she justified a new book of scripture by paraphrasing Nephi's prophecy that said there were "more nations than one."[20]

Parley Pratt was similarly sparing. Both in the original 1837 edition of his widely used tract, A Voice of Warning, and in his autobiography, he briefly mentioned the witnesses and moved on without comment, while dwelling at length on scriptural allusions.[21]

Archeological evidence weighed more heavily than the witnesses. When Parley Pratt revised A Voice of Warning before his death in 1857, he made much of the evidence accumulated by believers in the supposed Israelite origins of Native Americans. Pratt inserted nine pages of reports of Hebrew themes in Native American culture and lengthy accounts of the vast ruins in North and Central America. He recounted the story of Joseph Merrick finding a black strap that contained parchment with Hebrew writing from Deuteronomy and Ezekiel between the layers of leather. This kind of archeological evidence impressed Pratt more than the witnesses' testimonies.[22]

In the decades after the move to Utah, Mormon interest in the witnesses as evidence increased some.[23] Their testimonies joined the scriptures, healing, and archeology as elements in the rational defense of Mormon belief. From the 1850s through the 1880s, when the last of the eleven witnesses died, publication of their testimonies became more frequent. Mormon travelers to the Midwest stopped over in Kirtland to see Martin Harris or paid a visit to David Whitmer in Richmond, Missouri. When the two obliged their callers by affirming once again that they had seen the plates, the visitors took notes and returned to report their experience in meetings and eventually in newspapers.

More than two dozen visitors came to see Martin Harris between 1852 and 1875, the year of his death, inquiring about his testimony.[24] After their encounters, they told friends, recounted the story in sacrament meetings, and published their accounts in the newspaper. In 1870, Edward Stevenson, who had encountered Harris while a missionary, raised funds to bring Harris to Utah. After his arrival, people immediately inquired about his belief and asked him to speak—at least once in the Salt Lake Tabernacle. In Smithfield and, later, Clarkston, Utah, where he settled, people would drop by to ask the familiar question: do you believe in the Book of Mormon? His stock answer was to say no, I don't believe, and after the surprise had settled in, affirm that he did not believe, he knew the book was true.[25]

As Harris grew older, people were eager to hear his story before he passed away. A young man named John Godfrey met two friends in the street who told him they were on their way to Harris's house to hear his testimony, and he joined them. Harris's daughter-in-law announced them by saying, "Grandpa, some of the brethren have come to hear you bear your testimony." Another visitor was surprised to find two others ahead of him when he called. Harris seemed to enjoy retelling the story. A newspaper reported that "the old gentleman evidently loves to relate the incidents with which he was personally connected, and he does it with wonderful enthusiasm."[26]

David Whitmer, who outlived Harris by thirteen years, said he had been interviewed by "thousands of people, . . . believers and unbelievers, . . . gentlemen and ladies of all degrees and from many nations, sometimes 15 or 20 in a day." The Mormons came not to be convinced but for confirmation. James Hart, who called on Whitmer in August 1883, introduced himself by saying, "although I had no doubt of the truth of his published statement and testimony in the Book of Mormon, I should be pleased to hear the testimony from his own lips."[27]

For all the curiosity and inquiries, however, the witnesses were never at the forefront of the case for Mormonism. Their testimonies helped answer the question: did the plates really exist? The witnesses were evidence that they were once in Joseph Smith's possession. But missionaries did not lead with accounts of the plates being shown to eleven mortal men. The Church did not systematically collect and publish the witnesses' testimonies. Harris and Whitmer were visited sporadically, but as curiosities as much as sources of faith.[28]

Moral Guardians

The rational critics of Mormonism never took the witnesses seriously either. They were dismissed as family members and close friends who stood to benefit from the success of the Book of Mormon. Critics saw the plates as a concoction of a frenzied mind rather than an artifact whose existence required scientific assessment. They did not even bother to dwell on the absence of the plates and the lack of evidence that they existed. The story was ridiculed but not taken seriously enough to refute. The early critics were more concerned with the character of Mormons and their place in the history of civilization than the reality of the gold plates.

A typical response of Smith's critics came in answer to a letter from the Reverend Ancil Beach, a Methodist minister in Indiana. Beach wrote to the postmaster in Canandaigua, a market town fourteen miles south of Palmyra, asking about the Mormons. Probably he had met Mormon missionaries or known of a small branch in nearby Winchester, Indiana, and wanted to learn more. While Beach's letter has been lost, a January 1832 response from six leading citizens, including two judges, a pastor, and the postmaster himself, has survived, and indicates that his inquiry was about "the Character of the individuals who have published the Book of Mormon and who call themselves Mormonites."[29] Beach thought people in Canandaigua would know something about the Smiths.

The reply to Beach echoed the stories that Philastus Hurlbut later recorded when he visited Palmyra a few years later. Joseph Smith was "an idle worthless fellow," often employed in digging for money who "pretended to have found a box, in digging in the woods, containing some gold plates with Characters upon them." One of his followers, Martin Harris, a "farmer of respectable property," was considered by some "a deluded man partially insane."[30] The plates were not worthy of refutation.

More remarkable than the report itself was the premise of Beach's inquiry. When he wrote, he knew no one in Canandaigua. His letter was addressed simply to the postmaster.[31] Beach assumed that someone in Canandaigua would offer assistance and that his respondents' judgments would be trustworthy. Although unknown to him personally, Beach assumed the existence of a network of willing and trustworthy persons, not just in Canandaigua but by implication everywhere in the country.

The assumption of a network was borne out by the response. A group of citizens took the trouble to collect information about the Mormons to inform a stranger hundreds of miles away. The motives were not commercial or political. They had no known ties to Beach. The only conceivable motive is offered in the letter itself: "As it may serve the cause of truth and guard against imposition we cheerfully afford you the information in our possession."

Without hesitation, the six citizens took it upon themselves to act as the moral guardians of their community. They assumed it was their duty to halt a threatening "imposition." They bravely claimed that Mormonism was fast fading in New York—"In this State the movers in this project can do no harm"—but their concerns went further. "We should hope that their imposition, so gross, would not succeed in any part of our land."[32] They considered themselves part of a national society of knowing men whose duty it was to stop nefarious schemes like the Golden Bible.

It is probably safe to say that public reports of Smith's religion were nearly always intended for an imagined audience of upright citizens who took responsibility for protecting their communities from threats like Joseph Smith's.[33] As guardians of society, they saw themselves as joining forces "to counteract the progress of so dangerous an enemy in their midst."[34] They felt that besides proposing an explanation of the gold plates, writers must pass judgment on the perpetrators of the scandalous fraud. Beginning with the first notice of the Golden Bible in June 1829, the word "imposition" was used more frequently than any other to characterize Mormonism. The 1828 edition of Noah Webster's dictionary defined the word as "deception; imposture." It implied a scoundrel devising schemes to fool people, usually for his own gain. The six Beach letter-writers spoke of "honest and ignorant men who were deluded by the falsehoods published by the authors of the plan."[35] Someone had to step in to defend the public.

The critiques of Mormonism written for this imagined community shared an understanding of history that magnified the dangers of the Smiths' scheme. The writers assumed that Mormonism preyed on an impoverished and ignorant lower class, maliciously exploiting their susceptibility. In the South Bainbridge area, Abram Benton, an early critic, reported that Mormons proselyted "weak and silly women, and still more silly men, whose minds are shrouded in a mist of ignorance which no ray can penetrate, and whose credulity the utmost absurdity cannot equal."[36] Most of the Golden Bible reports rested on this informal sociology of knowledge. A letter of Palmyra residents to the Painesville *Telegraph* in March 1831 claimed that no one in their area took an interest in "the 'gold bible' question" but "the dregs of community, and the most unlettered people that can be found any where." The writers estimated there were about twenty converts in Palmyra, "and but two or three of them own any property"; around Waterloo, there were about forty, "three or four being men of property." In the residents' minds, property affected belief. These propertyless men not only accepted the Golden Bible;

"the whole gang of these deluded mortals, except a few hypocrites, are profound believers in witchcraft, ghosts, goblins, &c."[37]

The problem that Joseph Smith's imposition presented was not trifling. Abner Cole argued that the susceptibility of Mormon converts was a tale as old as time. In his second "Gold Bible" essay in January 1831, he opened with a frightening sentence: "The page of history informs us, that from time immemorial, MAN has more or less been the dupe of superstitious error and imposition; so much so, that some writers in derision have called him 'a religious animal,' and it often happens that the more absurd the *dogma*, the more greedily will it be swallowed, and the more absurd or unnatural the *tenet*, the more eagerly will it be embraced."[38] The capitalization of "MAN" implied that Cole meant human nature. All people were naturally susceptible to "superstitious error and imposition." "The author of the *Koran*" provided a parallel case of "ignorance and impudence." The British prophetess Joanna Southcott showed that no society was immune. "If an imposture, like the one we have so briefly noticed, could spring up in the great metropolis of England, and spread over a consi[d]erable portion of that kingdom, it is not surprising that one equally absurd, should have its origin in this neighborhood." No degree of civilization could choke off superstition. How could it when "every impostor since the creation, has owed his success to the ignorance of the people, and the propensity inherent in their natures, to follow every thing absurd or ridiculous"?[39]

Making matters worse, the plates raised doubts about all religion. Was Christianity itself a superstition like Mormonism, though of a more moderate variety? Did Mormonism prove that people would believe anything under the heading of religion, Christianity included? The free-thinking *Working Man's Advocate* chastised Christian critics for condemning Mormon extravagances when Christian beliefs were no more rational.

> From the serious and earnest manner in which some of the papers speak of the new religionists, we are almost inclined to think that their editors are really alarmed for the safety of their own faith. Ridiculous as is the idea that the founders of this new religion discovered their Bible inscribed on sheets of gold, which vanished as soon as it was translated, it is not more ridiculous than the stories of the origin of some other books that are now reverenced as holy by large portions of this earth's inhabitants; nor more ridiculous than the idea of a Christian editor, in a Christian country, solemnly writing articles to prove the inauthenticity of the "Golden Bible."[40]

A few writers postulated that the Book of Mormon was an atheistic plot to discredit all religion by making claims so ridiculous that the preposterous nature of religion was made obvious to all.[41] "It must have been written by an atheist, to make an experiment upon the human understanding and credulity."[42]

Eber D. Howe

Eber D. Howe, a printer in Painesville, Ohio, near Mormon headquarters in Kirtland, dealt with these broader issues when he published *Mormonism Unvailed* in 1834. Thirty-six years old at the time, Howe may have been questioning the Christianity of his New England ancestors. In 1838, according to his *Autobiography*, he "resolved to investigate the whole question of the hereafter, if any. The result was, in the fewest words possible, I became a skeptic." He was rescued from his doubts only by his eventual embrace of what he termed "spiritual science."[43]

Howe wrote out of unnerving personal experience with Mormons. He was shocked when people of standing in Painesville and nearby Kirtland and Mentor succumbed to Mormonism: Edward Partridge, a prosperous Painesville hatter, and Sidney Rigdon, a notable preacher. Worst of all, Howe's own wife, Sophia Hull, and sister Harriet were baptized Mormons in the early 1830s. These were not the poor and ignorant of Abner Cole's imagination, whose social position made them vulnerable to superstition. Respectable people believed the Mormon story. Howe's task, as he saw it, was to make his case so overwhelming that no one in his right mind could find Mormonism credible. He aimed "to satisfy every rational person, whose mind has not already been prostrated by the machinations of the Impostors, that the Supreme Being has had as little agency in the prosperity of Mormonism, as in the grossest works of Satan."[44]

Convinced though he was of Mormonism's fallacies, Howe still felt he was fighting an uphill battle. "Of all the impositions which 'flesh is heir to,' none ought to be more abhorred or dreaded, than those which come in the garb of sanctity and religion: But that none are more ardently seized upon and cherished, by a certain portion of mankind, all history goes to substantiate." For this son of the Enlightenment, credulity was the equivalent of original sin, a fault ingrained in human nature with no grace to remedy it. Credulity stood to defeat every attempt to establish the empire of reason. Howe seemed to be saying Mormonism could never be vanquished. He accepted as a tragic fact that "there is no turning a fanatic from his folly—that the distemper is more incurable than the leprosy—that the more glaring the absurdity, the more determined the tenacity of its dupes—and the more apparent you can render the imposture, the stronger become its advocates." He knew he could not defeat Mormonism or recover souls already in its thrall. He thought it impossible to "break the spell which has already seized and taken possession of great numbers of people in our enlightened country." At best he could "raise a warning voice, to those who are yet liable, through a want of correct knowledge of the imposition, to be enclosed within its fetters."[45]

Running through Howe's introduction to *Mormonism Unvailed* was the bitterness of a believer in the Enlightenment who sadly knew its limits. It frustrated him that the promise of a reasoned society could not be fulfilled.[46] The gold plates revealed the flaws and contradictions in human nature. That Mormonism, this most bizarre and ridiculous of human inventions, swept reason aside was a frightful commentary on human intelligence. Many of the critics shared his lament. Within the scorn and outrage they directed at the Golden Bible can be heard the frustration and anger of thwarted idealists. Belief in the plates showed once again that love of the marvelous would never be quenched.

Henry Caswall

Howe bemoaned Mormonism as a symptom of humanity's chronic irrationality. Other critics, hoping to discredit Joseph Smith here and now, picked at flaws and exposed contradictions. In claiming so much, Smith exposed himself across a broad range of miraculous happenings, and if any could be shown to be false, his whole story was undermined. As Smith grew in power and fame in his last years, critics bore down on one claim that they thought made him vulnerable: his pretensions as a translator. One of the marvels of his story was the translation of an ancient text without benefit of learning. If Smith could be shown to have faked translation, all the other miraculous events would be thrown into question.

Henry Caswall was one of the first to try. He saw in Smith's tale "the iniquity of an imposture, which, under the name of religion, is spreading extensively in America and in Great Britain. Mormonism needs but to be seen in its true light to be hated." Caswall's aim was to expose Mormonism and awaken "indignation against a cruel delusion and a preposterous heresy."[47] Born into a prominent English clerical family, Caswall had migrated to Ohio in 1828 to study at newly founded Kenyon College in preparation for a career as an Anglican clergyman. After graduating in 1830 and being ordained as a deacon, he held various minor clerical positions in Kentucky and Ohio, for a time serving as professor of sacred literature at a theological seminary. In 1837, he was appointed pastor of an episcopal congregation in Madison, Ohio, with twenty-two congregants and no chapel. In 1841, he joined the faculty of Kemper College, six miles west of St. Louis, but when he arrived to take up his duties, no divinity students had enrolled. Discouraged, he returned to England where his fortunes improved. He became a vicar in 1848 and later in life received an honorary degree from Oxford.[48] In 1839, Caswall published *America, and the American Church*, designed as a handbook for young Anglican clergymen contemplating a move to the United States. Listing the many Christian denominations, he observed that America has not given birth to any entirely new sect, "with the exception of the ridiculous Mormonites," who "are the victims, and to a certain extent, the actors, of one of the grossest impostures ever palmed on the credulity of man."[49]

On the eve of his return to England, Caswall decided to try his hand at exposing the absurdities of Mormonism. On the docks in St. Louis, he came across a shipload of Mormon converts, some of them from Preston, England, and, moved by their pitiable condition, lit upon a plan to catch Smith in his lie. Caswall removed his clerical garb and provided himself with "an ancient Greek manuscript of the Psalter written upon parchment, and probably about six hundred years old."[50] He would entice Smith to pretend to translate the text and, when he had committed himself, reveal the parchment's true nature and the prophet's duplicity.

On April 15, 1842, Caswall embarked from St. Louis for Nauvoo and two days later arrived in a city that at the time was excited by two literary events. One was the recent publication of the Stephens and Catherwood volume on Central America. The explorers' evidence for the veracity of the Book of Mormon still thrilled Mormon congregations. Caswall heard a Mormon preacher in the grove near the temple site assert that "in America there were the ruins of vast cities, and wonderful edifices, which proved that great and civilized nations had existed on this continent."[51] The other literary happening was the publication of extracts from Smith's translation of the Book of Abraham, which he had acquired in 1835 as a relic from Egyptian mummies.

Two installments appeared in the *Times and Seasons* in March 1842, less than two months before Caswall landed.[52]

Caswall's account of his visit in *City of the Mormons* made only fleeting mention of the Book of Abraham translation, but whether he knew it or not, that event lay behind the Mormons' eagerness to have their prophet examine the psalter. When they first saw the parchment, the citizens were sure that it must be one of the lost books of the Bible and insisted that only their prophet could understand its value. They begged Caswall to stay until Joseph returned. While waiting, they showed Caswall the framed parchments found with the mummies. Later that same day, Caswall dropped his pretense, explaining that his manuscript was in Greek and anyone who knew the language could translate it, but the Mormons would hear none of it. Their prophet must see it. Some of them offered to purchase the psalter at a high price.[53] Nauvoo seemed to have been infected with translation fever, speculating that every old text might contain stories like those unfolded in the Egyptian scrolls.

Caswall caught Joseph Smith in a rushed moment. He tried to be polite to his well-educated guest but apparently had other things on his mind. Caswall complained that Smith would not look him in the eye.[54] Perhaps sensing his hurry and hoping to force the issue of translation, Caswall dropped his pretense before the Prophet himself. He told Smith outright that the parchment he brought was a Greek psalter, but Joseph said otherwise, according to Caswall, declaring it "a dictionary of Egyptian Hieroglyphics." In a later account, Caswall added more details of the Prophet's response: "Pointing to the capital letters at the commencement of each verse, he said, 'Them figures is Egyptian hieroglyphics, and them which follows is the interpretation of the hieroglyphics, written in the *reformed Egyptian* language.'" The combination of an Egyptian character followed by interpretation was a natural reading for Smith because it was reminiscent of the Egyptian Alphabet and Grammar that Smith and his friends had put together in 1835 when they first acquired the Egyptian scroll. The Grammar and Alphabet featured individual Egyptian hieroglyphs followed by an English interpretation. In 1842, Smith seemed to see the Greek psalter through the lens of his experience with Abraham. Smith offered to purchase the psalter, and when Caswall refused, others asked him to lend them the book. Hopes for a new translation were running high, and the citizenry, including Smith, saw Egyptian everywhere. But the translation of another scripture was not to be. Smith had run out of patience, and other matters pulled him away. Walking to the front of the store where they conversed, Caswall watched him drive off as fast as two horses could draw him.[55]

After Joseph Smith departed, Caswall debated the citizens about their prophet, but his plan to expose Smith did not work out as he hoped. When the visitor confronted Mormons with Smith's statement about the psalter being Egyptian when it was actually Greek, they replied it must have been a human error without wavering in their belief in Smith's gift.[56] Caswall's test of Smith's translating powers proved inconclusive. The Mormons were too entranced by the Book of Abraham as a divine translation to worry about the Greek psalter.

Kinderhook

In 1843, a year after Caswall's visit to Nauvoo, a small group of conspirators in nearby Pike County, Illinois, devised a scheme that much like Caswall's aimed to test Joseph Smith's powers. They produced a collection of apparently ancient characters that were taken to Joseph Smith to translate, and eventually were revealed to be a sham.[57] Three men fabricated six small, bell-shaped brass plates, used acid to burn characters onto the surfaces, buried the plates eight feet underground in a bluff near a place called Kinderhook, seventy miles south of Nauvoo, and then a few days later with a few other local citizens, dug and pretended to discover the plates. Within a few days, the plates were taken to Joseph Smith to translate just as Caswall had brought the Greek psalter to Nauvoo, and as before Smith made a stab, once again relating the characters to ancient Egyptian.[58]

In its May 1, 1843, issue, the *Times and Seasons* gave over two pages to the Kinderhook plates (see Figure 5.1). The editors immediately saw the parallel to the gold plates and tried to turn them into evidence. The Kinderhook story shows, the paper declared, "that there are more dreamers and money diggers, than Joseph Smith, in the world," concluding that "this circumstance will go a good way to prove the authenticity of the Book of Mormon."[59] It was said that a Mormon accompanying the diggers leapt for joy when the small plates came to light. Simply finding another set of engraved plates seemed to support Joseph Smith's story. The editors of the *Quincy Whig* who first broke the story had made the same leap from Kinderhook plates to gold plates, heading their report "Singular Discovery—Material for Another Mormon Book," recommending that the plates be taken to the Mormon prophet. "If Smith can

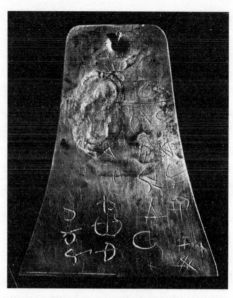

Figure 5.1. Photograph of the one surviving Kinderhook plate of the original six. They were found eight feet underground in Kinderhook, Illinois, in 1843. Courtesy of the Chicago History Museum.

decipher the hieroglyphics on the plates, he will do more towards throwing light on the early history of this continent, than any man now living."[60]

Coincidentally, nine years earlier Smith had been asked to interpret bones unearthed by his followers in the same county where Kinderhook was located. During the march of Zion's Camp from Kirtland to Missouri in June 1834, Camp members came across three stone altars on the bluffs overlooking the Illinois River on Pike County's eastern boundary. Digging down a foot or so, they found bones that Smith declared to be the remains of a famed Lamanite chieftain named Zelph who had once waged war in this region.[61] Kinderhook was located thirty miles to the west, on another set of bluffs overlooking the Mississippi. The plates, like the bones, came to Joseph Smith out of the ground, asking for an interpretation.

By the time the Kinderhook plates were discovered, the Mormons had reason to see them in a different light than that which illuminated Zelph's bones. Zelph came from the Book of Mormon world. The publication of the Book of Abraham in 1842 gave Mormons another history, the Egyptian culture of Abraham, to feed their imaginations. The past they thought of when they saw the Kinderhook plates was an amalgam of Abraham and the Book of Mormon. A few days after the *Times and Seasons* report, Parley Pratt wrote a friend that the newly discovered plates were "filled with engravings in Egyptian language and contain the genealogy of one of the ancient Jaredites back to Ham the son of Noah," mingling the Book of Abraham with the Book of Mormon.[62] Pratt probably got this reading from Joseph Smith, who, according to William Clayton, said the plates contained the "history of the person with whom they were found and he was a descendant of Ham through the loins of Pharoah king of Egypt."[63]

The historians Don Bradley and Mark Ashurst-McGee make the argument there was a direct tie between the Kinderhook plates and the Book of Abraham. One of the characters on the Kinderhook plates, they point out, bore a resemblance to a hieroglyph in the Egyptian Alphabet that Smith and his associates had compiled when translating the Book of Abraham.[64] A rough similarity to one of the Kinderhook characters was enough to identify the plates as Egyptian and provoke a speculative translation. The character according to the Egyptian Grammar meant of "the line of Pharoah," leading perhaps to "Ham through the loins of Pharoah" in the Kinderhook translation. A year after Caswall's visit, Smith was still preoccupied with Egypt. Reverting to the Egyptian Grammar, he mistakenly gave the Kinderhook plates an Egyptian reading much as he had Caswall's psalter.[65]

There was one significant difference between the Caswall and Kinderhook incidents. The Englishman immediately confronted Nauvoo Mormons with their prophet's error after Joseph mistakenly identified the Greek letters as Egyptian. Smith obviously had no translation gift, Caswall argued, if he could not differentiate the two languages. The more reticent Kinderhook conspirator did not reveal his forgery for thirty-six years. Not until 1879 did Wilburn Fugate announce that he had dreamed up the scheme with Robert Wiley and Bridge Whitton. Whitton cut the plates out of brass sheets, and the men engraved the characters in beeswax, filled the cuts with acid, and put the wax on the plates, etching the strange letters onto the metal. The three simulated ancient rust by covering the plates with nitric acid, iron, and lead. The night before the expedition, Wiley dug deep into the earth until he met a flat rock, under which he put the plates. The next morning nine citizens dug further. They overturned the flat rock and found bones, pottery, and the plates.[66]

Whatever the conspirators' purpose, Fugate's revelation of the scheme had little effect on Latter-day Saint belief. For a century after their appearance, Mormon scholars insisted on the authenticity of the Kinderhook plates. Not until one of the plates, which found its way to the Chicago Historical Society, was subjected to metallurgical analysis in 1980 and declared a nineteenth-century production did Mormon historians reluctantly admit they were forgeries.[67] The Kinderhook scheme had little bearing on Smith's claims to translate because the conspiracy was not revealed for so many years, but even the revelation of the plot failed to dent the Saints' belief. At the time, evidence based on the plates did not seem to weigh much in either direction. The Caswall and the Kinderhook incidents were more significant for revealing the Saints' enthusiasm for Smith's translations. The Book of Abraham prepared them for more discoveries. Hoping for another occasion for him to exercise his powers, they were disappointed but not disillusioned when he failed to bring forth another translation.

The Problem of Translation

Henry Caswall's Greek psalter and the Kinderhook conspirators' brass plates highlighted a problem with Smith's calling as a prophetic translator. After months of translating the gold plates, Smith came to the conclusion that his translations were not meant to end with the Book of Mormon, but what was he to translate?[68] An early revelation spoke of "records which contain much of my gospel, which have been kept back because of the wickedness of the people." Where was he to find those records? One of Smith's earliest revelations was a translation of a record written by John the Beloved which Joseph saw in revelation.[69] Were the texts to come by visions of parchments hanging in the air?

Initially, Smith had been unsure about the Book of Mormon plates. It took time to realize that he was to be their translator. Only gradually did he recognize that he was the one designated for that work.[70] In June 1830, three months after the Book of Mormon was published, he turned to another manuscript—the Bible—as a basis for translation. Smith treated the Bible as if it were incomplete or deficient, needing rewriting and expanding, He insisted on calling the revelation that became the Book of Moses a "translation of the Bible." For three years he worked through the Bible's pages, occasionally experiencing a burst of revelation, until the project ended around 1833. The resulting text was also labeled a "translation."[71]

Then in 1835, a new source of ancient writing arrived in Kirtland in the form of the Egyptian scrolls purchased from Michael Chandler. In this instance, Smith took them in his hands and knew in an instant that they were the writings of Abraham and the ancient Joseph, urging the Saints to buy them at considerable cost. The first recognition of their worth was followed by the arduous process of translation, which was not completed until 1842. Egyptologists later identified the scrolls as conventional burial documents having nothing to do with Abraham but that did not nullify the burst of inspiration when Joseph touched them—they had set off Joseph's exercise of his peculiar gift.[72] Smith may have had a similar burst of preliminary inspiration about the contents of the Book of Mormon when he first saw the plates in 1823. After his first visit to the hill, according to his mother, he gave his family descriptions of the ancient people who produced the record. A glimpse of the plates' import came suddenly at the beginning followed by a long process of translation.[73]

Judging from Joseph's responses to Caswall's psaltery and the Kinderhook plates, they dangled the hope of more translation. After seeing his work with the Abrahamic scrolls, Smith's followers were certain their prophet could recover the true meaning of Caswall's Greek letters and the Kinderhook inscriptions. Smith himself may have wondered if the psaltery and the plates contained scriptures like the Egyptian scrolls. The scrolls had fallen into his hands by chance; why not these two as well? A translator-prophet had to be alert for new texts. The psaltery might be an Egyptian alphabet like the one he and his comrades attempted to construct in 1835, and the Kinderhook plates were possibly a genealogy tracing the maker's ancestry back to Ham. Neither of these impulses was strong enough to warrant further pursuit, but they may have momentarily aroused a hope for more.

The encounters with Caswall's psalter and the Kinderhook plates were one kind of test for the conspirators. They wanted to prove Smith a pretender by showing he could not translate. They were another kind of test for Smith. He was searching for occasions to exercise his gift and had to be alert for moments when a burst of inspiration promised to release his powers. Both of these test cases came to naught. Hope for translating the psalter and the Kinderhook plates fizzled, and Smith made no further effort to pursue them.

James J. Strang

Two and a half years after the Kinderhook plates were uncovered, another set of plates appeared. On September 13, 1845, James J. Strang invited four of his followers to accompany him to a hill in Walworth County, Wisconsin, not far from the Illinois border, to dig for buried plates. A year earlier, Strang had proclaimed himself the successor to Joseph Smith, who had been killed in June 1844. In keeping with his new aspiration, Strang began exercising prophetic gifts. On September 1, 1845, an angel showed him "the plates of the sealed record" buried in an earthenware case under an oak tree on the hill and containing an account of an ancient people. Strang led the four men to an oak about a foot in diameter and then stepped back. The four dug through deeply rooted grass that showed no signs of having been disturbed and then through earth so hard it barely yielded to a pickaxe. About three feet down, they came to a flat stone, a foot square and three inches thick. Under the stone, they found a case made of "slightly baked clay" containing three plates of brass. Two of the plates had pictures on one side, one of a man with a crown and scepter and twelve large stars, and the other a "landscape view" of what the diggers took to be the nearby prairie. The reverse side of the two plates and both sides of the third were inscribed with characters of an unknown language.[74] (See Figure 5.2.)

Five days later, on September 18, 1845, Strang read a translation of the plates that he said he accomplished with the aid of a Urim and Thummim given to him by an angel. The words sounded like Moroni at the end of the Book of Mormon. "My people are no more. The mighty are fallen and the young slain in battle." Strang said the words had been engraved by "Rajah Manchou of Vorito," a name he seems to have modified to Voree as a name for the nearby countryside. A closing passage in the four-paragraph document seemed to foretell the Mormon situation after Joseph Smith's death. "The forerunner men shall kill, but a mighty Prophet there shall dwell. I will be his strength." His followers understood the fallen forerunner to be Joseph Smith and Strang the "mighty Prophet" whom the Lord would strengthen.[75]

The published account of the excavation was obviously shaped to verify Strang's claims to divine inspiration. The diggers took pains to highlight circumstances that foreclosed any possibility of his having planted the plates himself. "We examined as we dug all the way with the utmost care, and we say, with utmost confidence that no part of the earth through which we dug exhibited any sign or indication that it had been moved or disturbed at any time previous. The roots of the tree stuck down on every side very closely extending below the case and closely interwoven with roots from other trees. None of them had been broken or cut away." The four men were convinced by "every evidence that the sense can give" that the box had been in the ground

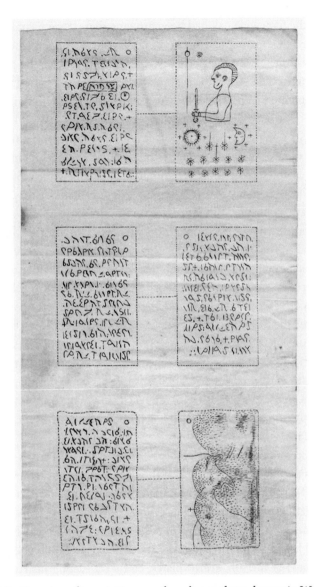

Figure 5.2. Drawing of inscriptions on three brass plates dug up in Walworth County, Wisconsin, on September 13, 1845, under the direction of James J. Strang and titled "The Record of Rajah Manchou of Vorito." Courtesy of John Hajicek, Independence, Missouri.

as long as the foot-wide oak had been growing there. Strang could not have manipulated the box because he "took no part in the digging, but kept entirely away from before the first blow was struck till after the plates were taken out of the case." Everything about the discovery supported their "faith in his statement as a Prophet of the Lord, that a record would thus and there be found."[76] The plates were the proof.

The use of a material event to corroborate Strang's inspiration suggests the avenues that Joseph Smith's plates opened to people searching for verification of divine intervention. Smith had created a new form of American prophethood. Like many others, it was apocalyptic, denunciatory, visionary, reformist, and ritualistic. But it was also evidentiary. He offered a new kind of device as a feature of his prophethood: a holy text inscribed on precious metal found in the earth. Smith's plates were fantastic and incredible; they were also material and sensory. Their very existence was evidence of supernatural forces at work. Strang's brass plates were a variant of Smith's. Not the plates themselves, but his vision of where they were buried was a miracle. He predicted the location of a box of plates that he could not have known by natural means or faked by burying the box himself. In both cases, the proof was sensory and earthy. The plates' story, both in its original form as told by Joseph Smith and in James Strang's derivative account, proved that angels and visions were real. Strang's biographer, Milo Quaife, suggests that "the finding of the Voree plates may well be viewed as the touchstone of Strang's prophetic career."[77]

The vision that preceded the plates' recovery followed Smith's script with scrupulous exactitude. "The Angel of the Lord came unto me James, on the first day of September, in the year eighteen hundred and forty five," he wrote of the revelation concerning the plates, "and the light shined about him above the brightness of the sun, and he showed unto me the plates of the sealed record and he gave into my hands the Urim and Thummim."[78] Light above the brightness of the sun, sealed plates, and a translating instrument were pure imitation. Strang was filling out a role, newly defined and made available to aspiring American prophets. By combining the material and the spiritual, Smith provided a template for prophethood in a skeptical time. Strang made the most of the combination. A revelation to his followers given in the voice of God admonished them to "serve and obey me and I will give unto him the plates of the ancient records which are sealed up, and he shall translate them unto you; and this shall be a witness between me and those that serve me faithfully."[79]

Strang's consuming desire was to assume Smith's authority over the Mormon people. His method was to assimilate Joseph's speech, methods, and voice. He spoke and wrote like the Prophet.[80] A number of people who knew and believed Joseph Smith found Strang to be convincing, including Joseph's mother, Lucy Smith, and his brother William. Virtually all of the two or three thousand believers who joined Strang in Wisconsin and on Beaver Island, Michigan, had once followed Joseph Smith. They saw Strang not as an innovator but an inheritor of the Mormonism that they had previously embraced.[81]

Strang did not disappoint them. To the end of his life, he read from Joseph Smith's script. A revelation to Strang instructed his followers who were building a house for him to "have a room for translations therein, for it is my will that thou translate ancient records, hiden truths, unto my people."[82] While receiving inspiration of many kinds, Strang's most striking revelation was the translation of another set of plates. In the Book of Mormon story, the migrating Lehi took brass plates of Laban with him containing the teachings of the Hebrew prophets. Strang said that he possessed those very plates and that they contained "The Book of the Law of the Lord," the name of a large ledger containing Joseph Smith's revelations and journal entries. A group of seven witnesses said Strang showed the plates to them. There were eighteen plates, nine inches long and seven and three-eighths inches wide. Echoing the testimony of the eight witnesses in the Book of Mormon, seven witnesses said they "examined them with our eyes, and handled them with our hands. The engravings are beautiful antique workmanship, bearing a striking resemblance to the ancient oriental languages."[83]

Using the Urim and Thummim, Strang translated the writing on the plates and published "The Book of the Law of the Lord" in a preliminary edition in 1851 and in a full edition beginning in 1856. The book presented itself as a systematic constitution for Israel written by Moses, kept in the Ark of the Covenant, and copied on to the plates of Laban. The forty-seven chapters of the text dealt with God, priesthood, sacraments, feasts, apparel, laws, marriage, all of it intended as a rulebook for organizing the Kingdom of God.[84] The Book of the Law of the Lord is unlike anything Joseph Smith wrote. It is more systematic, more legalistic, couched in the language of a law code rather than a prophecy, one of the few departures from his model's example.

Strang walked in Smith's footsteps to the end. Internal dissent troubled both prophets. Former Mormon leaders like William Smith and John C. Bennett stayed with Strang for a few months and departed. One of the first diggers, Aaron Smith, left Strang a year after uncovering the three brass plates.[85] Some grew restive with his control of dress, sexual relations, and alcohol consumption, harshly enforced on occasion by whippings. The Saints on Beaver Island also irked their neighbors. As the Saints' numbers increased, they dominated local elections. Strang was elected to the Michigan legislature. Using his political influence, he enforced unpopular measures. Many of the local settlers made their living by selling liquor to the Native Americans. Strang, who was attempting to preach to the Indians, objected and attempted to have the law against the liquor trade enforced. These resentful outsiders were complicit with disaffected followers in Strang's death. In 1856, two onetime followers shot him as he was about to board a steamer at Beaver Island.[86] It was a sad but suitable end for a man who wanted to be another Joseph Smith.

Despite Strang's charisma, his life as prophet did not bring him the triumphs he yearned for. His elaborate attempts to prove himself by way of two sets of plates did not validate his claims any more than the witnesses of Joseph Smith's plates decisively proved Mormonism. Caswall and the Kinderhook conspirators were no more successful. Their attempts at exposing Smith as a pretended translator got nowhere. The materiality of the plates seemed to offer a perfect opportunity for an objective test of Joseph Smith's claims, but the attempts at proving or disproving repeatedly fell short. In the Mormon case, evidentiary Christianity failed to fulfill its promise.

6

Fascination

Fiction, Lore, and Psychology, 1860–1910

Fayette Lapham

In the summer of 1830, a farmer named Fayette Lapham and his friend Jacob Ramsdell, curious about stories they had heard of ancient religious records, visited Joseph Smith Sr. at the Smiths' farm in Manchester, New York. Father Smith apparently gave the two men an account of his son's discovery of a seer stone, the visit of an angel, and the translation of the gold plates. Although intrigued, Lapham did not immediately tell the story in print; he waited forty years before publishing an account in the May 1870 issue of *The Historical Magazine*. By the time he wrote, attitudes toward the Mormon story were beginning to change. Had Lapham written his account immediately on returning home, he would likely have warned his readers against a dangerous imposture; in 1870, Lapham wrote to amuse.[1] He was one of a number of observers of Mormonism after mid-century who told the gold plates story to satisfy curiosity rather than arouse indignation.

Most early writers on Mormonism felt obliged to condemn the movement. An 1841 book titled *The Mormons, or, Knavery Exposed* said that "the exposure of the swindling transactions of the Mormons had the effect of banishing them from the borough of Frankford, where they had previously met with encouragement and favour. Were the same efforts made in every community where they attempt to practice their fraudulent and swindling hypocrisy, the same results must necessarily follow."[2] Abner Cole noted in his 1831 *Palmyra Reflector* essays that much of the writing on Mormonism "evinced a spirit of rancor," but he also linked Mormons to "the vulgar and ignorant from time immemorial" who were the dupes of "superstitious error and imposition."[3] The Painesville, Ohio, editor Eber D. Howe's aim in writing *Mormonism Unvailed* was to "raise a warning voice, to those who are yet liable, through a want of correct knowledge of the imposition, to be enclosed within its fetters."[4]

Lapham wrote from a different perspective. He made no effort to situate the plates in the history of religious frauds or to explain Mormonism's disreputable origins. He simply reported an interesting phenomenon. Lapham wrote about Joseph Sr.'s preoccupation with treasure-seeking lore without comment. Father Smith enlarged on the requirements for reception of the plates—the right kind of clothes, the company of the right person, a napkin to cover them—and the harassment of screeching devils meant to terrify his son. All this was recorded in cool, neutral language. In his very last sentence, Lapham did say that he and his friend "returned home, fully convinced that we had smelt a large mice," but that was all. That superfluous add-on aside, the essay was free of judgments about truth or propriety. Lapham recorded Joseph Sr.'s report of his son moving "a large boulder, of several tons weight" without comment. No questions were raised about the "set of gold plates" found in the hill.[5]

In the years when Lapham wrote, the supposed evils of Mormonism continued to be exposed in the anti-polygamy, anti-theocracy literature of the post-bellum era, but the outrage that motivated earlier writers was waning.[6] (See Figures 6.1 and 6.2.) *The Historical Magazine*, which published Lapham,

Figure 6.1. Frontispiece, E. D. Howe, *Mormonism Unvailed* (Painesville, Ohio: By the Author, 1834). Joseph Smith, holding either the gold plates or the Book of Mormon manuscript, receives a boot from a devil, making Smith his despised tool.

Figure 6.2. Frontispiece, Pomeroy Tucker, *Origin, Rise, and Progress of Mormonism. Biography of Its Founders and History of Its Church* (New York: D. Appleton, 1867). Pomeroy Tucker in 1867 was as hard on Joseph Smith as E. D. Howe in 1834, but the frontispiece showed a softening of attitudes. Rather than the tool of the devil, Smith appears as a radiant visionary recovering the plates under the watchful eye of a winged angel.

was one of hundreds of periodicals that published materials of general interest aimed at informing or amusing.[7] Lapham had no pretensions to discovering truth or situating the gold plates in the history of religious imposture; his report was purely personal. He and Ramsdell set out for Manchester merely to satisfy their curiosity.[8] In his essay, the gold plates passed out of the realm of fraud into the realm of fiction.

W. D. Purple

A few years later, a writer with the luscious name of W. D. Purple was also intrigued by what could be called the romance of the gold plates. Purple found the purported discovery of the plates a wonderfully amusing tale. A physician, he had lived in South Bainbridge, New York, in 1825 and 1826 when Joseph Smith came down from Manchester to work for Josiah Stowell, first as a treasure-seeker and then as a farm hand. Purple attended Joseph

Smith's 1826 trial on charges of glass-looking and may have contributed to the extensive notes on the trial. He later moved to Greene, New York, where he served as town clerk and postmaster. In May 1877, the *Chenango Union*, which served a number of small towns including Greene and nearby Afton (the more recent name for South Bainbridge), published Purple's reminiscence as "Joseph Smith, the Originator of Mormonism. Historical Reminiscences of the Town of Afton," based on his memories of the trial and his encounters with Smith and Stowell.[9]

In 1877, Afton was a tiny village buried in the back country of the upper Susquehanna Valley near New York's border with Pennsylvania. The May 3 issue in which Purple's reminiscence appeared offers a glimpse of life in Afton. As one piece of notable news, the paper reported that "another parcel of cheese sold at the Calvin Warner cheese factory last week at 14 cents per pound." More exciting was the report that "a dog kept by Walter Clark bit Marion Williams' little boy last week through the arm. We hear the arm is doing well." The piece added the editorial comment that "we hope Mr. Clark will dispose of his cross cur."

Small wonder that visiting lecturers were welcomed to Afton. As part of the "Smyrna Lecture Course," Thomas Randall had spoken the preceding Saturday on "Tramps," a talk judged the "most entertaining and instructive of any as yet." His efforts were appreciated. "Although the day was very rainy, and the roads very bad, yet the house was crowded to the utmost, and all were much interested, and listened attentively until the close of the lecture." Mr. Randall "brought out some splendid ideas, and favored more christian charity towards the tramp."[10]

Like that of the lecturer Thomas Randall, Purple's aim was to entertain and enlighten more than to warn or condemn. However he judged Joseph Smith at the 1826 trial, Purple saw his 1877 essay as a kind of literature, akin to the fiction of the innumerable "story-papers" and dime novels that were by this time selling millions of copies.[11] Only faint echoes of the disdain and anger of Howe and Cole were heard in Purple's prose. At the end of his essay, he spoke of "that prince of humbugs, Mormonism," but even those derogatory words lacked sting. A "prince of humbugs" was more clown than villain. Purple wrote with gentle sarcasm of "that wonder of the age, Mormonism," as if to invite his readers to look on with amusement rather than outrage. He introduced the topic by saying "we often saw in that quiet hamlet, Joseph Smith, Jr., the author of the Golden Bible." Smith was an inconspicuous figure in a bucolic scene, an "inmate of the family of Deacon Isaiah [Josiah] Stowell," not a threatening invader. Purple spoke slightingly of Stowell's fascination with hidden treasures, but lightened the picture by quoting from a popular lyric of the day, "*The Dying Words of Capt. Robert Kidd: A Noted Pirate, Who Was Hanged at Execution Dock, in England.*"

> *Ninety bars of gold*
> *And dollars many fold*[12]

Purple seemed determined to give a literary cast to the whole story. He observed that Stowell's fascination with treasure "adhered to him like the fabled shirt of Nessus," a reference to the shirt smeared with the toxic blood of the centaur Nessus that Heracles was tricked into wearing as revenge for a mortal wound he had inflicted. The diction was literary, with allusions to Greek myths and popular poetry. The holes the treasure-seekers dug were "nocturnal depredations on the face of Mother Earth."[13]

The heart of the story was Purple's account of Joseph Smith's testimony after his 1826 arrest as "a vagrant, without visible means of livelihood," which sustained the accusation that Smith practiced glass-looking, an illegal activity in New York. Here Purple's narrative slows down and the emotions intensify. Purple said the story of Smith's early life and discovery of his seer stones was so compelling, "I am tempted to give it somewhat *in extenso*." It began with Joseph learning of a girl who could look in a glass and see anything. Looking into her glass himself, he saw "a small stone, a great way off." The stone lay "under the roots of a tree or shrub as large as his arm, situated about a mile up a small stream that puts in on the South side of Lake Erie." He thought about the stone for several years until finally setting off to find it.[14]

Here Purple's story begins to sound like a fairy tale or a mythic account of a young man on a quest:

> He took a few shillings in money and some provisions with him. He stopped on the road with a farmer, and worked three days, and replenished his means of support. After traveling some one hundred and fifty miles he found himself at the mouth of the creek. He did not have the glass with him, but he knew its exact location. He borrowed an old ax and a hoe, and repaired to the tree. With some labor and exertion he found the stone, carried it to the creek, washed and wiped it dry, sat down on the bank, placed it in his hat, and discovered that time, place and distance were annihilated; that all intervening obstacles were removed, and that he possessed one of

the attributes of Deity, an All-Seeing Eye. He arose with a thankful heart, carried his tools to their owner, turned his feet towards the rising sun, and sought with weary limbs his long deserted home.[15]

It is hard to know what to do with such a narrative. In his trial testimony, did Joseph Smith tell the court about carrying the stone to the creek, washing it, and wiping it dry before sitting down to look? Such details are not in the extant court record, and we can't check Purple's narrative against other accounts because no one else told the story.[16] The literary allusions in the buildup to the account may forewarn us that Purple was digging into his imagination for some of the facts. Was he plying the storyteller's art as much as the historian's craft?

Near the end of his tale, Purple told of a treasure-seeking expedition that could serve as a narrative for John Quidor's 1832 painting *The Money Diggers*.[17] In Purple's account, Smith told Stowell of a box of treasure that robbers buried long ago and protected with a spell:

Digging was commenced with fear and trembling, in the presence of this imaginary charm. In a few feet from the surface the box of treasure was struck by the shovel, on which they redoubled their energies, but it gradually receded from their grasp. One of the men placed his hand upon the box, but it gradually sunk from his reach. After some five feet in depth had been attained without success, a council of war against this spirit of darkness was called.[18]

In this crisis, Smith devised a scheme:

Mr. Stowell went to his flock and selected a fine vigorous lamb, and resolved to sacrifice it to the demon spirit who guarded the coveted treasure. Shortly after the venerable Deacon might be seen on his knees at prayer near the pit, while Smith, with a lantern in one hand to dispel the midnight darkness, might be seen making a circuit around the pit, sprinkling the flowing blood from the lamb upon the ground, as a propitiation to the spirit that thwarted them.[19]

All this was attributed to the testimony of Jonathan Thompson at the 1826 trial. The court transcript has Thompson saying that on "account of an enchantment, the trunk kept settling away."[20] Nothing about a prayer near

the pit, or the lantern to dispel the midnight darkness, or sprinkling lamb's
blood in a circle. It is impossible to know what Purple heard in 1826 and what
he embellished fifty years later, but it is clear he was painting a scene. As he
wrote, "what a picture for the pencil of a Hogarth!" The money-digging venture was the work of people who "drew all their philosophy from the Arabian
nights and other kindred literature." Adding to the delight of his readers, the
story, worthy of the Arabian nights, had happened in their own town. "It was
declared under oath, in a Court of Justice, by one of the actors in the scene."[21]
Magic had once come to Afton.

Purple's stories enabled readers to toy with marvels, dabble in a world of
wonder, experience spells and seer stones, and still remain safely within the
regularities of ordinary life. Accounts like Purple's bring into view readers
tantalized by contacts with another world. In the very act of denying the
plates' existence, he kept them alive for his readers' pleasure.[22] At the end,
Purple reminded them that Mormonism was humbug, and then let them go
back to selling cheese and warding off cross curs.

Cave Lore

After mid-century, Latter-day Saints themselves heightened the romance of
the plates by adding details that had not appeared in earlier accounts. Instead
of downplaying the incredible, they embellished it. Beginning in 1855, accounts of a cave full of records began to appear. William Horne Dame wrote
on January 14, 1855, of a story told by W. W. Phelps about Joseph and Hyrum
Smith, Oliver Cowdery, and David Whitmer visiting the Hill Cumorah. "As
they were walking up the hill, a door opened and they walked into a room
about 16 ft square. In that room was an angel and a trunk. On that trunk lay
a book of Mormon & gold plates, Laban's sword, Aaron's brestplate."[23] All of
this was new to the historical record. None of the published accounts about
caring for the plates mentioned a hillside room where they were stored. The
cave story must have been circulating before 1855 for Phelps to mention it in
a meeting, but where it originated remains unknown.

The next year, Heber C. Kimball, then a member of the Church's First
Presidency, told a similar story in the tabernacle. Kimball spoke of "the vision
that Joseph and others had, when they went into a cave in the hill Cumorah,
and saw more records than ten men could carry. There were books piled up
on tables, book upon book."[24] These tales seem to have originated in stories

from Oliver Cowdery and David Whitmer, not from Joseph Smith himself. Their appearance suggests that after mid-century, the fabulous was becoming more appealing and the incredible less troublesome. Mormon storytellers felt safe to embellish the earlier accounts of the plates with fascinating details. It is possible that with the Utah Saints far removed from gentile society, tales that had remained private in Nauvoo and Kirtland came to the surface.

In roughly the same period, old-time residents of Palmyra were beginning to tell the same kind of story. Pomeroy Tucker, who was editing Palmyra's newspaper in 1830, commented in his 1867 book titled *Origin, Rise, and Progress of Mormonism* that "the work of translation this time had been done in the recess of a dark artificial cave, which Smith had caused to be dug in the east side of the forest-hill near his residence, now owned by Mr. Amos Miner. At least such was one account given out by the Mormon fraternity." Another version claimed that Smith translated "behind the curtain at his house, and only went into the cave to pay his spiritual devotions and seek the continued favor of Divine Wisdom. His stays in the cave varied from fifteen minutes to an hour or over—the entrance meanwhile being guarded by one or more of his disciples."[25]

Where and when Tucker heard these stories is unknown. He made no mention of the cave in an article he published in the (Lyons, NY) *Wayne Democratic Press* in 1858 titled "Mormonism and Joe Smith. The Book of Mormon or Golden Bible."[26] Cave stories may not have been circulating in Palmyra by then, but none of the affidavits collected by Philastus Hurlbut in 1833 mentioned a cave, nor, so far as I have been able to determine, did any other non-Mormon statements before Tucker's 1867 book.

By 1867, the cave not only merited inclusion in Tucker's work, it was mentioned in a Wayne County gazetteer. Hamilton Child, in a short summary of "the insidious monster, Mormonism," wrote that "Joseph Smith would repair at night to a cave in the hillside, and dictate to his amanuensis, (Oliver Cowdery) what he 'mysteriously translated from golden plates.'" From then on, a version of the cave story was standard in gazetteers, county histories, and newspaper articles on "Old Palmyra."[27] The cave apparently seeped into the memories of old-time residents who lived through the founding period. Between 1881 and 1887, William H. Kelley of the RLDS church and another researcher for an ephemeral publication called *Naked Truths about Mormonism* interviewed between them seven elderly citizens who each told a version of the cave story. Sometimes the cave was in Cumorah, sometimes in a hill two miles north called Miner's Hill after the owner of the property.

Sometimes translation went on in the cave, sometimes only meditation and revelation.[28] The cave became such a fixture that in 1893, a reporter from the *New York Herald* visited the cave on Miner's Hill with Orson Saunders. The reporter, speaking in the voice of Smith, later wrote that after the plates were obtained, "I carried them home and afterward hid them in a cave, where I began the first translation of the [i]nspired pages." By 1930 the cave had assumed the status of historical fact. In a 1930 history, *Palmyra and Vicinity*, by an old resident based on stories he was told, Thomas L. Cook said that Joseph dug a forty-foot-long cave, mounted a door at the entrance, and "just at twilight, for the next three months he visited the cave, always accompanied by two or more, but always entering the cave alone."[29]

There were actually more references to the cave among the reports of Palmyra old-timers in the years after 1855 than in Mormon sources, but the Mormon reports were much richer. The Palmyra reports emphasized the digging of the cave, the visits by Joseph Smith, the door, sometimes translation, and little more. The Mormon reports filled the cave with resplendent objects and significant events. Brigham Young had more to say than anyone about the cave's contents and purposes. A few months before his death in 1877, Young told a Farmington, Utah, congregation one Sunday that after translating the Book of Mormon, Joseph and Oliver took the plates back to Cumorah. As they approached, "the hill opened, and they walked into a cave, in which there was a large and spacious room." They laid the plates on a large table under which "was a pile of plates as much as two feet high, and there were altogether in this room more plates than probably many wagon loads; they were piled up in the corners and along the walls." The first time they visited the cave, the sword of Laban hung on the wall; "when they went again it had been taken down and laid upon the table across the gold plates." A few years earlier Young told the Saints in southern Utah that there was "great wealth in the room in sacred implements, vestments, arms, precious metals and precious stones, more than a six-mule team could draw."[30]

The stories were told with a purpose. The disposition of the plates after the completion of the translation had always been a puzzle. Elizabeth Kane, a friendly visitor to Utah in the 1870s, realized that she had embarrassed her Mormon hosts when she innocently asked where the plates were now. She "saw in a moment from the expression of the countenances around that I had blundered." The response from Brigham Young was that Cowdery had been to the cave with Smith and would not deny he had seen the plates. As if to drive home the point, Brigham Young then went into details about what

Smith and Cowdery saw on their third visit to the cave. "It was about fifteen feet high and round its sides were ranged boxes of treasure. In the centre was a large stone table empty before, but now piled with similar gold plates, some of which also lay scattered on the floor beneath."[31]

The little facts about the cave doubtless fed the Saints' taste for the fabulous, but the details also served to make the fabulous real. Young reported that as Oliver walked into the cave, "he did not think, at the time, whether they had the light of the sun or artificial light; but that it was just as light as day."[32] The source of the light remained a mystery, but Oliver's reflection that he had not noticed where light came from made his story credible. He was trying to figure out something he had actually seen. Measuring the number of plates in wagon loads sounded like the observation of someone who had been there. The same for the estimates of room size. Such observations would be natural for a person trying to evaluate a real memory. The details in cave lore made the plates palpable.

Lily Dougall

All through the last half of the nineteenth century, cave stories circulated among ordinary people in Utah and New York. Palmyrans passed along the lore as part of their local culture; Latter-day Saints retold tales heard from Brigham Young and Heber Kimball as bits of folk knowledge. Cave tales, in turn, were part of the larger collection of gold plates stories spread by writers like Lapham and Purple. They catered to a curious audienc rather than an indignant one. Theirs were minor voices scarcely heard in the roar of expos. és and condemnation voiced in the public sphere, but they were a beginning.

At the end of the nineteenth century, this informal, vernacular storytelling rose to a higher level. The Canadian-born writer Lily Dougall (1858–1923), an accomplished novelist, turned Joseph Smith's life into a substantial piece of fiction entitled *The Mormon Prophet* (1899). The work was important enough to justify a visit to Salt Lake City where she researched the Church archives and interviewed people who had personally known Joseph Smith. Her labors were well received. The reviewer for the magazine *Arena*, who spoke of Dougall's "well-deserved reputation" as a writer, said the novel "indicates steady increase of power."[33]

Dougall wrote at a propitious moment. In 1890, Church president Wilford Woodruff had declared an end to plural marriages, and in 1896 Utah was granted statehood. The barriers between this despised western religion and Christian America began to crumble. Freed of the burden of their offensive marriage practices and put on an equal footing with other states, Mormons had begun by 1899 to think of themselves as Americans. At the same time, on the other side of the divide, Americans began to think of Mormons as fellow citizens.[34] How was the nation to look upon this band of strange believers now that the barbaric polygamy saga was drawing to a close and Mormon theocracy was being dismantled? Could Mormons be embraced as fellow citizens? The January 1900 debate in the US House of Representatives over the seating of B. H. Roberts, the recently elected polygamist from Utah, epitomized the issue.[35] Were Mormons to be included in the national culture? The *Arena* reviewer noted that Dougall's novel was "made timely by the current discussion as to the seating of a newly-elected congressman from Utah."[36]

Dougall was one in a group of writers who addressed the Mormon problem at the end of the century. Among the others were two Yale graduates who published substantial histories in 1902 and 1903. William Alexander Linn came from a wealthy New Jersey family and graduated from Yale College before going on to a career in journalism and banking. In 1902, he published *The Story of the Mormons: From the Date of Their Origin to the Year 1901*, which received a sober and respectful review in *The American Journal of Sociology*. I. Woodbridge Riley wrote about Joseph Smith for his Yale PhD dissertation, published in 1903 as *The Founder of Mormonism*. Riley's Yale adviser George Ladd, a respected philosopher, wrote an introduction to the published version.[37] Two Yale graduates and a reputable novelist writing about Mormonism was attention at a level previously unknown. Not since the reform Baptist Alexander Campbell wrote an analysis of the Book of Mormon in 1832 had people of this standing examined Mormon history and beliefs.[38]

William Linn's book was the least original of the three. Linn summarized current knowledge without advancing anything new about the origins of the Book of Mormon or the nature of Mormonism. He adhered to the standard Spaulding theory about the book's origins. It was obvious, Linn thought, "some directing mind," other than Smith's "gave the final shape to the scheme." The mastermind behind the text and the Golden Bible hoax must have been Sidney Rigdon building on the romance by Solomon Spalding. Unlike Linn, Riley and Dougall found the Spalding hypothesis unconvincing.[39] Riley spent over twenty-five pages minutely analyzing the "Spaulding-Rigdon

Theory." He went through the hypothesis point by point, noting the lack of evidence and concluding that "these marks of the book are not the marks of the man Rigdon." Dougall dismissed the theory summarily, observing "that it [Book of Mormon] was an original production seems probable."[40]

The abandonment of the Spaulding-Rigdon hypothesis by two serious writers turned Mormon studies in a new direction. If Rigdon was not the mastermind behind the Book of Mormon, Joseph Smith must have been, and how could that be explained? How did this unprepossessing treasure-seeker compose such a complex text? That question compelled observers to speculate about Joseph Smith's mentality and temperament. What were the psychic sources of his visions and revelations? Abner Cole and Eber D. Howe, the first of the serious critics, saw no need to investigate Smith's mentality. They borrowed motives and mentality from historical stereotypes. Smith was an impostor and confidence man like other charlatans who troubled human society. With Rigdon gone and Smith the author of Mormonism, Dougall and Riley needed a more encompassing explanation. Both asked what light the newly emerging science of psychology might throw on visions and revelations.[41]

Although addressing the same question, the two took different approaches. Riley claimed that Smith obviously suffered from epilepsy. His description of the First Vision with its darkness and his inability to speak, followed by a bright light and then release could not have been clearer. Riley traced the inclination to mental disturbances back through the family line, finding that the Smiths had been mentally impaired for generations. Although cognizant of developments in psychological science, Lily Dougall took a more humanistic approach. She talked to William James about Smith's visions not long before James's Gifford Lectures at the University of Edinburgh, which became *The Varieties of Religious Experience*.[42] Dougall blended art with science, aiming to imagine Smith's psychology artistically rather than scientifically.

Dougall also wrote from a theological position. She spent her life breaking free from the strictures of her evangelical Christian father's hard-edge Christianity. She gravitated toward modernist doubts about miracles and to broad church toleration of a wide range of Christian beliefs.[43] She wanted to respect Mormons, even while distancing herself from their irrational belief in miracles and revelations. She was aware of the polemical, moralist tradition that preceded her. In her candid introduction, she acknowledged that "it has been earnestly suggested to me that to write on so false a religion in other than a polemic spirit would tend to the undermining of civilised life."[44] She was determined to find more in Mormonism than polygamy and to establish grounds for toleration and empathy.

Dougall allowed her beautiful young heroine, Susannah, to accept Mormonism of her own free will. The darling daughter of a stern Calvinist mother and a "reckless young Englishman of gentle blood," Susannah left Kingston, Canada, after her parents' deaths to live with her aunt and uncle Croom in Manchester, New York, the town where in the story Joseph and Emma Smith resided in 1830. The Crooms scorned Joseph Smith. Susannah's aunt Martha considered him "a blasphemous wretch," but Susannah came to feel differently when by chance she strolled by the Smiths' cabin and met Emma and Joseph. Susannah took kindly to Smith when the young prophet walked her part way home under an umbrella to shield her from a summer storm. On first meeting, Susannah told Joseph that she did not believe he saw angels or had gold plates, yet within a few weeks she was baptized.[45]

Dougall makes the leap by playing up Susannah's stereotypical female qualities: innate spirituality, empathy, and kindness. She is attracted by Joseph's gentleness and his boyish candor about his unworthiness. When he prophesies her future, Susannah listens. To this warm-hearted empathy, innate in her heroine, Dougall adds psychological insights about visionary mentality. By chance, Susannah stumbles on Joseph lying in a hollow at the Hill Cumorah, his face buried in a hat. He shows her "a curious stone composed of bright crystals, in shape not unlike a child's foot" and explains what happens when he looks.[46]

> All I know is that when I've been lying for a long time, feeling that I'm a poor fellow and haven't got no sense anyway, and the tears come to my eyes and gush out, feeling I'm so poor and mean, then when I lie and look and look into this peepstone, I see things in it, pictures of things that is to be, and sometimes of things that are just happening alongside of me that I didn't know any other way. I can't say how it may be; I only know when I see it that I am "accounted worthy."[47]

Still skeptical, Susannah asks Joseph what he sees. He replies that he has seen her standing in a room with another man. He holds up the stone and "Susannah stared at it to prove to herself that there was nothing remarkable about it." But as she looked, "the feeling of opposition seemed to die of it-self." In the following days, "phrases and sentences from the prophecy which Joseph Smith had pronounced clung to her mind." "She tried to tell herself that the man was mad; in childlike wonder she considered what might be the mystery of the vision within the stone and the prophecy if he were not mad." Having let the reader follow Susannah this deep into the vortex of Joseph Smith's mind, Dougall quickly adds that Susannah had never heard of "mental automatism" or "hypnotic suggestion," references to current scientific labels for psychological phenomena.[48]

Susannah is baptized under the impressions that Joseph and a young Quaker named Angel Halsey made on her soft, womanly heart. She is affected by Angel's simple, pure piety and his love and belief in her. He is convinced that she is destined to believe, and Joseph Smith goes further to say she is to marry Angel. Sensing that there may be truth in these prophecies, and fearing to resist God, Susannah, almost in a trance, slips into the water and is baptized. Later under the same spell she marries Angel. Her own kindness, her susceptibility to feelings, and her sympathy for the badly abused Mormons betray her. She is unable to resist.[49]

But within a few weeks her attitude and her character are transformed. The turning point comes when Angel rapturously reports the healing of Newel Knight. Afflicted with demonic possession, Angel reports, Knight was elevated from his bed after the demon is driven out and floats in the air. The report is too much for Susannah. The claim of elevation had to be a lie. Dismayed, she is transformed. From then on, she looks at every miracle, every revelatory outburst with skepticism. Susannah, now a drab but still beautiful follower, moves with the Saints to each new home. She now sees that the poor Saints have been misled. From her role as the spiritually impressionable young woman, she becomes the voice of reason, common sense, and reality. She interrogates Joseph Smith about his extravagant claims, causing him to back down and reconsider his own experience. After Angel is murdered at Haun's Mill, Joseph seeks her out and hints he would like to marry her. He seems to need her as a mother or a wife. He trusts her insight into his soul. Her conversion and life among the Mormons allows her to refute and correct Smith in the very act of mothering him. Eventually Susannah works her way free of the Mormons and returns to Manchester and her cousin Ephraim's love.[50]

Dougall stands at a turning point in investigations of Smith and his plates. She does not seek to expose or condemn Mormons, the aim of Cole and Howe, and she goes beyond Lapham's and Purple's simple wish to tell an amusing tale. Her aim is understanding and sympathy. She appreciates Joseph's gifts, even if in the end he is deeply misled. She imagines a Joseph Smith flooded with words whose origins he could not imagine, pouring into his mind from a source he could not resist. "His only choice lay between counting himself the sport of devils or the agent of Heaven; an optimistic temperament cast the die." Dougall knew enough about automatic writing to invoke the label but her greater achievement was to imagine the revelatory process empathetically.[51]

The Mormon Prophet was not widely read or cited. It was not an influential book. But it foreshadowed trends in twentieth-century studies of early Mormonism more accurately than Riley's *Founder of Mormonism*. Riley's epilepsy diagnosis appealed in a time when physiological psychology seemed like a promising path for psychic research, but its range was limited.[52] Epilepsy was of no help in understanding the gold plates. Riley had nothing to say about how the plates figured in Smith's psychic economy. The epilepsy diagnosis, moreover, was tied to fashions in psychological research. At the time, epilepsy was also offered as an explanation of St. Paul's Damascus vision too. As early ambitions for a broad application of the syndrome lost traction, their usefulness in understanding Joseph Smith faded as well.[53]

Dougall's imagination fared better. Her confidence in her ability to imagine the mentality of a prophet allowed her to account for the gold plates. Susannah bluntly tells Joseph that "it is very hard for me to believe, for instance, about the gold plates. How could they appear only to you and vanish again?" Dougall's Joseph explains them simply as a fact of his experience. "I'll tell you just how it was, even though it's not just the way other folks has got hold of it."

> The night that the angel came down three times and stood at the foot of my bed, and told me to go and get the plates and where they were to be found, my brain just seemed to go on fire. I could see things I never saw any other time. Why, that night I saw through the wooden wall and into the next room, just as if there hadn't been any boards there, and I saw all the air about me full of motes, just as they are in that sunbeam, and it was dark to other people. . . . I ran up the hill and worked into the hole, and there I saw the plates, just as the angel had said. I'll never forget to my dying day just what they looked like, and the sort of writing they had. I took them up and covered them up as the angel had said, and I carried them home and hid them, and told my folks. . . . When I looked again at the plates they just looked like bricks, but the angel told me that they were really the gold plates with the writing I remembered on them, but were changed lest any one should see them and die.[54]

By way of her empathetic imagination, Dougall turned bricks into gold plates.

The imaginative reconstruction of Smith's mentality proved to be more useful to writers in the next century than Riley's physiological psychology. Vardis Fisher, an Idaho writer from a Mormon background, followed Dougall in trying to reconstruct the First Vision. His 1939 novel, *Children of God*, won the Harper Prize and warm reviews when it came out. Carl Van Doren, the American literary critic, called it "a vast, brilliant, rowdy, understanding novel which ought to go fast and far."[55] In Fisher's pages, Joseph Smith is a sincere farmer with mystical tendencies who sees a vision of the Father and the Son. "They walked down the beam as down a highway of light." Later a conviction grows in Smith that God will tell him the origin of the Indians and "he must write a book." "To his happy amazement, a voice declares that the Indians are from the Twelve Tribes of Israel and had left upon golden plates a record of their past." The next morning, after dreaming in the warm sun for two hours, Joseph drifts away from his body to the Hill Cumorah. "Whereupon, quite out of himself in the transporting intensity of the vision, he went in a pilgrimage as swift as light to the hill and lifted the plates out of their ancient stone box." Returning to his body, Joseph resolves to "translate the everlasting gospel, as well as the records of the lost tribes" in fulfillment of the angel's promise that "the secrets of the golden history would be given to him."[56]

Fisher and Dougall did their best to imagine what it meant subjectively to see God and write the Book of Mormon. The natural tendency of story-telling was to present an empathetic account, allowing the lead characters at least a measure of sincerity. To imagine them as duplicitous from the start would reduce interest in their fate and cast a long shadow over the rest of the story. Fisher balked, however, when it came to the plates. It was one thing to imagine a vision of God or even an aspiration to write the history of the Indians. It was another to pretend to poessess golden plates. After Joseph tells his family about his vision of the plates, Fisher has Joseph's father express belief in their reality, warning Joseph to take care that the records not be stolen. At this point, Joseph must decide to go along with his father's naive faith or tell him that they were not a material reality, that he "would visit the records only in a vision." At the crucial moment, Joseph "let the opportunity pass" to tell the truth. He implicitly confirmed his followers' belief that "he would visit a hill and open a vault and look with mortal eyes upon plates of gold." Rationalizing the deceit to himself, Fisher's Joseph reflects that "perhaps, indeed, the plates *were* real; for in this, as in many other matters, he was still uncertain."[57]

Dougall likewise begins with a Smith who believes in his own plates but at the end has him confess his doubts. After one of her appeals for him to listen to reason, Joseph confesses to Susannah that he may not have seen the gold plates at all; they were just bricks. "As to them plates, I told you before I didn't have them as much in my hands as I said I did. I got wrong a bit there too."[58] As from the beginning, the plates were the hinge between two understandings of Joseph Smith, sincere visionary or deceitful fraud.

These writers were a few scattered voices in the cacophony of nineteenth-century writing on Mormonism.[59] At first, they were chiefly significant for suspending judgment, appealing to readers who were more curious than outraged; the "impostor" label disappeared from their pages. As time went on, mere curiosity became an urge to understand. No more a believer than Cole or Howe, Dougall took on the task of making visions comprehensible. Desiring to re-create the prophet as a believable and tolerable human type, Dougall went further than any previous commentator in making Smith accessible to broad-minded readers, even though in the end, the plates remained an illusion.

7

Art: 1833–2023

Poetry

W. W. Phelps, the loquacious newspaper editor and friend of Joseph Smith, was the first poet I am aware of to write about the Book of Mormon and the plates. Phelps's 1833 poem "An Angel Came Down" summed up what the Saints thought about the Book of Mormon in the first generation:

> An angel came down from the mansions of glory,
> And told that a record was hid in Cumorah,
> Containing the fulness of Jesus's gospel;
> And also the cov'nant to gather his people.[1]

Like all art about the Book of Mormon, Phelps's poem abbreviated a complicated story. Of all that might have been said about it, Phelps focused on the angel, the record at Cumorah, the pure gospel, and the gathering. In 1833 that was what the Saints were about: the record from Cumorah linked to the gathering of Israel. Those themes came out of Joseph Smith's revelations, but resonated with the rampant millennialism in Smith's America.[2] Smith's revelations took hold partly because millennial themes were so deeply engrained in the society around him. Phelps saw the record "hid in Cumorah" as part of this great cause.

> O Israel! O Israel!
> In all your abidings,
> Prepare for your Lord
> When you hear these glad tidings.[3]

The cultural environment has always influenced Book of Mormon art. The elements that went into a poem or a painting depended on the revelations but also on what seemed relevant at the time. From Phelps's early verses to this day, painters and poets have sought to understand the plates in terms of their own cultures, which meant that the depictions of gold plates were constantly shifting.

In the first decades, the history of the indigenous people was one of the relevant themes. The Book of Mormon appeared at a moment in the nineteenth century when interest in the origins of Native Americans was peaking in the United States.[4] No longer a threat in the Northeast (though fighting for their lives in other parts of the country), Indians became an object of curiosity and melancholic reflection.[5] Contemplation of their demise threw poets into contemplative reverie that the literary scholar Edward Whitley terms elegiac. "The elegiac mode in *Book of Mormon* poetry," Whitley explains, "traces its origins to the late eighteenth-century and early nineteenth-century Indian elegies by white poets who lament the demise of indigenous cultures while gazing longingly at the silent ruins of once-great civilizations."[6] William Cullen Bryant subscribed to the idea that American Indians of his time had destroyed a previous civilization of mound-builders in the Ohio River Valley.[7] In his 1832–1834 poem "The Prairies," Bryant meditated on the passing of these people.

> Are they here—
> The dead of other days!—and did the dust
> Of these fair solitudes once stir with life
> And burn with passion? Let the mighty mounds
> That overlook the rivers, or that rise
> In the dim forest crowded with old oaks,
> Answer.

Bryant imagines life among these people, but he is frustrated by their silence. They do not answer; he can only imagine their lives.[8]

Whitley points out that Bryant's perspective on the lost Indian civilization colored Mormon poetry about the Book of Mormon.[9] Mormon poets had more reason than most to reflect on the fate of the native peoples, and when they did, they often picked up on Bryant's melancholy. They could not, however, sustain his sadness when they knew of the "truth that's speaking from Cumorah's ground."[10] A hymn published in a Latter-day Saint hymnal in Manchester, England, and later attributed to Parley Pratt, mourned the Nephites as "nations long since dead, / who once had dwelt alone," but now there was cause to rejoice: the ancient people have spoken again.

> An Angel from on high,
> The long, long silence broke—
> Descending from the sky,
> These gracious words he spoke:
> Lo! in Cumorah's lonely hill
> A sacred record lies concealed.[11]

The gold plates broke the frustrating silence bemoaned by Bryant. As a voice from the dust, they answered his call, and "the long, long silence broke."

That mode of storytelling was not to last. Over the course of the century, the joyful news refrain faded in Book of Mormon poetry just as the longing for an answer from the dead diminished in American poetry. At the end of the century, a more somber variant took their places. The words about a nation long since dead in "An Angel from on High" foreshadowed a theme in poetry and drama that rose to a crescendo in the mid-twentieth century. Mormon poets came to dwell on the tragic fall of a civilization. Poetry in the William Cullen Bryant vein reflected on the disappearance of a people; poetry on the fall of civilization enlarged the scale to the destruction of a nation. Both reflected on loss, but the earlier poetry was elegiac; it mourned the disappearance of lovers in the woods and of workers of the soil. The later poems were epic; they addressed the downfall of a civilization. One was filled with pity and melancholy, the other with awe and horror.

The epic theme in human history is exemplified in a series of paintings from Joseph Smith's time by Thomas Cole under the title *The Course of Empire* (1833–1836). In five paintings, Cole traced the course of human civilization from primitive simplicity to imperial grandeur and finally to moral decay and destruction. The fourth painting depicted a glorious but corrupt city undergoing an onslaught from barbaric forces. The series was based on the premise that the histories of civilizations followed a pattern. As Cole wrote to his patron Luman Reed, "The philosophy of my subject is drawn from the history of the past, wherein we see how nations have risen from the Savage state to that of Power & Glory & then fallen & become extinct."[12] Fascination with rise and fall of empires permeated Western thought from the publication of Edward Gibbon's six-volume *The History of the Decline and Fall of the Roman Empire* (1776–1788) down through Arnold J. Toynbee's twelve-volume *A Study of History* (1934–1961), which traced the course of nineteen civilizations through the early stages of genesis and growth to turbulence and disintegration. These theories of growth and decline were particularly relevant in the new United States because of the common fear that democracies would in time fall into chaos and yield to a tyrant to re-establish order.

This frame of mind underlay Book of Mormon poetry from the late nineteenth century on. It led to a somewhat morbid interest in the last gasps of a dying civilization. One of Parley Pratt's poems hinted at the epic demise of the Nephites when their mighty army was reduced to twenty-four soldiers:

> O who that has search'd in the records of old,
> And read the last scenes of distress;
> Four and twenty were left who with Mormon beheld,
> While their nation lay mouldering to dust.[13]

Only a minor theme in Pratt's time, the fall of civilization became a constant refrain at the end of the century. Edward Stevenson's 1893 account of a visit to the Hill Cumorah used epic language that foreshadowed what was to come. Stevenson had toured Cumorah in 1871 as part of his effort to recover memories of the early days of the Church. Recalling his visit set off a meditation about Cumorah's place in history. What he chose to remember in 1893 were the final battles:

The great and mighty nation of the Jaredites, having departed from God and shed the blood of the prophets, became divided into bloodthirsty factions, who waged relentless and merciless wars against each other for many years; finally, after millions were slain, they arrayed themselves into two mighty opposing armies and mutually agreed to give each other four years in which to gather their entire forces of men, women and children around Ramah, and there make one last appalling death struggle for victory, but so well were these colossal armies matched in numbers, valor, fury and hatred that they continued to fight day after day till both sides were completely destroyed from the face of the land.

To add to the horror, not one nation but two bled to death at Cumorah:

The Lord again peopled the land and they too became haughty and lifted up in the pride of their hearts, renounced God and slew his prophets, and division, war and bloodshed again filled the land with horror. Once more were immense hosts arrayed into two great armies, the one called the Nephites, the other the Lamanites, and strange to say they also marshalled their forces, and undertook to make one last death struggle for victory or death. The battle ceased when the Nephites were destroyed, and again millions lay dead upon the fatal ground.[14]

Stevenson dwelt on themes that were to recur in poetry and drama for the next half century: bloodshed, the deaths of millions, and the tragic destruction of whole nations. In this scenario, the gold plates became a record of the final collapse and a warning to all future nations to beware.

Through the twentieth century, the mood captured in Stevenson's account spread widely among Mormon artists and poets. Just prior to 1893 when *Reminiscences* was published, Alfred Lambourne painted a Cumorah to match Stevenson's prose. Lambourne was an English-born convert who migrated to Utah and made his living as a landscape painter and writer.[15] His Cumorah depicted the hill as a great mountain, silhouetted against a burst of light on one side and a dark, stormy, lightning-riven sky on the other, much in the style of Frederic Church's paintings of sublime and terrible mountains. When the pianist Reid Nibley was later asked to compose music in response to a painting, he chose Lambourne's Cumorah. The painting, Nibley explained, "gives me pretty much the same feeling as my piano piece—tempestuous movement, harmonic colors shifting from dark to light and sudden changes in dynamics. There are unlimited possibilities for a story to go with the painting and music but the very name 'Cumorah' opens our imagination to the incredible events that occurred there."[16]

At mid-century, Nibley's and Stevenson's feeling about events at Cumorah came to full flower. The mood was dramatic, titanic, Wagnerian. The music chosen for the early performances of the pageant at Cumorah in the 1940s included Wagner's opening storm music to *Die Walküre* and the fourth movement of Tchaikovsky's *Pathétique* Symphony.[17] This mood had been building in Book of Mormon poetry since the beginning of the century. Poets dwelt on the violence, the struggle, and the epic passing of a nation. In 1909, Theodore Curtis in a poem titled "Cumorah" called the hill "tombstone of their nations gone!" He saw it as the burial site of a people "to prophetic ruin hurled . . . with their prehistoric story/written on your heart of gold." In 1915, J. M. White wrote a poem called "Hill Cumorah":

Fierce raged the fight; a wild, barbarian horde,
Thirsting for blood, surged like a stormy sea,
Around a little band, wielding the spear and sword,
Seeking to live and evermore be free,
Fast fell they there, as grass before the blade,
Until but one remained, who then in deep despair,
By night, in secret there, the tribal records laid,
Then died alone, last of his nation there.[18]

The plates were the one redeeming hope in the terrible history of two collapsing nations.

The high drama of epic history inspired Latter-day Saint poets throughout the twentieth century. Whitley writes that in "the eight book-length epic poems written about *The Book of Mormon* between 1904 and 1996, the overwhelming focus is on the triumphant rise of the Nephite civilization in 600 BCE and its devastating fall in 400 CE; the prophets and warriors who occupy the other 800 years (and 350 pages) of *Book of Mormon* history go largely overlooked."[19] This focus began with Lula Greene Richards's *Branches That Run over the Wall: A Book of Mormon Poems and Other Writings*, and continued to Michael R. Collings's *The Nephiad: An Epic Poem in Twelve Books*. All eyes were turned on the climactic downfall of the two civilizations.[20]

Clinton F. Larson, the most acclaimed Latter-day Saint poet at mid-century, gave the theme classic form in *Coriantumr and Moroni: Two Plays*. The extinction of the Jaredites dramatized in the Coriantumr half of the play stressed the brutality of the end scenes, the blood, the wounds, the degradation of love into crude animal lust. Sarah, the wife of Coriantumr, laments that where there were once cities and government, "there is nothing but the shadows of wings flickering through the ruins of our past." Ether, the keeper of the plates, moves in and out of the picture as the one moderating presence. Both parties value him and want him to record their battles as if acting on a stage. Sarah has heard of the "ancient men who kept those records you keep, and they never gave them up until they were sure that the memory of our people would endure." While battling to destroy each other, the hopeless warriors want to be remembered.[21]

The downfall of Nephite civilization in part two of Larson's drama poses the conflict in different terms. Mormon and Moroni partake of the high culture exemplified in their grand city Sherrizah with its great tower and in the ethereal Ruth, Moroni's betrothed. Both city and woman are refined and lustrous.

The plates that figure centrally in the Moroni half of the drama serve to refine the feelings of those who prize them; in fact, the plates become the deterrent of war. The plot of this second half turns on Mormon's waning taste for battle. He wants to preach to the Lamanites, not slaughter them, so much so that Moroni and the other military officials fear that Mormon is weakening. One comrade demands "where are these artifacts—these plates—that make you less a warrior than you were an hour ago?" Mormon replies: "I cannot tell you why, but they rest next to my conscience." In his devotion to the plates, Mormon stands alone. The generals are scornful of Isaiah. "Isaiah!" exclaims one, "the name trips like a mystic guess, unreal as moonlight winking out." Moroni shares the skepticism and speaks sarcastically of the plates' miraculous claims to have survived a thousand years.[22]

Mormon exercises enough influence to persuade the other officials to go with him to Cumorah to bury the plates and secure their safety. They seal most of the records in a cave. One small set remains outside, which for Moroni is a nuisance he would rather be rid of. Still he cannot escape his responsibility to guard the plates, and as his father knows his destiny is irresistible. Mormon tells an official to inform the Nephite remnant that "Moroni is the guardian; the records are safe, for now in his dream of faith the great fire breaks over him and in our sepulchre he keeps Sherrizah on plates of gold for the suns of a thousand years."[23] The city Sherrizah stands for the high civilization of the Nephites, now about to go to ruin. The city and the civilization it embodied will be preserved only on the plates of gold. Everything noble and good of Nephite culture is concentrated in those plates.

Painting

In Larson's poetic imagination, the plates carried that huge load. Perhaps not coincidentally, his fascination with the twilight of a civilization spread through the church at about the same time that *Coriantumr and Moroni* was completed in 1961. Until then, painters illustrating the story of the plates were slow to follow the poets. They focused on Moroni on the hill, with Joseph opening the box as the key moment in the plates' history. In the nineteenth century, C. C. A. Christensen depicted Joseph kneeling on a slope so steep he seems in danger of sliding out of the picture.[24] Edward Stevenson's *Reminiscences* featured an engraving of the same two characters standing before the stone box and the plates between them (Figure 7.1).[25] That moment

Figure 7.1. Joseph and the Angel Moroni, Edward Stevenson, *Reminiscences of Joseph, the Prophet* (Salt Lake City: Stevenson, 1893), 21. Until the mid-twentieth century, the portrayal of Moroni with Joseph on the Hill Cumorah, this one probably by Edward Stevenson himself, was the scene most commonly chosen by artists to depict the plates.

and those figures summed up what painters saw as the critical event to portray in the plates' history. The closing scenes with Mormon and Moroni seemed not to have registered. In 1883, Reuben Kirkham brought twenty-three scenes to a panoramic display of Book of Mormon history, which he displayed in more than 100 towns in the territory. Based on the surviving titles, none of the paintings showed Mormon passing the plates to Moroni or the last days of Nephite civilization.[26]

For nearly a half century after the appearance of these early images, Latter-day Saint artists paid almost no attention to the plates. The painters whom the First Presidency sent to Paris in 1890 for training came home to paint landscapes and portraits. No one (to my knowledge) chose to depict Book of Mormon scenes, much less the plates. In 1923, Lewis Ramsey painted the traditional Moroni showing Joseph the plates. An angelic figure stands on the hillside with Joseph kneeling by the open stone box.[27] Nothing of Moroni as warrior in the final moments of Nephite civilization captured Ramsey's interest.

That changed in 1951 when Adele Cannon Howells, general president of the Latter-day Saint children's auxiliary, personally commissioned Arnold Friberg to paint twelve Book of Mormon illustrations for the periodical *Children's Friend*. Born in 1913 to Scandinavian immigrants who would soon join the LDS Church, Arnold Friberg trained as a commercial artist at both the Chicago Academy of Fine Arts and the Grand Central School of Art in New York City. During his career as a commercial artist, he painted over 300 portraits of Canadian Mounties and created character, costume, and set designs for Cecil B. DeMille's *The Ten Commandments*. After completing the first eight paintings for *Children's Friend*, Friberg took a hiatus to work on DeMille's movie, returning to Salt Lake City only in 1957 to finish his Book of Mormon illustrations.[28]

Friberg brought to life the moment in the plates' history that poets had dwelt on for half a century. He dramatically portrayed the time when Mormon turned the plates over to his son against the backdrop of the Nephite holocaust, the episode that poets like Clinton Larson were dramatizing in the same years. Against that background, Moroni assumed a new character. He appeared as warrior rather than an angelic messenger. Earlier images gave him a modest body dressed in angelic garb. The prophet-warriors of the last battles were muscular men, often with weapons at their belts or lying close to them on the ground. Even when Moroni comes to Joseph in angelic garb, he possesses a massive physique. Howells had hoped Latter-day Saint children would find spiritual heroes, and Friberg supplied them.[29]

In the last of Friberg's Book of Mormon paintings, *Mormon Bids Farewell to a Once Great Nation*, the gold plates appear at the center of the scene (Figure 7.2). Mormon, who has been wounded in battle, lies with a bandage around his ribs, his right arm reaching toward the horizon where a conflagration rages. He appears to be making prophetic utterances, while supported from behind by his son, Moroni, still in full battle dress. Here the downfall of the Nephite nation is dramatized in the spirit of Wagner's death of the gods in the final scene of *Götterdämmerung*. By Friberg's own admission, he was a

Figure 7.2. Arnold Friberg, *Mormon Bids Farewell to a Once Great Nation.* © By Intellectual Reserve, Inc. Friberg invested the Book of Mormon with the high drama of Richard Wagner's operas.

Wagnerite. He fell under the spell of Wagner's music as many in Hollywood did in those decades.[30]

> I love Wagner. . . . I tried to capture the *Götterdämmerung* feeling such as Wagner could have captured in music! This is the end of a nation and an entire race. Mormon was . . . wounded . . . so they have laid him down there on the hilltop. Things like this one last leaf on the tree had their own little symbolism. You see the buzzards circling, because there is death all around. Blood on the sun! This is really Wagnerian tragedy.[31]

As in Larson's play, the plates are the last remnant of the dying Nephite civilization.

Friberg's paintings proved so popular that Church leaders inserted them into the Book of Mormon in 1962. Then, two decades later, the Church replaced *Mormon Bids Farewell to a Once Great Nation* among the Book of Mormon illustrations with artist Tom Lovell's *Moroni Burying the Gold Plates*, a solemn rendering of a white-haired Moroni praying over the plates before burying them on a snow-covered slope.[32] His pose is reminiscent of Friberg's famous painting of George Washington praying at Valley Forge.[33] Lovell (1909–1997), not a Latter-day Saint but a friend of Harry Anderson, a Seventh-day Adventist artist who had done a lot of work for the Church, welcomed the commission. Lovell also painted a widely circulated image of Moroni appearing to Joseph Smith in his bedroom. In a less extreme form, Lovell's angel Moroni carried on the Friberg tradition. Though dressed in white angelic garb, Moroni is a massive figure, clearly ready to strap on armor when needed.[34]

Friberg's style was echoed in other public representations of the plates in the 1960s and 1970s. Avard Fairbanks's two large bas-relief sculptures in the lobby of the Harold B. Lee Library at Brigham Young University completed in 1961 showed on one side of the entrance a large frieze of Lehi and Nephi with plates and on the other Mormon handing plates over to Moroni, all of them muscular men in the Friberg spirit. In the first, Lehi is a man of learning with the Liahona in his hand; in the second, Mormon is a warrior with a helmet and armor buckled on. Fairbanks takes an interest in the plates at the beginning and again at the end of the Book of Mormon.[35] That interest carried over to the Book of Mormon diorama at the 1974 World's Fair in Spokane. There, three dioramas told the story of the plates from Nephi to Joseph Smith. In the second diorama, showing the by now familiar scene of Mormon giving the plates to his son, Mormon describes "his people's destruction." The Spokane diorama showed the appeal of the defeated warrior in a failed cause. The narrator pointed to "one of earth's oldest riddles is what happened to the ancient pre-classic civilizations of America, highly developed cultures which appeared suddenly and just as suddenly disappeared 400 years after Christ."[36] The work of mid-century artists pivoted on the tragic moment.

Friberg's influence waned in the closing decades of the twentieth century. His muscular warriors lost their appeal. Paintings by Minerva Teichert, the New York–trained, ranch-dwelling artist, now rival Friberg's as the best-known illustrator of the Book of Mormon. Rather than showing the fall of civilization, her *Moroni: The Last Nephite* pictured Moroni in a cave laboring over the plates. She does have Moroni in armor with weapons in the background, but the most prominent feature is a large black pot over the fire where Moroni is cooking his supper (Figure 7.3). Teichert's Moroni is more domestic than militant. Her painting titled *Last Battle between the Nephites and the Lamanites* features five graceful figures in Indian headdress galloping across a battlefield on beautiful horses, armed to be sure but lovely in their militance (Figure 7.4).[37]

Figure 7.3. Minerva Teichert (1888–1976), *Moroni: The Last Nephite, 1949–1951,* oil on Masonite, 34¾″ × 47″. Brigham Young University Museum of Art, 1969. Teichert's Moroni is a warrior, but she catches him in a quiet moment cooking his supper and making an entry in his journal.

Figure 7.4. Minerva Teichert (1888–1976), *Last Battle between the Nephites and the Lamanites, 1949–1951,* oil on masonite, 35$\frac{15}{16}$″ × 48″. Brigham Young University Museum of Art, 1969. The violence in this battle scene gives way to the beauty of the horses and the grace of the warriors.

And so the story of the plates continued to evolve. Over a century and a half, artists and poets had turned their attention from one site to another in the plates' history. Through the nineteenth century, Moroni and Joseph at the hill struck artists as the critical moment calling for attention. Then Friberg and others joined the poets in painting Mormon and Moroni witnessing the last battles of their people on the eve of their nation's collapse. The plates became the digested essence of a dying nation's history, a message in a bottle about to be cast into the sea.

Global Faith

While poets and painters searched for which moments in Book of Mormon history to depict, another group of artists grappled with another question: how to translate a story that originated in the United States into a narrative that was intelligible to people around the world. The plates were discovered and returned in upstate New York. Their story had been elaborated for American audiences, depicted by American artists, and extolled by American poets. How would the plates travel to the rest of the world?

From the beginning, Church leaders had thought globally. Within a year of the Church's organization, missionaries had been dispatched to Native Americans and within a decade to Europe and the Middle East. Soon after, missionaries were preaching in the Pacific and Asia. Translations of the Book of Mormon appeared throughout the nineteenth century.[38] The problem of framing a global message from an American story was not new in the mid-twentieth century, but not until then did details such as how to describe the gold plates come up. How were the plates to be understood in cross-cultural terms? And how would Latter-day Saints in the heartland react to versions of the gold plates story coming back from abroad? Richard Oman, former curator at the Museum of Church History and Art (now Church History Museum), observes that the visual language of another culture "can be almost as enigmatic to those from a different culture as are unfamiliar verbal symbols."[39] Would a translation into native forms seem unintelligible or even sacrilegious in Utah?

The Navajo potter Lucy McKelvey's work *Echoes of the Ancient Ones* raised these questions in an acute form (Figure 7.5). It was one of eight clay pots by Native American potters in an exhibition at the Museum of Church History and Art in 1994. McKelvey had grown up on the Navajo

Figure 7.5. Lucy McKelvey, *Echoes of the Ancient Ones.* © By Intellectual Reserve, Inc. Lucy McKelvey situates the gold plates at the center of a design that is rife with indigenous symbols.

Reservation, served a mission for the Church of Jesus Christ of Latter-day Saints, and attended Brigham Young University. At BYU she met a Hopi man whose mother taught McKelvey Hopi pottery techniques.[40] Over decades, she learned to use native clays, oak-fired kilns, and pigments made from clay, hematite, and beeplant.[41] *Echoes of the Ancient Ones* thoroughly absorbed Book of Mormon stories into Navajo form and Hopi technique. As the exhibition's curator, Oman explained, "The migration to the promised land is represented by four Mimbres figures symbolizing Laman, Lemuel, Nephi, and Sam. The figures cross the waters on whirling logs such as those depicted in the Nightway Chant." The gold plates are not situated at Cumorah or in Meso-America but in the traditional home of the Navajo: "Hesperus Peak (the north mountain), Mount Taylor (the south mountain), Blanca Peak (the east mountain), and the San Francisco Peaks (the west mountain)." Radiating from the plates and the mountains are step patterns, the Navajo symbol for rain clouds, an expression of heavenly blessings. "Below the plates is an Avanyu, or plumed water serpent. This plumed serpent represents the traditional god of the Santa Clara Pueblo— the god that taught farming and was the arbiter of morals. The Avan[y]u is the equivalent of Quetzalcoatl of Meso-America."[42]

The plates occupy a central position in the design. They appear to be in a womb-like circle on one side of the pot with the tongue of the Avanyu pointing directly at them. All other designs swirl outward from the circle. But powerful as the design is, without directions from Oman, most white Latter-day Saints would fail to detect the Nephite story on the surface of the pot. McKelvey has made the plates entirely hers. She has absorbed them into her Navajo world at the risk of confusing her Anglo-American brothers and sisters. Her work raises the question: how can cultural translations be made accessible to the mother culture?

Hadi Pranato

Most global art does not absorb Mormon narratives so thoroughly into the native culture. Much of it is produced for the triennial International Art Competition sponsored by the Church History Museum, where it is caught up in various cross-currents. The native artists feel a need to cater to the preferences of heartland Latter-day Saints in order to be accepted, while the judges at the Church History Museum want to broaden their standards to include artists from around the world. On both sides, there is an inclination to accommodate.

This tendency to mediate the differences shows up in the batik portrayal of *Joseph Smith Receives the Gold Plates* by the Indonesian artist Hadi Pranato (Figure 7.6). Batik is created by drawing designs on cloth with a pencil and then dripping wax onto areas of the cloth the artist does not wish to dye. The cloth is then immersed in dye. When the desired shade is achieved, wax is removed from the fabric using heat. This entire process is repeated until the desired color and design are achieved. Extensive drying periods between each immersion may result in a six-month production process. Pranato, a third-generation batik artist, resided and worked in Yogyakarta, an ancient center of Javanese culture and the hub of Indonesian batik making. He was

Figure 7.6. Hadi Pranato, *Joseph Smith Receives the Gold Plates*, exhibited in "For Glory and for Beauty: LDS Batiks from Indonesia," Church History Museum, 1991–1992. Hadi Pranato highlights the gold plates with color and design.

a high-ranking batik artist employed at one of the city's finest studios, the Aidiyanto Batik Studio.[43]

Pranato depicts perhaps the most familiar form of the gold plates story: Joseph Smith receiving the plates from Moroni. The angel stands slightly above the Prophet gesturing toward Joseph dressed in a formal coat and tie holding the plates, all common conventions in such pictures. Pranato has learned from his predecessors, but this is no ordinary portrayal either. Moroni emerges from a gold arch in the shape of a traditional mandorla.

Moroni's robes and Joseph's cloak are swimming in sinuous organic forms. Most striking, the plates emit a brilliant aureole, brighter than anything in the picture. Joseph and Moroni are of about equal brightness. The most brilliant item in the picture is the gold plates.

Rather than absorbing the plates into his native Javanese culture, Pranato mediates the differences between his own culture and the culture of the Salt Lake City audience who will view the exhibition. He tells a familiar story but with strong elements of his own culture and art form. His batik embodies the effort at accommodation that comes when people of differing origins set out to speak a common artistic language. In this case, the gold plates are the beneficiary. Pranato makes them the star of the show.

Jorge Cocco Santángelo

No artist has painted the plates more frequently than the Argentinian Jorge Cocco Santángelo (b. 1936). To date, he has completed over a dozen sacrocubist and more representational paintings of the plates. His representational artwork challenges the Latter-day Saint artistic canon by painting the plates in settings rarely portrayed by other LDS artists, such as Jesus examining plates, while anxious Nephite scribes listen to his critique. Cocco has included eleven sacrocubist iterations of the plates held by the Angel Moroni in his *Angels Collection*. Despite the collection's title, it is the plates that are foregrounded in the center of each painting, with an angel behind them in a supporting role.[44]

Cocco joined the Church of Jesus Christ of Latter-day Saints in 1962 and subsequently received an award to study art in Buenos Aires. He spent seven more years in Spain exploring cubist modernists such as Pablo Picasso, Juan Gris, and Georges Braque. Cubists broke the visual field of the canvas into multiple planes, hoping to allow viewers to see their subject matter from many different angles.[45] Cocco began making representational paintings of Book of Mormon subjects while still experimenting with abstract art. The combination of these two approaches resulted in a style he labels "sacrocubism."[46]

In subject matter Cocco is conservative. Ten of eleven Moroni pictures in his angels collection depict Moroni with a horn, following the lead of Cyrus Dallin's Moroni on the peak of the Salt Lake Temple. This pose also links Cocco's angel to Torleif Knaphus's Moroni on the Hill Cumorah holding the plates in one of his arms (Figure 7.7). Both turn Moroni into the angel in the Book of

Figure 7.7. *Angel Moroni.* © Jorge Cocco Santángelo. Used with permission. Cocco depicts Moroni in a classic pose with plates and horn but in an unconventional style for Mormons, sacrocubism.

Revelation who restores the everlasting gospel to the earth. Cocco's angels have their heads back, horn to lips, authoritatively proclaiming the gospel.[47]

Cocco's departure from tradition is in artistic style rather than subject matter. He has virtually singlehandedly won over Latter-day Saint collectors to the cubism he learned in Spain. By the second decade of the twenty-first century, cubism was entirely domesticated in the American art world. It had become a staple of art sales, as familiar as impressionism. But Latter-day Saint collectors were slow to accept any form of modernism. They certainly resisted cubism in its heyday along with abstract art in any forms. For Cocco's cubism to be so warmly welcomed even at this late date was a significant accomplishment.[48]

Theater and Fiction

Almost all the depictions of the gold plates in poetry and painting came from the hands of Latter-day Saint artists trying to depict the essence of the founding stories. Mainly they spoke to an audience of believers. Not so with theater and fiction. Novelists and playwrights sensed the drama in the gold plates story and put it to their own uses. No iteration of the gold plates has had more exposure in popular culture than the brief references in the famed musical *The Book of Mormon*. First produced on Broadway in 2011, the musical comedy toured the United States from 2012 to 2020 and with long runs in Chicago, London, and Australia. Grossing over a billion dollars, it is considered one of the most successful musicals of all time. It was awarded nine Tony Awards including Best Musical and a Grammy Award for Best Musical Theater Album. *Entertainment Weekly* called it "a spectacular, rather perfect Broadway musical."[49]

The gold plates have only a bit part in a story about two eager young missionaries sent to Uganda to convert people who are beset by AIDS, poverty, and violence. The characters sing rather gaily about how the plates' motivated Palmyra residents to move west, but the authors mingle references to the plates with gratuitous sexual allusions so extreme they cannot be printed here.[50] The authors, Trey Parker, Matt Stone, and Robert Lopez, seemed determined to degrade the plates. Parker claims his intentions are innocent. "When someone goes, 'Oh, this group is really pissed off at what you said,' there's not a piece of my body that goes, 'Sweet!' " Parker observes. "That means I did it wrong. I'm just trying to make people laugh."[51] Earlier in their popular TV show, *South Park*, Parker and Stone had told the plates story straight, only lightly questioning Smith's refusal to show the plates, but in the musical, the authors pull out all the stops.[52] The willingness of audiences to laugh suggests the power of the plates to provoke contempt. At the end, the authors cover up their disdain by assuring the audience that the missionaries, for all their stupidity, are well-meaning and kindly.[53] But the point is clear: the apparent good feelings toward Mormons and their gold plates sometimes mask darker thoughts.

I know of no other place in American popular culture where the plates are subjected to such abuse, but even when shown more respect, they are often depicted negatively. In Tony Kushner's *Angels in America*, the plates come with the blessings of heaven. An angel tells the hero Prior about the plates under the tiles in his kitchen as part of a divine call to reconcile people to

God. But for Kushner, linking the plates to God is not a positive endorsement. Prior is disgusted with God's disinterest in human suffering. He is writing against God and the angels, putting the plates on the wrong side. Prior is instructed to prophesy to his generation just like Joseph Smith, but he refuses and to punctuate his refusal returns the plates to the angel and curses God. Kushner rejects everything the plates stand for.[54]

James Rollins's gold plates in *The Devil Colony* are marvelous and magnetic, but in the end dangerous. Buried in the mountains of Utah, they contain the advanced scientific knowledge of a nation of ancient Jews who migrated to the New World centuries ago and communicated with early Founding Fathers about forming a fourteenth colony. Lewis and Clark were sent to aid them. Before the destruction of their civilization by a mysterious French enemy, the plates were deposited underground and protected with a nanotechnology that will destroy the earth if triggered. Rollins's plates are charged with intelligence, but they also are a threat. If they fall into the hands of evil persons, the knowledge they hold could be used to rule the world. The guardian nanotechnology has to be neutralized or it will destroy everything.[55]

Among modern writers, the Latter-day Saint novelist Orson Scott Card stands out for his positive take on the plates. In Card's Alvin Maker fantasy series, a golden plow that Maker forges stands in for the gold plates. To endow the plow with power, Maker, a Joseph Smith figure, climbs into the fire himself, and this process comes to symbolize how a holy city must be built. People must give themselves to the process of creation. The plow (the plates) show the way. Card plays up the magic implicit in the plates story. He imagines a world where many people have "knacks," magical gifts. Card would like to re-enchant the world, reversing the secular impulse to drain the world of magic.[56]

The four stories suggest the ways the plates can figure in the modern imagination. Parker, Stone, and Lopez look at them as alien objects in the modern, scientific world. So foreign are they, the plates can only be ridiculed or despised. Kushner, Rollins, and Card welcome the enchantment that the plates bring with them into the world. They fill their stories with magic: the appearance of an angel is the crashing climax of part one of Kushner's drama; Rollins makes the remnants of superhuman intelligence and mysterious powers of destruction the hinge of his plot; and Card bestows mysterious making powers on Alvin Maker. Magic is possible in a world where the plates are a reality. All three authors play upon the plates' hybrid nature, part heavenly, part earthly to create worlds where the protagonists engage with superhuman forces. Even though Kushner and Rollins ultimately repudiate the plates, the re-enchantment achieved with their help enables both authors to explore dimensions of human experience otherwise beyond their reach.

Only Card feels at home with these mysterious powers. Kushner wants to send the angel packing; Rollins fears the plates' mysterious force and spends the whole novel stopping them from destroying the world. Both authors want to rid the world of the powers the plates introduce. The plates only seem to rest in peace in the mind of Card, the Latter-day Saint whose gold plow points the way to a utopian social order. Elsewhere they are as alien as they were when first brought to the attention of newspaper readers in 1829.

Conclusion

The gold plates have always been freighted with meaning, but the meaning keeps changing. All those who pictured them, wrote about them, used them in stories or poetry added their bit. In Joseph Smith's mind, they began as a treasure and soon became a holy record cared for by an angel. Early Latter-day Saint poets wished to absorb the plates into the sad story of a lost people now at long last speaking from the dust. Later poets and painters dwelt on the tragic history of two fallen civilizations, perhaps hoping to ennoble the Book of Mormon by linking it to recurring stories of rise and fall. In the late twentieth century, Latter-day Saint global artists dealt with the contemporary issue of negotiating cultural divides. How can a founding narrative set in America speak to all segments of a global religion? Recently, the plates have figured in the work of writers of differing persuasions who wish to introduce magic into their imagined worlds. So far the magic is bad for writers outside the Mormon realm and good for those inside.

The story of the plates in art does not conclude. As the wheels of the ambient culture keep turning, the plates acquire new meanings—magical, ominous, divine. Doubtless at this very moment, their place in the world is shifting.

8

Instruction

1893–2023

Torleif Knaphus

In the winter of 1901, Torleif Knaphus was studying art in Oslo when a roommate pressured him into going to a concert sponsored by the Latter-day Saints. After attending a few Sunday services, Knaphus concluded that "this was the only true Church of God" and was baptized three months later in an icy fjord. In 1906, he passed up an art scholarship in Rome to emigrate to Utah where he was hired to make carvings for the Tabernacle and the Salt Lake temple. In 1913, Knaphus, now married with two children, studied art at the Académie Julian in Paris before returning to Utah at the outbreak of World War I. Between 1915 and 1927, Knaphus worked on temples in Hawaii, Alberta, and Arizona, with more to come. He also sculpted the figure of Moroni for the monument on the crest of the Hill Cumorah.[1]

Knaphus's career as a Church-sponsored artist once again draws attention to the large role art has played in telling the story of the gold plates. In his case, the emphasis was on public relations, or perhaps more accurately, instruction, rather than pure expression. He was concerned to guide people into the best way of thinking about the plates. His work falls into the same category as the art of illustrators who try to make the story of the plates believable and attractive to the rising generation. In his monument of Moroni on the Hill Cumorah, Knaphus hoped to capture the imagination of the American public.

When Knaphus learned in 1928 that the Church had purchased the Hill Cumorah, he began sketching a design for a monument even before he was commissioned. According to a close friend, he carried seven sketches to the top of Ensign Peak just north of Salt Lake City, laid them on the ground in the dark, prayed, and saw an angel pointing to one of them. The next morning, he took the sketches to the Church office building where the Church Authorities selected the same one. By then, Knaphus had become a competent sculptor and was a trusted artistic resource for the Church, a natural choice to design the monument. The statue of Moroni on the crown of the hill was dedicated in 1935.[2]

The Cumorah monument was a sequel to the granite shaft erected to mark Joseph Smith's birthplace in Sharon, Vermont. The birthplace monument was dedicated on December 23, 1905, the hundredth anniversary of Smith's birth. The Church leaders considered it a public relations triumph and were quick to purchase the Hill Cumorah as soon it was available, hoping for a repeat performance.[3] Both events occurred in the wake of Church president Wilford Woodruff's announcement in 1890 that he was no longer authorizing plural marriages. In a single stroke, the aspect of Mormonism that had dominated its public image for over three decades was removed—or at least much reduced. For the previous thirty years, a primary aim of the Church's defenders had been to demonstrate that women were not downtrodden, that Mormons had wholesome family lives, and that the Church was not an oppressive institution.[4] After 1890, the Church was positioned to take a new tack. Rumors of plural marriages lingered on after 1890 (not without foundation), but the policy change opened space for defenders of the faith to propose a fresh image of Mormon life and belief, one that was more cultivated, orthodox, and wholesome. For the next half century, the Church worked hard to redefine itself in the public eye—including finding a reputable role for Joseph Smith's gold plates.[5]

Within a year after President Woodruff's announcement, Church leaders began planning an entry in the 1893 Chicago World's Fair, a great gathering of peoples and nations intended to educate the public about the industrial and cultural achievements of people around the world. Utahns felt they had a right to tell their story along with the others. In Chicago, the Parliament of Religions thwarted B. H. Roberts's attempt to explain Mormon beliefs, but the Tabernacle Choir won a prize in the choral group competition, a thrilling achievement for a people accustomed to being thought of as crude and degraded.[6] The dedication of the Joseph Smith birthplace monument provided another opportunity. Susa Young Gates published a lengthy account of the dedication, emphasizing the grace of the attendees, the eloquence of the speakers, and the beauty of the monument. She emphasized that the Mormons carried off the dedication to their founding prophet with dignity and aplomb. It was an occasion for Mormon pride, showing Church members to be anything but relics of barbarism.[7]

The dedication party returned to Utah by way of Palmyra where they visited the Hill Cumorah, foreshadowing the erection of another monument there.[8] In 1915, Church president Joseph F. Smith called Willard Bean and his wife Rebecca Peterson Bean to move to Palmyra. They were asked to make friends with the locals and wait patiently until the opportunity to purchase the hill arose. In 1923, Willard Bean purchased half of the hill on behalf of the Church. Five years later, when he informed Church leaders that, after long delays, the owners of the other half were ready to sell, the First Presidency wired him to make the purchase immediately.[9]

In view of these events, Knaphus knew the monument commission was an occasion to make a significant statement about Mormonism. The monument would convey the meaning of Cumorah to the world. To choose the exact place for the monument, Knaphus drove along nearby Route 21 to be sure Moroni would be visible from the road.[10] He may also have understood that the Moroni statue would suggest how the Saints should think of themselves when they stood in the public gaze. Who were they and what did they stand for? The aim of the Cumorah monument was to tell the Mormon story for the twentieth century.

Every artist creating a historical moment makes decisions, and Knaphus made some bold ones. He felt licensed to depart significantly from the historical record. For one, he left Joseph Smith out of the picture. Smith and others appear on the brass plaques on three sides of the monument's base, but not in the large sculpture at the top of the column. There the ten-foot Moroni, covered with gold leaf, stands alone (Figure 8.1). In Joseph Smith's history, Moroni never appears alone, only in conversation with the prophet. C. C. A. Christensen's 1878 portrayal followed the convention of showing Moroni on the hillside with Joseph kneeling beside the stone box.[11] Knaphus lifted Moroni off the ground with no one beside him and his arm raised as if addressing the world. Nowhere in Joseph's account of his visions does Moroni address the world. Nor does he carry the plates in his hand as he does on the monument. Knaphus's sculpture was not meant to re-enact a historical scene; it depicted Moroni's role in the Restoration of the gospel.

The Knaphus Moroni is reminiscent of the angel weathervane fixed to the steeple of the Nauvoo temple in 1846. Nauvoo's horizontal angel is more in flight than Knaphus's erect Moroni, but both carry a book and both proclaim the gospel.[12] Both the Nauvoo weathervane and Knaphus's Moroni evoke the

Figure 8.1. Torleif Knaphus, *Angel Moroni on the Hill Cumorah*, 1935. © By Intellectual Reserve, Inc. Knaphus's Moroni at Cumorah is a preacher rather than the messenger who brought the plates to Joseph Smith.

angel mentioned in Revelation 14:6 who flies in the midst of heaven "having the everlasting gospel to preach unto them that dwell on the earth."[13] By putting the gold plates in one arm and raising the other to proclaim the gospel, Knaphus cast Moroni as Revelation's angel. He was a character from the Bible as well as from the Book of Mormon. Knaphus knew no better way to make Moroni and the plates acceptable to the Christian world than to give him a part in both books.

John Henry Evans

In 1933, two years before the Moroni statue was dedicated on Cumorah, John Henry Evans published an admiring biography, *Joseph Smith: An American Prophet*, that cited the Sharon and Cumorah monuments. Evans's was the first biography written by a believing Latter-day Saint to be published by an outside press. He lauded Smith's rise from ignorance and poverty to become "mayor of the biggest town in Illinois and the state's most prominent citizen . . . the founder of cities and of a university." Smith wrote a book "which has baffled the literary critics for a hundred years . . . and developed a religious philosophy that challenges anything of the kind in history." Evans ended his page of praise by noting that "already a granite shaft pierces the sky over the place where he was born, and another is in course of erection over the place where he received the inspiration for his Book."[14] Evans saw his book and the two monuments as engaged in the same project—to honor Joseph Smith and make Mormonism respectable.

Evans, however, approached Moroni and the plates differently than Knaphus did. Evans apparently felt that Joseph Smith's story could be told with almost nothing said about the plates or the angel. In his account of the Book of Mormon, Evans finessed Moroni and the plates entirely. Evans said that early in life Joseph Smith disappeared from his family's village. Then, under the subheading "THE BOOK OF MORMON APPEARS," Joseph suddenly returns. "Three years later," Evans wrote, "Joseph turned up in Palmyra with a wife on one arm and under the other a bulky manuscript." Evans said nothing about the visit of Moroni or the retrieval of the plates. Only later in the book is the plates' story told and then only in a long excerpt from Smith's history, not in Evans's own words.[15] This remarkable omission by the man who had previously written *One Hundred Years of Mormonism*, a believer's Church history, is puzzling. Evans was an orthodox writer. A committee of Church leaders, including two apostles, who reviewed the earlier book found "the facts therein to be true and correct" and recommended it for use in "our Sunday Schools and other Church institutions of learning."[16] Why a later work that suppressed Moroni and the plates and other visionary episodes in Joseph Smith's life?

Near the very end of the biography, Evans made a labored attempt to explain the plates, but he wrote as if his audience consisted of skeptical outsiders. He never claimed that the plates were more than an imagined possibility. "The plates were tangible things—if they existed at all." Evans may have held back because the biography was published by Macmillan, a non-Mormon press. Writing for the general public, he wanted to create a Joseph Smith who could be admired for his achievements as a religious leader without requiring belief in miracles. "In his capacity of seer and prophet, rather than as the founder of a religion," Evans wrote, "he will continue to pique curiosity."[17] Revelation as a seer and prophet was a curious aside, not a revolutionary breakthrough. The plates and angel were intriguing but not essential. What mattered to Evans was the construction of an institution. He pointed to Knaphus's Moroni monument as evidence of Smith's ongoing influence rather than his role as translator of the Book of Mormon.

Evans wrote in the aftermath of the general recasting of Latter-day Saint history that began immediately after the Manifesto. Cyrus Dallin's monument to Brigham Young unveiled at the 1893 Chicago World's Fair and finally dedicated on Main Street and South Temple in Salt Lake City in 1900 removed all traces of Young as a polygamist and a prophet. He was the great colonizer who led his people out of bondage and worked to civilize the West and bring it into the American republic.[18] The monument gave no indication that he or his people were even Mormons. They were pioneers, to be honored for their achievements, not their religion. As the veils dropped at the dedication of the monument in 1900, the band played "America."[19] Evans was probably there.

He wrote near the climax of an intellectual movement that had riled the Church for thirty years. In the early decades of the twentieth century, a growing body of ambitious Latter-day Saint scholars had left Utah for eastern universities to receive training in the social sciences and humanities. Especially at the University of Chicago, they struggled to reconcile their religion with their studies, seeking to shape a Mormonism more in line with contemporary biblical criticism and liberal scientific values. As one of them, the Chicago-trained philosopher E. E. Ericksen, argued in his dissertation, this generation was "placing the institutions of their fathers on the dissecting table for analysis."[20] When the scholars returned to Utah, many of them to join the Church's education system, they resolved to bring Mormonism up to date. Evans was not one of the university-trained skeptics, but he felt their influence and sought to define a Mormonism that could survive their doubts. The intellectuals preferred a Joseph Smith without revelations. Ericksen's *Psychological and Ethical Aspects of Mormon Group Life*, published in 1922, also summarized Mormon history without mentioning Moroni or the gold plates.[21] A dozen years later, Evans followed suit. For some intellectuals of this generation, mystical or spiritual experiences were better laid aside. Perhaps Evans hoped that all varieties of Mormons could agree on Joseph Smith's remarkable achievements as a religious leader without the gold plates in the picture.

Preaching the Gospel

The stripped-down version of Mormon history was not to prevail. In the struggle between honoring Moroni and concealing him, the promoters won. Progressive Mormon intellectuals were sidelined, and the plates remained central to Joseph Smith's story.[22] In the systematic teaching programs that emerged after World War II, Knaphus's Moroni proclaiming a message from heaven was the Moroni ingrained in missionary and Sunday school lessons. LeGrand Richards, who had been president of the Southern States Mission between 1934 and 1937, developed an outline of lessons for use in proselyting that was published in 1950 as *A Marvelous Work and a Wonder*.[23] Over the next three decades, the book sold 1.5 million copies and was translated into eighteen languages.[24] It quickly became the standard summary of gospel principles for an entire generation.

In the first chapter of the book, Richards noted that a radio commentator once said that the most important news he could imagine was that a dead person who once lived would return with a message from God. Richards reported that "in the western part of the state of New York in 1936 they [the Latter-day Saints] erected a monument upon the Hill Cumorah to such a person, Moroni, a prophet of God, who lived upon the American continent four hundred years after Christ."[25] The reference suggests the impact that Knaphus's monument had made. It seemed to be a touchpoint regarding the public face of the Church. But the connection went deeper than that. Richards followed Knaphus's lead in proposing a Moroni who was as much a Bible character as a figure in the Book of Mormon. Richards lavished attention on the biblical prophecies of the book. He was especially fascinated by Ezekiel's prophecy of a "stick of Joseph" that at some time would join the "stick of Judah" to become a single book of scripture. Richards elaborated on all the promises to Joseph's seed scattered through the Hebrew Bible and then asked, "Where is the stick of Joseph?" To this line of reasoning, he added the Isaiah story of a learned man who cannot read a sealed book and Christ's comments about "other sheep" whom he must bring. The chapter on fulfillment of Bible prophecies of the Book of Mormon took up twelve pages, one of the longer chapters in the book.[26]

The Northwestern States Mission plan formally distributed in 1949 for use by all the missionaries in the Northwest played up the same scriptures. Richard Lloyd Anderson, a missionary who developed the plan, gave more attention to the witnesses than Richards, but still based his case mainly on Bible scriptures. Anderson (soon to enroll in Harvard Law School) told missionaries how to "Sum Up and Clinch" the argument. "Review the Bible prophesies, gaining admission on each individually. Does the Bible prophesy of the Book of Mormon? Is it necessary to believe both if we believe either one? What does this agreement mean? Does it mean you have a responsibility to read the Book of Mormon?" Anderson felt he could demand agreement because of the underlying premise that the Bible was God's truth. At the opening of the discussions, the missionaries ask, "We both believe the Bible, don't we?" and the investigator replies, "Why, of course." The Bible was their common ground.[27]

Over the next four decades, missionary teaching plans rapidly evolved. The creation of the plans moved out of the hands of individual mission presidents into the control of the missionary committee of the Church, which pared down the lessons to a few general principles. In 1952, the Church missionary committee published A Systematic Program for Teaching the Gospel, which incorporated much from Richard Lloyd Anderson's plan into its six lessons. In 1961, the missionary committee replaced A Systematic Program with A Uniform System for Teaching Investigators. In both cases, the Book of Mormon was presented as the fulfillment of biblical prophecy.[28]

Changes were soon to be made, however. Trends in the religious world were undermining the logic of the earlier programs. A later set of missionary lessons, the Uniform System for Teaching the Gospel, published in 1986 offered only a few lines on the recovery of the Book of Mormon. "As a witness of Christ, Joseph Smith received authority to teach the gospel. He also brought forth additional scriptures. He was commanded to translate the writings of ancient prophets. These writings are found in the Book of Mormon: Another Testament of Jesus Christ." That was all. Nothing about Moroni, the gold plates, or the witnesses. Smith simply "brought forth the Book of Mormon." As for reasons to believe: "Read in the Book of Mormon and pray to know that it is true."[29] No mention of the Bible scriptures that meant so much to LeGrand Richards and Richard Lloyd Anderson. The Bible had lost its place in the logic of the lessons.[30]

The current plan, *Preach My Gospel*, published in 2004, explains why the Bible is an unsteady base for teaching. "People's beliefs about the Bible vary widely. Some believe that the Bible is absolutely perfect, without error, and that it is all we need to be saved. Others think the Bible is literature worth studying, but they deny that it is evidence of Christ's divinity and miracles or direct revelation from God. Some choose to ignore the Bible, and others have never seen the Bible or had a chance to read it."[31] With the foundation of Bible literacy now gone, the teaching plans had to adapt.

Preach My Gospel added to the lean version of the plates story but not by much. The story of recovery is summed up in a few sentences: "Joseph Smith was directed by a heavenly messenger named Moroni to a hill where gold plates had lain hidden for centuries. These gold plates contained the writings of prophets giving an account of God's dealings with some of the ancient inhabitants of the Americas. Joseph Smith translated the contents of these plates by the power of God." Nothing is said about witnesses, and biblical prophecies are merely listed. No argument is offered in support of the book in the manner of Richard Lloyd Anderson or LeGrand Richards.[32]

Instead, *Preach My Gospel* relies on a dispensational framework to explain the book's purpose. Throughout history, truth has been revealed, and truth has been lost. Christ taught the gospel, but it was diluted and distorted over time. That is where the Book of Mormon comes in. "Knowing that doubt, disbelief, and misinformation would remain after centuries of darkness, our loving Heavenly Father brought forth an ancient volume of holy scripture comparable to the Bible, which contains the fulness of the everlasting gospel of Jesus Christ."[33] And how is the book to be evaluated? "In order to know that the Book of Mormon is true, a person must read, ponder, and pray about it. The honest seeker of truth will soon come to feel that the Book of Mormon is the word of God."[34] Everything else follows from that. "Knowing that the Book of Mormon is true leads to a knowledge that Joseph Smith was called as a prophet and that the gospel of Jesus Christ was restored through him."[35]

That is the foundation on which *Preach My Gospel* rests. Moroni and the gold plates have nearly disappeared from the story. The plates do not figure as the stick of Joseph to join with the stick of Judah, as Ezekiel would have it. They are not attested to by witnesses. The Book of Mormon restores what has been lost through apostasy—close to what Knaphus thought—but without reference to Book of Revelation's angel flying through the midst of heaven. The plates and the angel are incidental details. The essential thrust is to teach revelation. "In answer to our prayers, the Holy Ghost will teach us truth through our feelings and thoughts."[36] Newly baptized members are to learn about the plates and the origins of the Book of Mormon from some other source.

Instruction

Within the Church, however, new members and children growing up in the late twentieth century have access to ample information about the plates. The minimal accounts in the missionary plans did not carry over to inside teaching materials. Manuals and history books went into detail about the plates' discovery and appearance. One exception was Lowell Bennion's *Religion of the Latter-day Saints*, published in 1939 for use in the Church's Institute of Religion for college-age young people. Bennion wrote in the last phases of the John Henry Evans period when progressive Church scholars considered Moroni and the gold plates non-essential. Bennion emphasized the goodness of Mormon teachings rather than angelic visits and supernatural powers of translation. He said of the book, "The Book of Mormon is essentially religious, yet it also contains a thread of history running throughout the entire c. 1000 years of Nephite civilizations."[37]

Aside from Bennion's version of the gospel, the Church's teaching manuals did not pull back from Moroni and the plates. William E. Berrett, a leading figure in seminary program for high-school-age students, showed no such reluctance about telling the plates story in his 1936 volume, *The Restored Church*. Berrett opened his discussion by noting that a traveler on New York State Highway 21 headed south from Palmyra "would pass directly by the most impressive monument in the northern part of that state." "Surmounting the huge granite shaft is a representation of the angel Moroni. Six great flood lights play upon the unusual work of art."[38] Like Knaphus, Berrett relished details that liberal expositors of Mormonism had passed by. He devoted forty-eight pages to accounts of uncovering the plates, their appearance, their weight and engravings, the ancient breastplate, translation, and the three and eight witnesses.[39] A successor volume, *Church History in the Fulness of Times*, a 1989 history aimed at college students, likewise incorporated all the latest scholarship on the plates as well as referring to the Isaiah and Ezekiel passages that earlier missionary plans had dwelt on.[40] The discrepancy between the omission of the angel and the plates in missionary teaching programs and their abundant presence in manuals for internal use points to some uncertainty about the appeal of the plates stories. Are they too difficult for investigators to comprehend? Are they irrelevant?

The many other players in the teaching business have shown no reluctance to promote the plates. The electronic media revolution prompted the Church and a host of commercial vendors to pump out an endless array of pictures and performances telling the story of the plates for instructional purposes. A visit to the Church website helps to gauge the extent of this effort. Besides the static visuals going back to Arnold Friberg and his fellow artists, the Church now lists an array of videos.[41] There are sixteen collections on subjects ranging from "Sharing the Gospel" to "Youth," among them "Book of Mormon Teaching Videos," "Book of Mormon Stories," and "Book of Mormon Videos."[42] In addition to official Church productions, the independent apologetic institute Book of Mormon Central (now Scripture Central) employed Katie Payne to illustrate a video covering various episodes in Book of Mormon history.[43] All are available to Sunday school teachers and instructors in the Church's teaching programs for high school and college students. They provide a multitude of occasions for the plates to make an appearance.

In this vast array, twentieth-century interest in the end of civilization did not disappear. The dying civilization of the mid-century poets and painters showed up again in the Church's brief video *Moroni Invites All to Come unto Christ*. Moroni, bearing a sword, wanders alone and desolate and finally constructs a stone box for preserving the plates.[44] In her Book of Mormon Central series, Katie Payne models her "Moroni Greets a Dying Mormon after the Final Nephite Battles" after Friberg's depiction. The wounded Mormon lies on a rock, his hand on the plates and a burning temple behind him (Figure 8.2).[45] Clark Kelley Price's *Moroni Buries the Plates* showed no warriors, no burning buildings, but the haggard Moroni stands alone on a desolate rocky landscape with a sword nearby on the ground, implying a civilization that had exhausted itself through war.[46]

Although old scenes persisted, in the first decades of the twenty-first century new themes began to emerge. Artistic depictions of translation, for example, had to adapt to the emerging scholarship. Through most of the twentieth century, Latter-day Saints had assumed that Joseph Smith translated by looking at the plates through the crystals in the Urim and Thummim. Depictions had shown Joseph, sometimes behind a curtain, peering through the crystals at the plates. Some had him looking directly at the plates with his unaided eyes as if he had learned the language.[47]

Figure 8.2. Katie Payne, *Moroni Greets a Dying Mormon*. Used with permission. Echoes of Arnold Friberg are seen in Payne's digital rendition.

These visualizations were called into question by the early twenty-first century as scholars pointed to sources indicating that Smith had used a seer stone placed in a hat to exclude the light. He looked in the stone while the plates lay on a table wrapped in a cloth. A Gospel Topics essay on the Church's website explained that Smith did not even look at the plates as he translated.[48] Not everyone accepted this reading of the sources, but a number of artists attempted to depict the scholars' conclusions. Gary Earnest Smith, who has regularly pictured scenes from Church history, earlier painted Smith translating with a pair of spectacles and the plates visible on the table. After the new scholarship began to circulate, Smith painted Joseph looking in a hat while Emma takes down dictation and the plates lie wrapped in cloth on the table. Most recently, Anthony Sweat, a professor of religious education at BYU, has painted several pictures depicting translation with the seer stones in the hat (Figure 8.3). The plates take a subservient role in the paintings. They are either absent or sit on a table wrapped in cloth. The Church-owned bookstore Deseret Book published a collection of Sweat's paintings in 2020, putting the more scholarly informed image into wider circulation among Latter-day Saints.[49]

On another front, the question of ethnic identity came to the fore with the increasingly sharp focus on race in American culture. What did the

Figure 8.3.   Anthony Sweat, *By the Gift and Power of God.* Used with permission. Anthony Sweat, a teacher of religion at Brigham Young University as well as an artist, depicts Joseph Smith translating with a hat, seer stone, and wrapped plates.

Nephites look like? Arnold Friberg's characters were vaguely Anglo-Saxon or even Nordic. Elspeth Young depicted Nephi's brother Jacob like a wealthy patron of the arts from seventeenth-century Germany or the Netherlands with white skin, well-combed hair, and a maroon velvet robe.[50] Minerva Teichert, on the other hand, who frequently wore a headband herself, usually gave the Lamanites a Mesoamerican look: leather pants, bows and arrows, sometimes feathers.[51] Teichert's Nephite characters were indeterminate with vaguely classical armor. Katie Payne's extensive series for Book of Mormon Central showed Moroni as distinctly Meso-American (Figure 8.4).[52]

Figure 8.4. Katie Payne, *Moroni Buries the Plates*. Used with permission. Payne's Moroni has an ethnic identity.

Were the plates a record of a people much like modern white Americans? Or did they come from a people who might appear to some readers as "other"? Depictions of non-white people might force white people to hear the word of God from people who were other than themselves and thus require a broadening of sympathies. Artists unavoidably took a stand in modern debates about inclusion when they made their choices.

Fun

Church publications of gold plates images were only a fraction of the whole production on the subject. Professional cartoonists turned Mormon and Moroni into characters with dialogue balloons over their heads.[53] In the early 1960s, Fritz O. Alseth illustrated an entire apologetic work by Jack West titled *Trial of the Stick of Joseph* with a cartoon caricature of Joseph Smith arguing his case before a judge.[54] Michael Allred, a highly respected cartoonist, temporarily left his lucrative commercial work in 2004 and 2005 to publish a comics version of the Book of Mormon, titled *The Golden Plates*. Three more volumes appeared in 2017, bringing the total to six. Collectors can purchase a book featuring all six issues with 207 full-color pages.[55]

The need for instructional materials mobilized an army of commercial enterprises. Plates came in all sizes and many forms. The Book of Mormon

Foundation offered a model for $258.75.[56] PioneerPlaysets marketed on Etsy sold a budget version for $12 and the Temple Store a 3D printed replica for $4.99. "These large gold plates are a beautiful treasure that you can display and store your special things in. The top or lid is a page that you can open to reveal a large compartment."[57] Plates came in cardboard and felt. You can learn how to make a brass plates cake, and plates can be made of Rice Krispies and butterscotch chips.[58]

Many gold plates ideas appear on blog sites from people trying to build a following. A single divorced mother with two sons said she quit her computer programming job to start a cleaning business and set up a blog with ideas to accompany Primary lessons. She explained how to attach tin foil to a wall and let the children engrave the foil like Moroni engraving the gold plates.[59] An origami specialist offered instructions on how to teach your kids to fold the sacrament meeting program into gold plates.[60] You can purchase gold plates pins, tie clips, and cufflinks.[61]

The more professional sites market the plates in the language of commerce. The sellers of a "3/4-scale" printed gold plates box with secret compartment assure their customers: "This seller consistently earned 5-star reviews, shipped on time, and replied quickly to any messages they received," and "Arrives by Aug 15–18 if you order today." To manage the $89 price you can "Pay in 4 installments of $22.25."[62] People accustomed to online purchases apparently feel no incongruity in mixing commercial language with the purchase of a replica of a holy book.

Labeling these replicas as "kitsch" or simply "tacky" does not do justice to the motives of their makers. They aid parents in passing along their values to the next generation, the deep purpose of education at all levels. Parents want their children to understand and believe and know the job is not easy.[63] Parents are not doing battle with skeptics and enlightened rationalism. They are in competition with a massive popular culture that threatens to take over their children's minds. They are not fighting for belief so much as for attention. Will their children take an interest in the stories of their parents' religion? They need to make the narratives exciting as well as believable. One purchaser of a PioneerPlaysets set of plates happily reported success: "This was everything I hoped for and more. My 5 year old is obsessed with the golden plates. After weeks of begging me to make some, I found these. He is absolutely excited and has been carrying them around since we got them, and has been 'burying' them so he can find them like Joseph Smith."[64]

The desire to engage kids pushed creators to concoct novel devices in hopes of capturing their interest. One marketed by Deseret Book for $16.99 was called "A Flashlight Discovery Book." All you had to do was "shine a light behind the pages and be dazzled as hidden images show up before your eyes. ... Children of all ages will be delighted to illuminate the pages to see what Lehi saw in vision, what Nephi used to build a ship, where Moroni hid the golden plates." All you need is "the book, your family, and anything that shines a light—even your cell phone!"[65]

Conclusion

The references to Torleif Knaphus's Moroni monument diminished by the end of the twentieth century. The thrill of that huge presence standing in public view near New York State Highway 21 gradually faded. Knaphus's attempt to make Moroni into the angel in St. John's Revelation flying in the midst of heaven bringing the gospel to the earth also has receded. For a time, LeGrand Richards and Richard Anderson argued that the Book of Mormon fulfilled prophecies in Ezekiel and Isaiah, making their Moroni, like Knaphus's, a figure in biblical history and the plates a key event in the history of Israel. That tactic worked so long as missionaries could count on their investigators' faith in the Bible. When it became apparent that such belief was spotty at best, proselyting programs drew back from citing biblical prophecies as evidence. In the current missionary manuals, belief in the Book of Mormon rests on pure faith. No evidence is offered other than the whisperings of the Spirit.

On the other hand, the coverage of the plates in instruction manuals within the Church has not diminished in the least. The brief effort in the 1930s to promote Joseph Smith as a religion-maker and city-builder rather than a prophet and revelator gained little traction internally. Churchgoing children today hear the familiar stories about the plates as they always have, learning their history just as they learn about the Declaration of Independence in school. In the face of modern disbelief, the official Church has not backed away from the gold plates. Knaphus's Moroni still stands on the crest of the Hill Cumorah, holding the plates in one arm and lifting the other to preach the gospel to the world.

9

Scientific Approaches

1900–2023

In 1986 someone wrote to the "I Have a Question" department of the Church's *Ensign* magazine asking: "Why were the Book of Mormon gold plates not placed in a museum so that people might know Joseph Smith had them?" Versions of the question had shadowed the plates from the beginning. Why not let people see this fabulous object? Monte Nyman, a professor of ancient scripture at Brigham Young University, answered that the plates' high monetary value would distract people, and to benefit from the Book of Mormon, readers had to have faith first.[1] The question leads to speculation about another possible career for the plates. What would have happened if they had been turned over to a museum to be brought under scientific inspection and put on public display? There they could have been studied by historians, anthropologists, and archeologists as well as satisfying the curiosity of visitors.

Artifaction

It is possible to imagine this unlikely event because of a fabulous object of a similar vintage and Egyptian connections that was acquired by a museum in the same decade that the gold plates entered the Mormon story. In January 1819, the British Museum installed the massive bust of the younger Memnon in its Egyptian collection. The Memnon statue made of pink and gray granite, eight feet, nine inches high and six feet, eight inches wide, and depicting the Pharaoh Ramesses II, had guarded the entry to a burial site in Thebes, Egypt. Its acquisition inspired Shelley's sonnet "Ozymandias" about a fallen statue with its face half sunk in the sand and the famous line inscribed on its base: "Look on my Works ye Mighty, and despair!"[2]

The great statue's appearance among the museum's other Egyptian antiquities in January 1819 culminated a process that the historian Elliott

Colla has called artifaction.[3] If placed in a museum as the *Ensign* inquirer wished, the gold plates, like Memnon's head, would have become an artifact subjected to the indignities and glorification that come to objects in a modern museum. Artifaction is a way of turning objects into knowledge by scientifically analyzing and categorizing them. Once collected, a pot buried in the sand for centuries is treated with great care. The sand is meticulously brushed from every crevice, measurements taken, materials chemically analyzed, comparisons made to similar items. Then it is stored in a cabinet in a dark cool room with temperature and humidity controls to prevent deterioration. Artifaction transforms an object from a forlorn item lost in a waste into an object of study and admiration. If applied to the gold plates today, if only in the imagination, artifaction would answer all the questions about the plates that modern science could devise.

Artifaction of the Plates

Were the gold plates to turn up in a museum, what story would they tell? It took at least two decades after installation of the Memnon head to realize its identity. The curators and directors did not know if it was a giant curiosity, a work of fine art, or a clue to a great culture. In dealing with the plates, the Smithsonian curators would have to decide on a story and assemble a suite of suitable artifacts for context. The problem would be which story to choose. There are at least four possibilities.

1. The Joseph Smith story of a naive boy led by an angel to a precious, ancient record that he was required to translate. This is the story told by the Church History Museum and Brigham Young University. It is the story undergirding the faith of millions of Latter-day Saints. Its historical parallels would be in stories of prophets writing the Bible and the Quran. In the museum, companion pieces would be drawn from holy books of all kinds.
2. The critics' stories of an imposture contrived to deceive the public. This version remained the unspoken assumption behind most secular histories of the plates through most of the twentieth century. More recently, secular scholars try to avoid judgment about deception. They portray the plates and Smith's visions as a religious expression like that of other visionaries down through time, but the story is still made up.

3. Abner Cole's story of gold plates evolving from money-digging. A variant of the imposture stories, Cole's account embedded the plates in folklore about treasure-seeking. Initially, believers denied the influence of folk magic on Smith, but in recent years his early involvement has been generally acknowledged, opening the door to references to counterfeiting, hermeticism, and folk magic in an exhibit of the plates.[4]

4. The plates as an instance of ancient record-keeping on metal sheets. The search for parallel artifacts aims to sustain the believers' story of a naive boy led to the plates. Identifying similar plates makes Joseph Smith's plates seem less fantastic and more a part of history. Latter-day Saints have extended the search for metal plates to the whole world. Curators persuaded by the ancient metal records argument would add inscribed plates from around the globe to the exhibition cases.

Versions of these narratives could have guided the treatment of the plates at a museum. It was not to be, of course, but throughout the twentieth century, advocates of the four stories have elaborated their theses and assembled evidence to make their respective arguments. By various ingenious methods, they have subjected the absent plates to artifaction. Considered as a group, the four stories sum up how modern people think about the gold plates.

The Joseph Smith Story

Through the years, the advocates of the Joseph Smith story have been as inclined as any to employ scientific methods to extract knowledge from the plates. To demonstrate the plausibility of the official Church story, the defenders of Smith's account try to prove the accuracy of small details on the assumption that if enough circumstantial evidence can be accumulated, the whole story gains credibility. They have, for example, made hypothetical measurements to answer questions about the space available for writing the Book of Mormon on the plates. Could a book that printed to 584 pages in the first edition be squeezed on to a stack of metal plates six inches wide and eight inches long and only a few inches deep? The entire stack was said by observers to be four to six inches high, but Smith said two-thirds of the plates contained a history that was sealed shut. Subtracting the sealed part left only an inch or two of plates on which to inscribe the entire history.[5] If the Book of Mormon would not fit on the plates, the Smith story was thrown into question.

The problem was addressed by a former Baptist minister, Janne Sjodahl, who migrated to Utah from his native Sweden in 1886 as a thirty-two-year-old widower. After a mission to Palestine, he took a position at the *Deseret News* in 1890, to be followed by editorial assignments with the *Millennial Star* in England and the *Improvement Era*, the Church's official magazine. A thin, energetic intellectual, Sjodahl wrote fifty-four articles while at the *Era*, a great many of them on historical and archeological evidence in support of the Book of Mormon. He joined other eminent Latter-day Saint intellectuals in believing that religion, and particularly Mormonism, was entirely compatible with science. "For truth is truth, wherever found." He thought that if information from Book of Mormon was combined with the problems puzzling archeologists, it would be possible "to form a theory in which all this material can be united."[6]

In a 1923 article on "The Book of Mormon Plates" in the *Improvement Era*, Sjodahl attempted to answer the question of space. He opened with a demurral in the spirit of scientific humility. "As far as I know, we have no data from which to calculate, with any degree of accuracy, the number of plates contained in the original volume of the Book of Mormon." This is not the language of faith or religious polemics: "data," "calculate," "degree of accuracy." Sjodahl aimed at logical rigor, careful measurement, attention to assumptions. When selected from the varying descriptions of the plates' size, he chose the smallest number, four inches rather than six, to make proof as hard as possible for himself.[7]

To demonstrate that a stack of plates slightly more than an inch thick (1/3 of 4 inches) could hold the book, Sjodahl conducted an experiment. He asked a friend who knew Hebrew to write fourteen pages of the Book of Mormon onto paper the size of one of the gold plates. By writing very small letters, the friend crammed all fourteen pages on to one sheet. Multiplying the numbers, Sjodahl concluded that the entire book could be written on twenty-one plates using both sides. If the Hebrew letters were not so cramped, he argued, the book would fit on forty-eight plates. How many unsealed plates were there in the stack of four inches? People who saw the plates said they were about the thickness of common tin which would be about fifty to an inch. The total number available in the one and a third inches in the stack devoted to the Book of Mormon, then, was sixty-six or sixty-seven plates, more than the forty-eight required to write the larger Hebrew letters. Playing the role of objective observer, Sjodahl did not drive home the authenticity of the Smith family story based on the plates' sufficient size. He claimed only that "there is ample enough margin to allow for large, readable characters, and the necessary thickness of each plate." He wrote in the restrained spirit of artifaction, doubtless judging that in a scientific age that tone was more persuasive than religious polemic.[8]

Sjodahl's attempt at scientific precision did not end with his generation. His essay was examined and confirmed in 2001 by John Gee, an Egyptologist and linguist at Brigham Young University. Gee noted that most Hebrew writing was larger than Sjodahl had assumed. But that was only true for writing with brush and ink on papyrus. Hebrew writing on objects was on the scale Sjodahl had hypothesized, and so his conclusion held.[9]

Through the century, other questions arose. The weight of the plates received similar analysis, the underlying question being Joseph Smith's ability to carry them home. Forty to sixty pounds seemed feasible for a muscular young man.[10] But a solid block of gold the size of the plates would weigh 200 pounds. Only by allowing for the space between the plates and the possibility that they were an alloy and not pure gold could the weight be brought within reason. The metal of which the plates were made therefore became a subject of interest. In 1966 in the *Improvement Era*, Read H. Putnam argued for tumbaga, an alloy of gold, silver, and copper known to have been worked in Central and South America in antiquity.[11] Tumbaga weighed half as much as gold and still could be hammered into sheets less than .02 inches thick, allowing for enough plates to hold the text of the Book of Mormon. They would weigh as little as a manageable fifty-three pounds. The problems of weight, size, and suitability for engraving all were resolved by hypothesizing tumbaga as the plates' metal.[12]

Instead of gradually petering out as the twentieth century went on, the analysis of weight, size, and material, all part of artifaction, reached a high point in 2015 with the publication of *Ziff, Magic Goggles, and Golden Plates: The Etymology of Zyf and a Metallurgical Analysis of the Book of Mormon Plates* by Jerry D. Grover, a civil engineer and Utah County commissioner for twelve years as well as author of *Geology of the Book of Mormon*.[13]

Grover brought an astonishing array of scientific disciplines to bear on metallurgical questions about the Book of Mormon. He devoted more than half of his book to the pursuit of Ziff, the name for a metal taxed by a Book of Mormon ruler along with gold, silver, copper, brass, and iron.[14] Ziff is one of a small number of Book of Mormon words that have no English translation, and Grover assumed that the word in the original text sounded like the letters in the translation. Grover's search in Near Eastern lexicons led him to "zyf," a Semitic word for a metal, as a possible source for the Book of Mormon word. According to Grover, the strongest candidate for the correct translation of ziff was tumbaga, the gold-copper-silver alloy found in South America that had previously been suggested as the actual "gold" of the plates. Smith could not offer a correct translation because tumbaga was a Spanish word, not in use in the English-speaking world until the nineteenth century. Coming upon the Semitic "zyf" on the gold plates, the translator, lacking a word in his own vocabulary, was thrown back on transliteration to "ziff."[15]

Grover went on to explore the implications of tumbaga as the plates' material. With his usual thoroughness, he compiled all the known descriptions of the plates to see if tumbaga measured up. A couple of observers of the plates, including Joseph Smith's wife Emma, mentioned that when she thumbed the edges of the plates as you would the pages of a book, they rustled. That sensation seems unlikely for metal plates, but not if they were thin enough. Grover ordered a set of copper plates of various thicknesses (gold was too expensive) and subjected them to a rustle test. He found that anything over .01 inches was too stiff, but under that thickness, the plates rustled when thumbed. He ordered a bench test of gold alloy plates that had to be thinner still, .007 inches, but at that thickness they would rustle. Even plates that thin, he found, could be engraved without pushing through to the other side. Grover conducted other investigations such as how much the plates weighed. He found that if the tumbaga was 87.6% copper, 11.8% gold, and .6% silver, the plates would weigh sixty pounds or less, the estimate observers had given in the time of Joseph Smith.[16]

Grover's methods enabled him to answer many questions a curator would pose upon acquisition. The question is why he devoted himself to such long and complex labors. He says in the introduction, "I am not a Book of Mormon apologist; I am actually a bit tired of the research that is primarily directed at responding to critics." "My approach is simply to objectively inquire and then provide whatever scientific information I can."[17] He never draws a lesson about Joseph Smith from his research, nor claims that the Book of Mormon is a true historical record. Instead, he implicitly assumes it. Grover treats the Book of Mormon as biblical archeologists treat the Bible, as a document with flaws and limits but still an actual history. Grover does not argue that the golden plates existed; he simply treats them as if he could sit them on his workbench to be measured and analyzed.

Most of twentieth-century Mormon research on the Book of Mormon has operated on these assumptions. Every passage in the Book of Mormon can be scrutinized, even doubted or dismissed, but always the text as a whole is treated as a historical document, not a nineteenth-century fabrication. To enter the complex world Grover constructs around the plates, readers must accept the plates' reality.

In recent years, apologetic scholars have also turned their attention back to the three and eight witnesses whose testimonies of the plates have been published in every edition of the Book of Mormon since 1830. Recently, an independent organization, the Interpreter Foundation, has launched "a massive undertaking" to tell the witnesses' stories again as the basis of a rational defense of the gold plates. The project includes a full-length movie entitled *Witnesses* and a two-hour documentary called *Undaunted: Witnesses of the Book of Mormon* featuring thirty-two interviews with scholarly experts.[18] The project emphasizes the steady refusal of the witnesses to deny their story even at the price of losing the respect of their contemporaries. The Interpreter Foundation's extensive effort, involving modern media and many approaches, implies that the witnesses' testimonies have not been given the respect they deserve. The testimonies have not persuaded skeptics nor played a significant role in the Latter-day Saint defense of the faith. The Interpreter project attempts to reawaken Latter-day Saints to the importance of the testimonies and perhaps persuade skeptics to think again.[19]

Imposture

Although they labored over small details like the size and weight of the plates, the supporters of the Smith family story always sought to buttress Joseph Smith's account. The plates were large enough to contain the Book of Mormon text; the pile of plates was not too heavy for a young man to carry; metal plates could rustle as Emma said. As they wrote, the Mormon scholars knew their favored account had many rivals, foremost among them the charge of imposture. The immediate response of the Palmyra papers in 1829 was that Smith and his fellow conspirators had contrived the plates as a money-making scheme. The plates, the Book of Mormon, and Smith's revelations were the work of confidence men, attempting to capitalize on the gullibility of the poor and ignorant. Much has changed since 1829, but until recently imposture remained the predominant explanation for the gold plates in the world at large. They had to have been a figment of Joseph Smith's imagination. What other explanation could there be?

The difference in the twentieth-century view of imposture compared to that of the nineteenth century is a reduction in vitriol. Throughout the nineteenth century, Mormon leaders from Joseph Smith on were considered insidious and unprincipled con men. They imposed their fantastic religion on people for the sake of power and gain. For the good of everyone, the religion had to be brought down.[20] That assumption prevailed until the end of the century, when Lily Dougall's novel *The Mormon Prophet* introduced an empathetic note. Rather than condemn Smith, Dougall tried to understand him. Although in the final analysis, the plates were an imposition, she wanted to know why he believed his own revelations. Twentieth-century historians ask what psychological forces lay behind Smith's effort to form a new religion. The result is greater sympathy for the prophet's efforts.

Fawn McKay Brodie, reared a Mormon, had a novelist's temperament and an affinity for psychoanalysis, the right combination for contriving a twentieth-century account of Mormon origins. Her biography of Joseph Smith was almost instantly accepted as a persuasive analysis of his early revelations; her Smith was a believable impostor. She was less successful in explaining the gold plates. Like Eber D. Howe in 1834, she thought that the very diversity of the reports about the plates suggested they were a half-formed idea that gradually crystallized. "No two of Joseph's neighbors had the same version of the story," she noted. She disparages the report of Peter Ingersoll, a neighbor who seemed to know Smith well, as "a savagely cynical account." In Ingersoll's account, Smith tells his family that his frock full of fine white sand is the Golden Bible. When they are credulous enough to believe, he decided to "carry out the fun." Although dismissive of Ingersoll initially, Brodie in the end comes back to a similar explanation: "Perhaps in the beginning Joseph never intended his stories of the golden plates to be taken so seriously, but once the masquerade had begun, there was no point at which he could call a halt. Since his own family believed him (with the possible exception of his cynical younger brother William), why should not the world?"[21] The plates, Brodie suggests, were not the product of some severe psychological crisis or cultural dilemma or a powerful idea. They resulted from an unexpected reaction to a chance comment. In Brodie's telling, the plates and all that followed from them were barely motived. They persisted in Smith's imagination—and drove his life for many years—because people around him believed an offhand remark. In her telling, the Book of Mormon began as a lark.

Brodie had more to say about the witnesses to the plates. Their testimonials, in her view, marked Smith's discovery that he had a gift. "At an early age," she writes, Joseph had "the talent for making men see visions." This talent first manifested itself when Oliver Cowdery envisioned John the Baptist coming to ordain Joseph and himself. It happened again when the three witnesses saw the angel holding the gold plates. Some writers had claimed the witnesses signed the testimony because they were in on the plot to deceive the gullible. Brodie wrote that they "were not conspirators but victims of Joseph's unconscious but positive talent at hypnosis." He had no fears they would expose the plot. As a natural and unconscious hypnotist, "he had conjured up a vision they would never forget."[22]

The eight witnesses seemed less subject to hypnosis than to bullying. Brodie offers Governor Thomas Ford's description of their witness as "one of the most plausible descriptions" of the event. Ford, formerly governor of Illinois, had heard from "men who were once in the confidence of the prophet" that Smith told the eight men that the plates were in a box. When the lid was opened and there was nothing, he set them to praying for two hours "with fanatical earnestness; at the end of which time, looking again into the box, they were now persuaded that they saw the plates." Brodie proposes Ford's description as only a possibility but has no other explanation. She admitted that "it is difficult to reconcile this explanation with the fact that these witnesses, and later Emma and William Smith, emphasized the size, weight, and metallic texture of the plates." Why were there so many reports of touching or lifting the plates? "Perhaps," she hypothesizes, "Joseph built some kind of makeshift deception."[23]

Among modern biographers, Dan Vogel has taken up Brodie's suggestion most directly. Vogel, the editor of a five-volume collection of original sources on this period, sought to remain true to the earliest records whether from his friends or his enemies. Vogel was well aware of the many accounts of people feeling or lifting the plates.[24] They were seen under a cloth, stored in a box, kept under bedcovers, transported in a barrel of beans, held on a knee.[25] Respecting these accounts, Vogel theorizes that "the would-be prophet constructed a set of plates to be felt through a cloth." Contemporaries later said the plates were the thickness of common tin; Vogel speculates that perhaps they were tin. "The construction of such a book would have been relatively easy" for the son of a cooper. During the hours he was up on the hill to retrieve the plates while Emma waited in the wagon, "he could have easily set up shop in the cave on the other side of the hill or in some corner of the forest." "Using a pair of metal shears, it would have been easy to cut a number of 6 × 8-inch sheets," and bind them together with wires or rods. Perhaps one reason Joseph did not bring the plates home on September 22 was that he had not quite completed the job.[26]

In the text of the biography, Vogel presents the manufactured tin plates as only a plausible hypothesis, but the footnotes make clear that he wants the hypothesis to be taken seriously. In the notes, Vogel describes tin plates with the thoroughness of a curator examining an artifact. He assembles descriptions of the size of the plates and explains such matters as what form tin came in. "Tinplate was usually available in 10 × 14-inch sheets. Cut into 5 × 7-inch plates, at approximately 1/8 of an inch thick and allowing for space due to unevenness, there may have been perhaps six plates to an inch." To fit the usual description of the plates, Smith would have manufactured thirty-six plates, or if they were thinner, 1/16th-inch thick, there would have been perhaps seventy-two plates. Then, much like Sjodahl and Grover, Vogel moves on to weight. A solid block of tin the size of the plates would have weighed 74.67 pounds. "If one allows for a 30 percent reduction due to the unevenness and space between the plates, the package would then weigh 52.27 pounds," putting the weight into the range of the firsthand descriptions. Vogel here contributes his bit to artifaction of the plates.[27]

Vogel devotes only a few paragraphs to the manufacture of tin plates. He is far more interested in locating the plates psychologically. Where did they fit in Joseph Smith's mentality and Smith family dynamics? His answer is that Joseph Smith suffered from the religious differences that divided his mother and father. Joseph Smith Sr. leaned toward Universalism, which downplayed the atonement of Christ and promised ultimate salvation to everyone. Lucy Mack Smith, coming from a more traditional Puritan background, was attracted to Presbyterianism. These disagreements came to a head when Lucy and three of the children joined the Presbyterian congregation in Palmyra and Joseph Sr. stayed home. Joseph Jr. suffered intensely from these family disputes and desperately wanted to help his father. Unfortunately, Joseph Sr., leaning toward rational skepticism, had little interest in his son's vision of God.[28]

The primary meeting ground of father and son, Vogel suggests, was in the field of folk magic and treasure-seeking where both were adept and active. "Joseph's line of authority with his father was his gift of seeing." That laid out a path. "Perhaps for the good of the family and his father's future welfare, Joseph might call upon that influence to bring his father to repentance and give his family the religious harmony they so badly needed." Joseph needed a story of treasure that would appeal to his father, combined with religion to bring him in harmony with his mother. During the night of September 22, 1823, young Joseph mused about an angel and gold plates with a history of ancient inhabitants. This was a story "not unlike the folkloric accounts of treasures and spirit guardians," lore he knew well. The next day his father sent Joseph home when he showed signs of exhaustion. Climbing over a fence, he fell unconscious to the ground. "It was here, midway between his father in the field and his mother in the house that Joseph decided to make his midnight musings reality." "He hesitated, knowing that he would be plunged deeper into deception and fantasy but saw it as the only way." Later he told the family of seeing the plates on his visit to the hill. "If Joseph's first vision failed to secure his father's full attention, this recital did. Unlike the vision of Jesus which tapped into his mother's visionary heritage, Joseph's 1823 story emerged from the symbols available in Joseph Sr.'s world—seer stones, dreams, guardian spirits, and enchanted treasures."[29]

Vogel's Joseph is a conscious fraud but one driven by pain and anguish. Smith's story was deeply motivated by the desire to redeem his troubled father. At first Joseph thought merely telling the story would be enough. Reports of conversing with a messenger would satisfy the family; he would not have to actually retrieve the plates and pretend to translate them. Vogel speculates that not until September 1827, when his life seemed to be headed into a tailspin, did Joseph think seriously about procuring the plates. "He would renounce, but not deny, his former activity as a seer and redefine his calling as a purely religious one. Joseph the magician would become Joseph the seer, called of God to translate the golden plates." On September 22 that year, Joseph went to the hill with Emma, extracted the plates from the box, and a few days later brought them home.[30]

Vogel suspends the plates between Joseph's father's folk magic and his mother's Christianity. Vogel is less clear about the origins of the idea of the plates. Why did the buried treasure take that particular form? "The inspiration for Joseph's gold plates—the 'Golden Bible' as some later called it—is uncertain," Vogel writes, and then ticks off possible sources. Joseph could have read in First Maccabees about the Jews writing on "tables of brass"; hammered brass plates sometimes turned up in Indian mounds; Moses received commandments written on tablets of stone. But that is all. The distinctive physical features of the plates in Joseph's imagination go unexplained. Vogel effectively tells of Joseph's anguished decision to make his musings about the plates a reality but says nothing about why he turned to gold plates to connect with his father.[31] Why the history of an ancient people written in a strange language on metal?[32]

Brodie and Vogel bypassed the plates, wanting to know why Smith contrived his tale of buried plates, not where the idea came from. In a book on three revelatory figures in American religious history, Ann Taves asks another question: is it possible that Joseph Smith believed in the plates even though they had no material reality? Taves, a professor of religious studies at the University of California, Santa Barbara, has taught about Mormonism and been instrumental in establishing a Mormon Studies program. In *Revelatory Events: Three Case Studies of the Emergence of New Spiritual Paths*, she examines the achievements of Bill Wilson, cofounder of Alcoholics Anonymous; Helen Schucman, author of *A Course in Miracles*; and Joseph Smith. In a chapter titled "Materialization," Taves summarizes her position on the gold plates in a sentence: "I will assume for the sake of argument that there were no plates, or at least no ancient golden plates, and at the same time take seriously believers' claim that Smith was not a fraud."[33] She is no more interested than her predecessors in where the idea of plates came from, but she is deeply interested in how Smith came to believe the plates were real. She wants to argue that he was not an impostor.

Taves sets a high bar for herself. She would like to imagine a prophet who is neither out to deceive people for his own gain, nor self-deluded. "We have to explain how the plates might have become *real* for Smith as well as his followers. The challenge, however, is not just to explain how they might have become real for Smith, but how they might have become real for him *in some non-delusory sense.*" Can it be said that Smith saw plates without being self-deceived? Through Smith, Taves investigates issues relevant to all religious visionaries: "What exactly does it mean to say someone has eyes to see things that are not?"[34]

Taves finds a model for the plates in the Book of Mormon story of the Brother of Jared taking molten stones to the Lord to be touched and luminated. In the book of Ether in the Book of Mormon, a small band of people are commanded to travel by boat after the confounding of languages at the Tower of Babel. Unable to provide light for the vessels, their leader, the Brother of Jared, takes sixteen small stones to the Lord and asks him to touch them. When the Lord does, they light up. Taves thinks Smith began with something he made like the stones. Making the plates "involved creating what was in effect a representation of the plates, perhaps using sand and later tin or lead," and then taking them to the Lord. "In the same way that the Book of Mormon depicts Jared's brother's solution to the lighting problem as a demonstration of his faith, so too Smith may have understood himself as demonstrating his faith by figuring out how to recover the ancient plates, that is, by taking homemade plates to 'the top of the mount' (the Hill Cumorah) and imploring the Lord to transform them into the ancient golden plates he saw in his 1823 dream-vision."[35]

She knows this opens Smith to charges of fraud and deception, citing Vogel's statement that the plates were "'the most compelling evidence' that Smith consciously misdirected his followers." But Taves deflects this line of reasoning by making another comparison. "Smith's logic . . . may have been less like an adept deceiving his subjects and more like a Catholic priest making Christ present in the Eucharistic wafer." "The comparison . . . allows us to consider the possibility that Smith viewed something that he had made (metal plates) as a vehicle through which something sacred—the ancient golden plates—could be made (really) present. In both the Catholic and Mormon case, the sacred character is visible only to those who believe." And it is sincere belief. "The priest doesn't just pretend that the wafer is the body of Christ. Standing in for Christ, he says, referring to the wafer, 'this is my body.' Nor did Smith claim that the plates were a representation of ancient gold plates; he claimed that they really were."[36]

This may be about as far as a sympathetic outsider can go in crediting Joseph Smith's story. Although Taves does not accept the reality of the plates, she has moved well beyond the imposture tradition. Since 1829, skeptics had accused the Smiths of deceit and villainy. In the twentieth century, the most sympathetic observers have considered Smith self-deluded. Taves's Smith is neither devious nor deluded, neither a villain nor misled. He is engaged in a serious spiritual quest. By an exercise of faith, he sought to make a lowly material contrivance, a pile of tin sheets, serve a high spiritual purpose.

Money-Digger's Treasure

The most extensive theory of the gold plates in Smith's time came from the newspaper editor Abner Cole in the *Palmyra Reflector* in 1830 and 1831. As recounted in a previous chapter, Cole thought the plates evolved from the

Smith family's treasure-seeking practice. The Smiths, like many treasure-seekers, Cole proposed, first sought to extract buried treasure from the clutches of a guardian spirit. Then seeing a better opportunity, Smith claimed to recover gold plates overseen by an angel. In Cole's theory, the first prepared the way for the second.

Twentieth-century historians have not returned to Abner Cole's theory, but they have identified treasure-seeking as a central occupation of the young Joseph. Fawn Brodie described him as "a likable ne'er-do-well who was notorious for tall tales and necromantic arts and who spent his leisure leading a band of idlers in digging for buried treasure." She derived this picture from what she called "the most coldly objective description of young Joseph that remains," the court record of his March 1826 trial in which Josiah Stowell's nephew accused Joseph of being "a disorderly person and an impostor," because he had assisted Stowell in searching for Spanish treasure. The Hurlbut affidavits supported this depiction. "Joseph's neighbors later poured out tales of seer stones, ghosts, magic incantations, and nocturnal excavations."[37] Brodie's Joseph was mostly a treasure-seeker. The gold plates were enveloped in this magical culture.

Well into the second half of the twentieth century, treasure-seeking was a key marker of histories by outsiders. By contrast, very little of the Smiths' money-digging filtered into biographies by Latter-day Saints. Treasure-seeking, they felt, unjustly besmirched the character of the prophet and his father. Believing historians did recount Smith's own admission that he had looked for treasure for his friend Josiah Stowell, but the Hurlbut affidavits and the court minutes from the 1826 trial for glass-looking were dismissed as bogus evidence contrived by an embittered Hurlbut (he had been excommunicated) or by enemies of the Church.[38] Seeking for treasure in the night, using spells and magic stones, seemed entirely out of keeping with Joseph's call by an angel to translate a book of scripture and found the Church of Christ.

In the late 1970s, the wall that barred treasure-seeking from Latter-day Saint accounts of their prophet's early life began to crumble. Latter-day Saint historians became aware of a growing body of historical literature on the practice of magic in early modern England. Even the learned were fascinated until the end of the seventeenth century when the oncoming Enlightenment began to drive magic from the realm of respectability. After that, it still flourished among common people in Europe and America. American historians found magical practices especially in New England

and Pennsylvania into the nineteenth century. Yankee farmers everywhere hunted for treasure.[39]

Rereading the Hurlbut affidavits in view of this research, it became clear that the Smiths' neighbors, many of them Christian believers, were digging for money too. Treasure-seekers had not defected to a scandalous superstition; they were devout Christians. Put in this light, the element of shame that had attached itself to the money-digging stories dissolved. Rather than turning away from respectable religion to practice folk magic, the Smiths and their neighbors were manifesting another form of belief in the supernatural. The folk magic in their lives no longer appeared as a character flaw or a shameful indulgence in foolish superstition, but as a common practice in rural society.

These days, nearly every historian of early Mormonism acknowledges the treasure-seeking in Joseph Smith's early life. Folk magic no longer seems toxic. In 2013, the Church's "Gospel Topics Essays" about Book of Mormon translation acknowledged that Smith used a seer stone as well as the Urim and Thummim in translating. It was the same stone he used "to look for lost objects and buried treasure."[40] The Church's new official history *Saints* has Smith recovering a stone "to search for lost objects or hidden treasure." "Joseph's gift for using the stone impressed family members, who saw it as a sign of divine favor." As his reputation spread, Josiah Stowell hired him "knowing Joseph had a gift for using seer stones." The book accepts the once contested 1826 trial record in which Joseph explains how he found the stone and Josiah Stowell testified that he knew Joseph had power to see things "by the aid of the stone." The angel had to admonish Joseph to "quit the company of the money diggers" before he could receive the plates.[41] In its display on the Restoration, the Church History Museum in Salt Lake City displays a photograph of the seer stone that Joseph Smith reputedly used to translate.

The trend has been so strong it has provoked a backlash. L. Hannah Stoddard and James F. Stoddard feel that "progressive historians" have betrayed the true story of Joseph Smith. The progressives have denigrated Smith's character and given way to the false accusations of his enemies. He was not a money-digger, and he did not use the stone to translate. The Urim and Thummim, the device provided by the angel, was the only instrument used in translation.[42] The old stories are the true ones. A kindred historian, Jonathan Neville, argues that Joseph Smith used the seer stone in a pretended demonstration of the translation process enacted for his friends to satisfy their curiosity. In actuality, he always relied on the Urim and Thummim for translation.[43]

Apart from these advocates of traditional views, magical practices have been so thoroughly integrated into the current understanding of folk belief that the Smiths' involvement has come to be seen as perfectly natural. Historians dispute mainly how much and how long did Smith use magic in his quest for the plates. Michael Quinn, a believing though alienated historian, made the case for magic so thoroughly infusing Smith family culture that it could be considered their fundamental "worldview." His analysis, however, fails him at one point. He has no more to say about the origins of the gold plates idea than Vogel or Brodie. Quinn offers just one paragraph on occult sources for the plates themselves. There was an occult tradition for plates of brass, he notes. And "an eighteenth-century book of Rosicrucianism stated that the number one, 'engraven on Brasse, . . . bringeth a Spirit.'"[44] There were a few other references to brass plates or books bound in brass or gold. That was all. Why the treasure took the form of a history written on gold plates is not explained. He makes a case for magic in the story of recovery, not for the magic sources of the plates themselves.

Although there would be arguments over the balance of magic and religion in a museum exhibit of the gold plates, virtually all historians today would acknowledge a magical context. All would agree that the plates floated between two worlds, a guardian spirit and treasure in one and an angel and an ancient record in the other. For a time, secular thought worked to separate magic from religion. By the twentieth century, Latter-day Saints themselves came to believe that treasure-seeking was a primitive superstition at odds with a heaven-sent angel bearing news of an ancient scripture. But as incompatible as the two accounts seemed for a time, it is now recognized that they had not been so distant in 1827. To many in Joseph Smith's generation buried treasure, seer stones, and guardian spirits were as real as angels and ancient records.

Ancient Record-Keeping on Metal Plates

One reason historians have had trouble explaining where the gold plates idea originated is that plates are not found in the Bible. There is virtually no evidence that Hebrews kept historical records on plates, while in the Book of Mormon record-keeping on plates is almost routine. Laban had plates; Lehi kept his history on plates; Nephi made at least two sets of plates.[45] Down through Nephite history, one group after another wrote on plates until at the end, Mormon seems to have had stacks of plates to rummage through. Since none of this shows up in the Bible, Mormon historians have scoured the Near East for evidence to back the Book of Mormon practice. The urge to discover plates has become so strong that Mormons stumbling across plates in Korea or Spain see them as applicable evidence.

The first indication of a taste for plates came when the Kinderhook plates were brought to Nauvoo in 1843. The *Times and Seasons* exulted that "this circumstance will go a good way to prove the authenticity of the Book of Mormon."[46] The pursuit of plates revived in the twentieth century when a general interest in scientific evidence for the Book of Mormon was on the rise. In a 1927 *Improvement Era* article, the redoubtable Janne Sjodahl pointed to the gold plate worn by the High Priest on his crown in Exodus 39:30 "on which certain words were engraved." Although a far cry from a history on plates, the priest's plate showed Israelites knew the art of engraving on some hard substance.[47]

In 1936, a newly returned missionary from Great Britain, Gordon B. Hinckley, published a report meant to respond to the "many people who cannot see as reasonable the assertion made by Joseph Smith that the records from which the Book of Mormon was translated were engraved on gold tablets." During a visit to the British Museum, Hinckley had seen "small, thin slabs of polished wood" with writing on them; "glistening ivory sheets" bearing writing; "25 leaves of silver" with writing in "the Sinhalese character" from the early nineteenth century; and of special interest, a gold tablet, two inches wide and six long with a "dedication of Temple to Osiris."[48] The essay was a twentieth-century indication that the Mormon interest in records on plates that first surfaced in 1843 in the Kinderhook episode was still alive.

In 1940, Franklin S. Harris, president of Brigham Young University, newly returned from a year as agricultural adviser to Iran, reported on the prize among all the discoveries of plates by Mormons. "Anyone who is interested in the Book of Mormon," he said in opening an article in the *Improvement Era*, "naturally pricks up his ears whenever gold plates are mentioned." As a guest of the government he was advising, Harris was told of an artifact in the new Museum of Archeology in Tehran. His hosts showed him plates excavated just seven years earlier in the main hall of Darius' palace at Persepolis. They consisted of two metal tablets covered with writing that proclaimed that Ormuzd, the greatest of the gods, had bestowed the land from Scythia to Kusha (Ethiopia) on Darius.

To Harris's delight, the plates were stored in a stone box and buried under the floor. Harris observed that "this experience makes it much easier for us to visualize the stone box with its gold plates taken from Cumorah."[49] Although the writings were not exactly a history and the provenance was a century later than Lehi, the plates of Darius came closest to the Book of Mormon gold plates of any of the plate finds for the rest of the twentieth century (Figure 9.1). In 1957, Harris's son published a compilation of sixty-two instances of ancient writing on metal plates and noted that the Darius plates were "one of the most striking examples of the recent discovery of plates."[50]

Paul Cheesman, professor of religious education at Brigham Young University, began his quest for Book of Mormon archeological evidences in the late 1960s. Cheesman received enthusiastic support from one apostle, Mark E. Petersen, and mild interest from other General Authorities.[51] Petersen published his own account of parallel plates in 1979 as *Those Gold Plates*. Cheesman followed in 1985 with *Ancient Writing on Metal Plates*, dedicated to Petersen. Cheesman's aims were simple. As he said in the Preface, "at

Figure 9.1. Stone case with foundation tablets of gold and silver from the Apadana Palace in Persepolis. Courtesy of the Oriental Institute of the University of Chicago. Commonly called the plates of Darius, the tablets are the closest parallel to Joseph Smith's gold plates yet to be discovered.

the time of Joseph Smith's remarkable discovery in 1830, there was probably no knowledge of writing amongst the American Indians, or of any written on metal." The Book of Mormon claimed both: a writing system and metal plates with writing on them. Cheesman's work consisted primarily of lists of ancient American writings either still extant or referred to in historical sources. He made no effort to connect the texts to the Book of Mormon save for the technology of writing. But he accomplished his goal of showing that ancient people in the Americas did indeed write. To this basic point, he added evidence that they wrote on thin sheets of gold, bound the sheets with metal rings, and stored them in stone boxes. "No more can critics of the Book of Mormon deny that ancient records were kept on metal plates." In his desire to authenticate the Book of Mormon, Cheesman pushed his evidence to claim that "the writings themselves often indicated Old World origins," and particularly a Hebrew connection.[52] This was more than the artifacts allowed, but his basic point was sound. Mayans certainly and others less definitely did write and use metal as a medium.

Cheesman died in 1991 and no one quite like him arose to take his place. The trained archeologists, anthropologists, and linguists typified by John Sorenson, Wells Jakeman, and H. Curtis Wright were taking over.[53] These scholars were no less eager to prove the Book of Mormon than Cheesman or Ferguson but conformed as best they could to scholarly standards. In 2007, William Hamblin, a professor of ancient history at Brigham Young University, published an essay entitled "Sacred Writing on Metal Plates in the Ancient Mediterranean" that exemplified the effort to speak authoritatively in a scholarly voice.[54] Hamblin set himself apart from the enthusiasts by limiting his survey of plates to Hebrew, Phoenician, Greek, and Italic cultures in the central and eastern Mediterranean where interactions with Lehi's Jerusalem would have been conceivable. He implicitly recognized that remote examples in distant places, often featured in Cheesman's and Petersen's writings, were irrelevant. Hamblin was aware as well of locating examples in the right time as well as the right place. In cultures that were constantly evolving, examples of late writing did not prove that plates were used in 600 BCE Jerusalem. After lining up his long list of examples, Hamblin argued that "the evidence leaves no doubt that the Hebrews had a long-standing tradition dating at least to the First Temple period (i.e., well before 587 BC) of writing sacred texts on metal plates for amulets, inscriptions, and literary documents." But to make that claim, he had to use the words "sacred texts," or as in the article's title "sacred writings," rather than histories. Laws, rituals, prophecies, and documents like treaties were inscribed, but not the lengthy narratives found on Nephi's plates.[55]

In a 2019 *Dialogue* article "The Gold Plates and Ancient Metal Epigraphy," Ryan Thomas pointed out the weakness in the apologists' case. Thomas found plenty of plates scattered through the Near East and the eastern Mediterranean from the third millennium to the fifth century BCE, but the inscriptions were generally short, mostly building inscriptions, legal decrees, treaties, incantations, and memorials. They were intended for public display, not for archives as a record on deposit. They were meant to remind or inform the public, not record the story of a people. The very abundance of plates among the Nephites set them apart: "At least six metal plate collections representing lengthy independent documents" are mentioned in the text, Thomas wrote of the Book of Mormon. The plates were meant to be national histories; "the plates of brass are labeled the 'record of the Jews.'" There were no parallels in the Near East. The Book of Mormon plates were not put on public display but went in an archive for storage of the information. Many authors added to the record, down through the generations, interweaving "multiple literary genres" in long narratives.[56] Nephite gold plates brought to light a rich and energetic writing culture quite unlike any in the known examples from the Near East. All in all, while the Mormon writers have located many inscribed plates in the general vicinity of sixth-century BCE Jerusalem, there is not enough evidence to make Joseph Smith's gold plates completely at home there.

But if not there, where do the gold plates fit in history? Are they more at home in Joseph Smith's America? The most serious modern students of Joseph Smith's culture, Fawn Brodie, Dan Vogel, and Michael Quinn, gave no answer. They located only a handful of possible precedents for the plates, none of which they argued for. The modern origins of the plates idea was never identified. The most serious attempts at proposing sources appear in the work of Michael Reed, an independent scholar, and Sonia Hazard, an accomplished religious studies expert. Reed scoured literary sources in Smith's era in search of references to ancient metal plates and found a lot of them.[57] He collected examples of metal plates from modern American sources just as Cheesman, Hamblin, and the Mormon plates-searchers gathered examples from antiquity. The two research agendas were mirror images of one another, Reed's to show that the gold plates came out of Smith's time, Cheesman's and Hamblin's to show they belonged in the ancient Near East.

Reed's research leaves little doubt that nineteenth-century sources mentioned metal as a writing medium among ancient peoples. Certain instances such as Hesiod's works were repeatedly described as inscribed on lead. But Reed does not account for the richness of Book of Mormon writing as described by Ryan Thomas. Even if Smith learned from Bible dictionaries that metal was a possible medium for ancient writing, that falls short of the Book of Mormon's gold plates.[58] As Thomas pointed out, the Book of Mormon featured long narrative histories, an archive of plates, many authors, many genres, a tradition of history-writing. That elaborate culture of record-keeping is not found in the nineteenth-century sources.

Sonia Hazard takes another approach. She is a leading figure in a new technique for approaching religion labeled "new materialism," which proved useful in this book to explain how the gold plates drove Joseph Smith toward translation. New materialism attributes more influence to material objects in shaping culture than has previously been allowed. Within an assemblage of people and things, people have experiences or form ideas that would not occur without the objects. Things in effect generate a force field that affects how people think and feel. Thinking this way, Hazard asks what objects in Smith's field of activity might have generated the idea of the gold plates. She confronts directly the question: what is the source of the gold plates in Joseph Smith's mind? "From what source, above and beyond his initial vision, did Smith derive the physical details of dimensions, weight, textual orientation, imagery, and so on? Could such a thickly detailed object (indeed, one that bears little resemblance to anything other than printing plates) be dreamed up?"[59]

Hazard's hypothesis is that Smith might have seen the metal plates that printers use to print books and that view sparked his own idea of gold plates. Printing plates are about the same size as the gold plates, have writing on them, are about the right weight, and, in the case of copper plates, are a similar color. Hazard proposes a list of eight resemblances that might have been suggestive. She can imagine Smith's wonder on running across printer's plates, a new technology to the area in the 1820s, and reacting by envisioning gold plates, an image linked to his own treasure-seeking.[60] Hazard does not want to reduce the gold plates to this one encounter or to downplay Joseph Smith's visionary imagination. "Cultivating an attention to the powers of material things is hardly to domesticate the Mormon story, nor to take everything away from its enchanting power. Quite the opposite. It might encourage us to find wonder in the everyday mysteries of the material world itself, like Joseph Smith did."[61] She proposes a naturalistic argument that grants full play to imagination and marvels.

The soft spot in her rigorously constructed argument is the actual encounter with printing plates. A diligent and ingenious researcher, Hazard finds that printers in Rochester were using plates by 1823, when Smith reported his first encounter with the gold plates. By 1827, when he said he retrieved them, printers in Canandaigua just ten miles away employed plates. "Beginning in 1824, Smith would no longer have had to board the public stage to Rochester to see stereotype plates. He needed only visit Canandaigua, ten miles south of the Smith farm, right down the main postal road—called Canandaigua Road, now Route 21—and enter the shop of the ambitious printer James D. Bemis, hailed as the father of the Western New York press."[62] But still, there is no direct evidence in any source that Smith saw a printing plate. It is at best a possibility. Nor does the hypothesis account for the complex role of the plates in Nephite culture. Why the abundance of plates? Why their function as bearers of long and elaborate histories? None of that came from a printer plate. Once again, the gold plates overflow the categories devised to explain them.

The gold plates seem to inhabit a world adjacent to but not identical with either the ancient Near East or nineteenth-century America. The absence of a secure historical context would complicate the task of our imagined curator preparing the gold plates for display. Surely she would fill nearby vitrines with examples of ancient metal plates drawn from the lists compiled by Hamblin, Cheesman, and Harris. Among the plates would be examples of tumbaga craft from Central and South America to suggest the plates' likely material as viewed by Putnam and Grover. The curator might wish to display tin plates to suggest the set that Vogel thinks Smith likely contrived, and of course, to satisfy Hazard, some nineteenth-century printing plates from a printer's shop. Perhaps the curator would want to include a few treasure-seeker tools as a reminder of the importance of treasure-seeking in Smith family life.

None of the settings drawn from the work of modern historians, however, would be entirely persuasive. The Book of Mormon itself did the best job of defining the plates' identity. There the plates were the medium for recording a people's history. Within the book, it is clear why the plates were created and why a record was inscribed. Perhaps in the Smithsonian exhibit, the plates would be surrounded by passages from the Book of Mormon. The plates would feel most comfortable in the world they created for themselves.

10

Global Perspectives

This book has traced the history of the gold plates in the minds of artists, critics, believers, and scholars from September 1823 when the plates first appeared in the Smith family down to the present. It took time for the idea of an angel and a golden book of records to fully register with the Smiths, but by 1827 when Joseph brought the plates home it was fully formed. In succeeding chapters, the book analyzes the role of the plates in the Book of Mormon, their part in moving Joseph Smith to translate, and then their effects on the Smith family and their friends. Critics and apologists almost immediately deployed arguments to dismiss or to defend the plates. In the late nineteenth century, the attacks lightened and the plates were seen less as a dangerous imposition and more as a fabulous fantasy. In the twentieth and twenty-first centuries, the plates took on many forms in popular literature and art and were subject to scientific analysis both by critics and apologists. This sequence of appearances and arguments constitutes, in my way of thinking, a history of the gold plates.

Historicism

A historical approach governs the book's inner logic as well its organization. The form of analysis has been historicist, meaning the book seeks to illuminate how each manifestation of the plates is caught up in a chain of events in which one thing leads to another. "Historicism is the doctrine that all historical phenomena can be understood historically," argues intellectual historian Dorothy Ross, "that all events in historical time can be explained by prior events in historical time."[1] This means that each particular use of the plates is determined by something that happened before.

Although not applied rigorously to every single fact, this way of thinking uncovered two gaps in the gold plates story. One was the origins of the idea of the plates in Joseph Smith's mind. Where did he get the conception of a set of plates containing the history of lost civilizations and engraved in ancient characters?

No satisfactory answer has been found other than an angelic visitation. But there is also a gap in believers' story of the plates. What prepared Smith to accept the idea of an ancient history inscribed on golden plates and delivered by a messenger from heaven? Latter-day Saints have assumed that he immediately realized that an angel had led him to the record of an ancient people, but what prepared him for such a leap? The sources indicate that for a while he thought he was uncovering a treasure like the gold coins that the family had sought in their treasure-seeking expeditions. It took time for the angelic story of a buried history to replace the guardian spirit story of buried treasure.

Although history is a natural way to understand the many appearances of the gold plates over the past 200 years, it is not the only way. Another is to take a more global approach, ranging through time and space for comparisons. If we expand the search beyond the plates' immediate environment, what other objects in other times and in other parts of the world resemble the gold plates? This approach is frequently put to use by religious studies scholars who think in terms of types or recurring patterns. Rather than look for cause, they are more interested in how similar phenomena function in different times and places.

Found Manuscripts/Pseudepigrapha

There are, for example, numerous pretended histories that were supposedly written by ancient authors, lost or buried, then discovered by chance and published to the world as a voice from the past. Solomon Spaulding, the supposed author of the text that Sidney Rigdon was said to have pirated and turned into the Book of Mormon, wrote a book based on the discovery of a lost manuscript. Spaulding engaged in the literary fancy of having dug up an ancient writing in Conneaut, Ohio, around 1812, which he then translated from the Latin. It told the story of Fabius, a Roman legate, blown off course while en route from Rome to Britain who recounted his adventures among North American Indian tribes with names like Kentucks and Ohians.[2] The novel did not foreshadow the Book of Mormon, as Philastus Hurlbut, the industrious researcher who was attempting in 1834 to discredit Joseph Smith and came across Spaulding's work, hoped it would, but the story of the book's discovery resembled Joseph Smith's recovery of the gold plates. The "Manuscript Found" is an example of a category in which the gold plates can find a place.[3]

One of the most famous of found manuscripts in the century before Joseph Smith was the Scottish poet James Macpherson's alleged translations of epic poetry supposedly written by the Irish bard Ossian. When Ossian's poems were published beginning in 1760, observers lavished praise on the work. Thomas Jefferson thought Ossian "the greatest Poet that has ever existed." Thoreau compared his work to the Iliad. The erudite Samuel Johnson, on the other hand, thought Macpherson was "a mountebank, a liar and a fraud" and labeled the poems a forgery. Johnson turned out to be right. Macpherson was a talented poet who thought to add allure of his work by presenting it as an ancient poem.[4] Apparently for similar reasons, Horace Walpole published *The Castle of Otranto* in 1764 as a story supposedly translated by William Marshal, from the original Italian of Onuphrio Muralto.[5] By Joseph Smith's time, presenting a work as translation of a recovered manuscript was a device available to novelists, poets, and historians.

The practice of enhancing a work by attributing it to an earlier author had a long history. In his book-length study of literary forgeries, Anthony Grafton writes of the sixth-century BCE mythographer and historian Acusilaus of Argos who "supported his rich account of gods and demigods and men by asserting that he drew it from bronze tablets discovered by his father in their garden." That was the beginning of an immensely fertile tradition, Grafton says. Acusilaus "thereby created one of the great topoi of Western forgery, the motif of the object found in an inaccessible place, then copied, and now lost, as the authority for what would have lacked credibility as the work of an individual." Grafton uses the harsh term "forgery" for these creations. Others conceive of them as a legitimate literary form that speaks in the voice and under the name of a dead author. The form came into its own in the fourth century BCE when cities and temples invented records of their heroic pasts. Such accounts flourished in both Greek and Hebrew contexts when contests for religious authority created a need for documentary proof backing one theological position or another.[6]

Works based on found manuscripts linked to the Bible are grouped together under the title pseudepigrapha, false writings, a misleading name bestowed by critics of the Bible. They were called pseudepigrapha because they pretended to be authored by a biblical figure and spoke in that prophet's voice. Actually, according to James Kugel, "the most common form of biblical commentary" in ancient Israel took the "form of a rewriting." The Apocalypse of Abraham was not a forgery but an attempt to make the

Genesis story more applicable.[7] These scripture-like texts were taken seriously during the early centuries of the Christian era when they jostled for inclusion in the Christian and Jewish canons. They had a biblical ring and echoed biblical themes but for reasons both theological and political did not make it into the canon. They had names like The Apocryphon of Seth, The Inquiry of Abraham, The Testament of Job, The Apocryphon of Ezekiel.[8] A Book of Enoch discovered in Ethiopia in 1773 was translated into English by Richard Laurence and published in 1821. Pseudepigrapha multiplied during the nineteenth century. They were labeled as forgeries just as the Book of Mormon was, but they added to a category of found religious manuscripts in which the gold plates can be included.[9] Locating them there does not suggest causation. Joseph Smith did not translate the Book of Mormon because he learned about pseudepigrapha and decided to make one of his own. But if the question is "where should modern scholarship locate the plates," found manuscripts constitute a broad category in literary history in which the Book of Mormon fits.

Relics

While helping to explain the text, identifying the Book of Mormon as an example of a found manuscript is not enough. The plates also ask to be situated in religious history as a holy object. They are depicted in Joseph Smith's history as precious and ancient, a gift from an angel, bearing prophetic truth otherwise closed to human view. In the long history of religious creativity, where are the parallels to this peculiar configuration? History is littered with icons, temples, and historical remnants of divine actions. What revered items in religious history do the plates most resemble?

Are the plates like the relics of holy persons that populate many religious cultures, objects of veneration that connect the present to the past? The ashes from Buddha's funeral pyre were divided into small portions and widely distributed. The ashes were deposited into thousands of stupas (some said 84,000) that serve as places of meditation throughout the East.[10] In classical antiquity, the bones of heroes were venerated. In Catholic Christianity, relics of holy people were much sought after for their power to heal. The relic itself was not the source of power, but a bone or a fragment of fabric gave access to the saint who interceded with God on the supplicants' behalf. The scriptural precedent was St. Paul's handkerchief that was used to heal an ailing person when Paul could not come himself. The handkerchief was a conduit between the sick, Paul, and God.[11]

Belief in relics ran high in medieval Christianity. The Second Council of Nicaea in 787 CE decreed that every church should contain a relic. To meet the demand, many fragments of the cross were found across Europe and many boards from the crib of Jesus. The bones, hair, and clothing of holy people were zealously acquired and guarded.[12] The Church wisely did not test every claim, but let people derive what assurance they could from the relics' miraculous properties. While opposing superstition and the commercial traffic in relics of saints, the Council of Trent in 1563, instructed bishops to teach that "the holy bodies of holy martyrs . . . are to be venerated by the faithful; through which bodies many benefits are bestowed by God on man." A Roman catechism noted that "the blind and cripples are restored to health, the dead recalled to life, and demons expelled from the bodies of men."[13] Stories of healings in the lives of the saints were collected in volumes of hagiography such as the *Legenda Aurea*, or *Golden Legend*.[14]

Do relics and the plates have anything in common? Relics rested on faith in the virtues of a holy person whom God honored by performing miracles in the relics' presence. Like relics, the gold plates also had strong associations with a righteous person. Mormon is said to have made plates himself, personally inscribed them, and poured his heart out on their pages. His work was fittingly called the Book of Mormon. But if the plates were truly Mormon's, they did not work like a relic. They did not give access to a saint who then could plead with God to act on behalf of a supplicant. Mormon was not honored for his holiness and nearness to God or used as a conduit to heaven. He was notable for having written a history of a branch of Israel, and that was all. The plates brought people to God through the words they contained, not because of the virtue of the man who wrote them.

From early times, relics hallowed the places where they were deposited. Constantine built ornate basilicas over the tombs of Peter and Paul, the early Christian apostles. After St. Polycarp's death by burning at the stake, early Christians in Smyrna "took up his bones, which are more valuable than precious stones and finer than refined gold, and laid them in a suitable place, where the Lord will permit us to gather ourselves together."[15] A particularly potent relic could draw visitors from distant places. Within Latter-day Saint culture, the gold plates endowed the Hill Cumorah with the gravitational force of a shrine. After the hill was purchased by the Church in 1928, it became a pilgrimage destination for Latter-day Saint families. Thousands of visitors came each year to show their children the site where Joseph Smith uncovered the plates.[16] But Cumorah did not evolve in the manner of Catholic shrines. People did not come to be healed or to see a miracle. When the Church began to develop Cumorah, they turned the hillside into a theater where Book of Mormon history could be re-enacted. In the 1930s the church instituted a pageant titled *Truth from the Earth*. Thousands gathered year after year to view the unfolding of Nephite civilization and the recovery of the plates in modern times.[17] Rather than experiencing a miracle of healing, Mormon pilgrims received a history lesson. Cumorah's developers pursued a Protestant emphasis on the word rather than a Catholic belief in miracles of the body.[18]

Stone Tablets

Although linked by their attachment to past religious figures, relics and plates diverge in many ways. Their respective internal workings are at odds. One connects with a virtuous person in search of miracles; the other offers a history providing enlightenment. In the search for a type, the plates come closer to the stone tablets on which the Ten Commandments were written. Joseph's plates and Moses's tablets both bore words coming from God. One was a set of relatively brief standards of behavior and worship and the other a lengthy history, but because both came from God, they are treated similarly. Both have been the subject of close examination even though long gone. Each of the sacred texts excites devotional attention and scholarly exegesis.[19] Moreover, the interest goes beyond the words on the tablets and plates. The stories of obtaining the two are nearly as important as the objects themselves. Moses' climb up Mt. Sinai bearing stone tablets and Joseph's retrieval of the plates from Cumorah have become iconic narratives embedded in scripture. Neither object was easily acquired. Moses smashed the first set when he found the camp of Israel in wild debauchery and had to climb the mountain again with another pair of weighty tablets. Joseph Smith had to return to Cumorah four times before he could take the plates from their hiding place. The objects themselves have long since disappeared, but the tortuous stories of their acquisition constitute essential parts of Mormonism's and Judaism's founding narratives. The parallels in tablets and plates allow us to imagine a category of material bearers of sacred words.[20]

Besides the similarities in treatment and origin, both texts suffer from complications. Smith lost the pages of his original translation and had to translate another set of plates to fill in the gap. Instead of retranslating the same pages as before, he substituted a translation from another set of plates, meaning there were two texts covering the same period. Moses similarly doubled up on the words written on the stone tablets. The first words written by God were lost when Moses smashed the tablets and had to go back with another set. According to Deuteronomy, God inscribed the first set with the Ten Commandments and, in popular belief, the Ten Commandments were inscribed again, but Exodus 34 says the second inscriptions were ritual instructions rather than the Ten Commandments. The original Ethical Decalogue was replaced by a Ritual Decalogue.[21] Christians and Jews are left with two possible texts coming from the tablets just as Mormons are left to wonder about the lost 116 pages. Both the commandments on the second tablets and the second version of Lehi's history are troubled texts.[22]

To these large puzzles, scholars of ancient Israel add inquiries similar to the questions asked of the plates. Jewish scholars have speculated about how much space was required to hold an inscription of the Ten Commandments in stone. Were the stone tablets large enough to hold all the text, the same question posed by critics of Joseph Smith. Jewish and Mormon calculations of size then lead to the related question of weight. Just as the weight of the gold plates has been endlessly calculated to determine if Joseph could have carried them home from Cumorah, Jewish scholars have asked if the stone tablets were too heavy for Moses to have carried up Mt. Sinai.[23]

Gold plates and stone tablets share many similarities of purpose and a number of parallels in their histories. They begin to diverge in their treatment after reception. The tablets were installed in the Ark of the Covenant, a magnificent, large portable box constructed with the most elaborate materials, shittim wood, gold overlay, hovering golden cherubim, the whole covered with a veil. The ark was consecrated with holy ointment and guarded with great care. The Lord spoke to Moses from the ark.[24] The plates were also scrupulously protected, and attention given to their preservation, but the containers had none of the grandeur of the ark of the covenant. The plates were kept in a box, stashed under the floorboards, hidden in a stack of flax, and transported in a barrel of beans. They were buried in the woods and kept under bedcovers. Even when believed to be in the hands of an angel, the plates were carried in a mere knapsack. They were an honored history, written by men of God, but they were not kept in splendor. Even the lore about them pictured the plates returned to a cave to lie in silence with the other records from which Mormon drew to write his book.

The Sinai tablets, moreover, were vested with fearful powers. When the feet of the priests who carried the ark touched the waters of Jordan as Israel crossed, the river dried up. After the bearers of the ark containing the plates circled Jericho every day for a week, the walls collapsed, and Israel conquered its enemies. The ark thereafter was carried into battle, exuding its terrible force. When touched by someone other than the designated bearers, the trespassers, despite their wish only to prevent the ark from falling, were struck down.[25] Martin Harris attributed some of the same frightening power to the plates. He said he dared not look on the plates without divine permission for fear he would be smitten. But that seems to have been his own extrapolation from the precedent of the Ark and scriptures about the dangers of looking on God's face.[26] The instructions to Joseph Smith never mentioned the dangers of looking on the plates. He was simply told not to show them to anyone. Nowhere in the Book of Mormon were trespassers warned against looking. The prophets took no precautions against someone mistakenly catching a glimpse. The eight witnesses saw them quite casually, hefting them and turning the pages without special preparations or the promise of protection. The plates were never used as a talisman to intimidate enemies or strengthen believers. The plates were more mundane and less forceful than the stone tablets. They were a utilitarian object that bore a sacred history and were esteemed for the holy words they contained, nothing more.

Plates and stone tablets share a divine purpose—to convey the mind of God in writing—without coinciding exactly. The stone tablets had been touched by the finger of God and bore some of His mighty power; the plates had been inscribed by prophets but served as a record not a talisman. The same issue separates the gold plates from the gold plate of Enoch in the lore of Royal Arch Freemasonry. According to the story, the ancient Enoch was taken up into a high mountain where he saw a triangular gold plate on which ineffable characters were engraven. Enoch was told not to divulge the pronunciation of the words but to build an underground temple with nine arches stacked on top of one another. In the top or royal arch, he was to deposit a facsimile of the gold plate with the ineffable characters written on it. Thousands of years later, some master masons uncovered a hidden vault in Solomon's Temple leading to the royal arch where Enoch's gold plate lay. Nearby was an ancient book and the Ark of the Covenant. With the help of Solomon, the masons translated the secret code on the gold plate and in this way passed down the name of God to generations of masons. The gold plate, the engraved characters, the passage through time resonated with Smith's gold plates, but not the contents. Enoch's plate with the name of God on it was more of a talisman not the historical record of an ancient people.[27]

There is another connection with the Hebrew Bible. In the Book of Mormon, the plates are associated with other holy items, the Liahona, the sword of Laban, the brass plates. These objects, passed from prophet to prophet along with the plates, were hallowed by their key roles during Lehi's exodus from Jerusalem to the Americas. The Liahona was the mysterious compass mounted on a globe that pointed in the direction the migrants were to take. The sword of Laban, admired by Nephi for its exceedingly fine workmanship, was used to decapitate Laban when he refused to turn over the brass plates.[28] The brass plates themselves were stolen by Nephi from Laban's treasury to provide Lehi's family with knowledge of sacred history and so sustain their civilization. This group of honored objects, later augmented by the gold plates of Ether and two translation stones, provided company for the gold plates.[29]

The collection resembled the objects from the Hebrew exodus named in the Book of Hebrews to accompany the tablets of the covenant: the golden censer, Aaron's rod that budded, and the golden pot for manna. These were kept behind the second veil in the tabernacle in the space called "the Holiest of all."[30] The gold plates and the tables of the covenant were sustained by association with historically notable objects, much like royal regalia sustains a monarch's crown. The holy objects, passed from prophet to prophet, created a divine aura around the sacred records.

Terma

Although parallels between plates and tablets are strong, perhaps a still closer comparison can be made to Tibetan Buddhist *terma*. Terma and plates both bore a message from past prophetic figures, both were hidden in the earth and recovered by religious teachers, both were valued primarily for their teachings, and both lent authority to those who found them. "Terma" means treasure and refers to messages secreted by past Buddhist masters for the enlightenment of future followers. Many are attributed to Padmasambhava, an eighth-century master, and his consort and fellow master Yeshe Tsogyal. Padmasambhava came from India to instruct Tibetan students, and when he foresaw the need for tutelage in times to come deposited terma in the earth, in lakes, rocks, and trees, and sometimes in a future mind. They began to be discovered in the eleventh century by treasure revealers called tertöns who taught the wisdom of the past master to a new generation of students. Buddhist teachings in general were passed along by gurus whose authority was derived from the notability of the masters they had studied with. Tertöns claimed authority through the terma, which connected them to notable masters in the past. The teachings partly came from the artifact itself, which was said to be written in a language only the tertöns could interpret. But translation was less important than spiritual influence. The physical object awakened the terma in the mind of the tertön. Seeing or hearing symbolic words caused the discovery of the terma, the treasure, in the tertön's intellect.[31]

The contents of the terma covered the whole range of Buddhist teachings and practices: prayers for all purposes, chapters on the lives of the masters, explanations of mantras, advice about how to live, Buddhist philosophy, and mind training. The most famous example of a terma in the West is *The Tibetan Book of the Dead* compiled by Walter Evans-Wentz, an American traveler in the Himalayas who chanced on a collection of terma, had them translated, and published them in 1927. Evans-Wentz studied theosophy, published a book on Celtic fairy folklore, and studied the Egyptian Book of the Dead, which was the source for the title of his Tibetan publication. He was of the opinion that deep common themes united many religions. His purpose in publishing *The Tibetan Book of the Dead* was to illustrate these themes in their Tibetan form.[32]

The manuscripts that fell into Evans-Wentz's hands were the work of a treasure-seeker named Karma Lingpa who extracted the texts on yellow paper from the Gampodar Mountain in the fourteenth century. Titled the Bardo Tödöl, they were instructions on how to conduct oneself during the Bardo, the period after death and before judgment and reincarnation. If managed rightly, the Bardo is a time when the soul can prepare itself for a higher form of existence. The literal translation of Karma Lingpa's work is "Liberation in the Intermediate State through Hearing."[33]

Although better known in the United States and Europe than in Tibet, the Tibetan Book of the Dead is relevant because one of the scholars who has studied the text, Donald Lopez, compares it to Joseph Smith's Book of Mormon. "The story of Joseph Smith holds many elements in common with the founding of a great religion," Lopez writes. "There is a visitation from an angel; the revelation of scriptures—indeed, scriptures inscribed on tablets in an ancient language; there are believers and unbelievers; there are prophecies fulfilled." There were other nineteenth-century revelators in addition to Smith, notably Mary Baker Eddy and Ellen White, Lopez acknowledges, but none quite like Smith:

> One of the things that sets Smith apart from these other founders is that his vision bore a physical form; he dug it from the earth in upstate New York. It is this element of Smith's revelation that connects him, in one of the uncanny parallels so beloved by Evans-Wentz, to *The Tibetan Book of the Dead*. For this Latter Day Saint was also a latter day treasure discoverer (*gter ston* in Tibetan), a latter day Karma Lingpa for America. Like Karma Lingpa, he unearthed texts from the soil of his native land. Like Karma Lingpa, he died an early and violent death. Like Karma Lingpa, he left a long and complicated legacy.[34]

The parallels go beyond the details of recovery, Lopez argues. They both make a connection to the past:

> The fabrication of lineage is what, from the perspective of historical scholarship, Tibetans had done for centuries. The fabrication of lineage is what, from the perspective of historical scholarship, Joseph Smith had done. In each case, the bodily resurrection of texts from native soil provides a connection to a sacred past. America is no longer merely the destination of immigrants whose scriptures came from a distant Holy Land; sacred scriptures of the Christian faith are buried in American soil; Carthage, Illinois is a place where martyrs died; Kirtland, Ohio is a place of pilgrimage.[35]

Lopez sees Joseph Smith as an American tertön conveying the wisdom of past masters through the translation of ancient texts.

Similar as they are, terma and plates are far from a perfect match. The plates were something less than the stone tablets inscribed by the finger of God, but they were something more than a yellow scroll bearing the teachings of a past master. The materiality of the terma counted for little. Paper or small objects like rocks or leaves could serve. Mind terma functioned with no material at all. The tertön discovered the teachings in his mind stream.[36] In the instances where material objects were involved, the material bearing the coded text was given little attention. This was quite the opposite from the gold plates, where materiality was everything. The plates were described in detail, the length, breadth, and depth of the stack, how they were bound together, the writing on the surface. The message from the past was not found in the mind stream of the prophet but had to be translated through a lengthy and arduous process. Once in hand, the plates were carefully guarded, their location specified, their observation limited. Unlike the long-buried scrolls of terma whose material existence was of little importance, the reality of the plates was a major issue for believers and skeptics alike.

The gold plates then do not line up perfectly with any of their likely kin among divinely invested objects. The plates stand apart from relics, stone tablets, and terma. They are their own configuration of craftsmanship, language, and divine purpose. And still, considering all these objects together, the plates are not alone in the universe. Unique in their details, the plates belong in the company of material things that have connected people to divine purpose and ancient wisdom. Like all their predecessors, the plates were a form of instruction and a source of godly power, linking the present to the past and earth to heaven. In 1827, when preaching was the chief form of religious influence and the Bible the foundation for belief, Joseph Smith introduced a new object into the ecology of faith. In making the gold plates a cornerstone of his founding narrative, he evoked ancient models whose religious resonance he could only have vaguely understood.

Enchantment and Myth

Turning from the past to the present, the recent scholarly fascination with "re-enchantment" has dangled the possibility of still another resting place for the plates. A century ago, the German sociologist Max Weber argued that increased intellectualization and rationalism in Western societies meant that among people of learning "the world is disenchanted." "[T]here are no mysterious incalculable forces that come into play." Belief in God, angels, and demons had been extinguished, meaning, of course, that the gold plates were doomed. Against Weber, dozens of scholars for the past twenty years have been arguing "that enchantment has never been lost." It has persisted as an ingrained and felicitous feature of the human imagination, even among scientists. The scholarship not only cites examples of revived enchantment but find its effects beneficial. Could that mean that the plates will receive renewed attention as a form of enchantment?

On the whole, acknowledgment does not seem likely. Much of the re-enchantment literature is explicitly not religious as the word is traditionally understood. Most proponents wish to avoid lapses into what they consider naïve religious belief. They do not want to revive superstition and fantasy. The overarching purpose of modern re-enchantment is communion—between humanity and nature, between people of differing cultures, between the self and the cosmos. The advocates look to enchantment for connection and empathy. The plates serve such purposes only vaguely. They are far too material, too defined, too religious. They are the wrong kind of enchantment.

The plates resonate more persuasively with classic adventure myths. Their coming into the hands of an uninformed farm boy is redolent of tales in which a simple youth finds himself possessed of magic powers and ventures into the world to face his destiny. Smith can be seen as another rendition of Joseph Campbell's *Hero with a Thousand Faces*. Smith's story is reminiscent of Bilbo Baggins in *The Hobbit* who stumbles across the ring of power and wonders what to do with it. Later, in *The Lord of the Rings*, he passes it to Frodo, a brave but simple soul who bears the ring to its final obliteration in the Cracks of Doom. In his reliving of the age-old story, the young Joseph Smith took on far more than he was prepared for when he brought home the gold plates. He was no more ready than Frodo to assume the burden. Smith too was an innocent, inexplicably chosen to fulfill a towering mission like so many heroes over the centuries. It was a story to stir the imagination of all who relished the adventures of unsuspecting heroes setting forth to save the world.

Doubtless, still more meanings could be piled on the plates. There is no single way to understand them. The plates have been seen as a treasure, as a record, as a fearful talisman of God, as evidence, as word from a dying civilization, as the "stick of Joseph," as a toy. Tony Kushner sees them as an unwelcome token from an absent God; Trey Parker, Matt Stone, and Robert Lopez as a joke; James Rollins as the bearer of advanced science; Orson Scott Card as the foundation of a better world. Scholars are just as ingenious. Sonia Hazard compares the gold plates to printer's plates and Ann Taves to the host in the Eucharist. It seems there is no end to the possibilities.

All of these contexts may partially explain why, after two centuries, the plates still figure in many imaginations. Despite their controversial beginnings, the plates have held their place among the world's strange marvels. Some credit must be given to the plates themselves. From the moment word spread of their presence in the Smith household, they were memorable, even when only imagined. It mattered little that their existence was disputed. As described, they were beautiful: hammered gold, dusky with age, bound with large rings, engraved with fine characters in an unknown language, bearing the history of lost civilizations. Everything about the plates was strange: their origins, their materiality, their mission, their invisibility. Two hundred years later, the mystery lingers on, inviting reflection and inquiry and more than a little wonder.

The Composition of the Plates

After summarizing more than 450 years of Nephite history, Mormon, the main author of the Book of Mormon, interrupted his work to comment on a discovery. As "I searched among the records which had been delivered into my hands," he wrote, he stumbled upon another set of plates written by Nephi and his successors. Liking what he found, Mormon added them to the record he had already made. The new plates covered the same period, but their "prophecies of the coming of Christ" pleased Mormon so much that the duplication seemed worth it.[1] In the plates Joseph Smith received were two accounts of the same period: Mormon's abridgment of one set of plates written by Nephi and his successors and this other set of plates also written by Nephi and his successors and customarily called the small plates of Nephi. Both told the Nephite story from the departure from Jerusalem around 600 BCE to King Benjamin's reign around 130 BCE.

The incident complicates the understanding of what Joseph Smith's gold plates actually consisted of within the world created by the Book of Mormon and Smith's accounts. The recovery stories imagine them as a stack of plates bound with rings and forming one unified collection. Actually, they were a composite of three collections with different origins and purposes. Mormon's editorial comment distinguished two of these collections. One was the abridgment he had been making of Nephi's record; the other was the small set of plates by Nephi that Mormon placed alongside his own abridgment, like a modern author inserting a chunk of original source material into a history book she was writing. The third collection was an ancient vision from a group scattered at the time of the Tower of Babel that Moroni transcribed on to his record.[2]

The Words of Mormon, which describes the discovery of the small plates of Nephi, came along in Joseph Smith's translation at the very moment that he was going through a manuscript crisis. After translating Mormon's abridgment down to early in the Book of Mosiah, Smith lost the manuscript that his scribe Martin Harris had recorded. Harris had pled with Smith for permission to show the manuscript to his unbelieving wife, hoping to convince her that the project was real. Smith reluctantly agreed and was devastated when Harris reported that the 116 pages of manuscript had disappeared. According to Smith's account, the angel took away the plates and the interpreters, and translation halted for nearly ten months.[3] When Smith resumed again in the spring of 1829, a revelation informed him that he was not to retranslate the lost portion of the large plates of Nephi, but to substitute a translation of the small plates that covered the same period.[4] Smith did not go to work on the small plates immediately, however. First, he and his new scribe Oliver Cowdery took up where Smith and Martin Harris left off in Mormon's abridgment and continued on to Moroni and the end of Nephite history. After they had finished the last part of the history, they then went back to the beginning and translated the small plates of Nephi that covered the history lost with the 116 pages—from the departure from Jerusalem down to King Benjamin around 130 BCE.[5]

The small plates then conveniently came along at exactly the moment when the first manuscript was lost, enabling Smith to solve his problem. He could substitute a translation of the small plates for the lost pages of Mormon's abridgment. A revelation in the spring of 1829 warned Smith that if he tried to retranslate the large plate, his enemies would alter the text and prove him to be a fraud. The possibility worried him enough that the preface to the first edition of the Book of Mormon in March 1830 told readers about the commandment not to retranslate the part that was stolen. "For Satan had put it into their hearts to tempt the Lord their God, by altering the words, that they did read contrary from that which I translated and caused to be written; and if I should bring forth the same words again, or, in other words, if I should translate the same over again, they would publish that which they had stolen" and prove him false.[6] The small plates saved Smith from the embarrassment of not being able to duplicate the text he had already dictated to Harris.

The coincidence of Mormon discovering the small plates at the very moment Smith lost the abridgment cannot help but arouse suspicion. Were the Words of Mormon anything more than Smith's transparent attempt to escape his plight after the loss of the 116 pages? It looks like a device, but if Smith was retrofitting the text to get out of a tight spot, he worked hard at making the small plates convincing. Inside the Book of Mormon, the small plates are more than a contrivance to replace the lost 116 pages. They were a potent political document in Nephi's long-standing feud with his brothers. Nephi forged the small plates just after his father died and when he had split with his brothers Laman and Lemuel.[7] The book of First Nephi and the first five chapters of Second Nephi were an extended apologia for his part in the breakdown of brotherly relations and the division of Lehi's family into feuding nations. The moral of story after story was that Nephi acted with the blessing of God and his father Lehi, while Laman and Lemuel had resisted both. The small plates were not just the physical carrier of the story but a strategic document in the internal dynamics of the Nephite drama.

Political aims drove the writing so long as the brothers lived together. After the separation, the story's underlying purpose shifted, and Nephi's record became a different kind of book. As the Lamanites became a more distant threat rather than an ever-present reality, the need for justification of Nephi's rule faded, and the small account changed. Instead of an indictment of Laman and Lemuel, it provided instruction on the coming of the Messiah, the last days, and the end of Nephite civilization. The small plates could indeed have been an invention to rescue the floundering translator, but the plates were no make-do patch job. The text conformed itself to the changes in Nephite history. At first the small plates intensified the basic Mormon plot of Nephite versus Lamanite and when that issue faded turned to the Nephites' evolving needs.

Among Latter-day Saint scholars, the small plates have raised questions. Problems arise, for example, in trying to reimagine exactly how Mormon dealt with the small plates, an interloper in the otherwise orderly process of abridging the large plates of Nephi.[8] What did Mormon mean when he said he would put them "with the remainder of my record"?[9] Did that mean he added the small plates to the stack containing his abridgment? Did Joseph Smith recover a set plates with both large and small plates bound together in the rings? The independent scholar Jonathan Neville argues that Mormon did not add them to his stack, and the small plates were not among the plates Joseph Smith recovered from the stone box. The small plates came to him later in the translation period as a second installment. Neville thinks Joseph Smith translated Mormon's abridgment from the plates he recovered from Cumorah while living in Harmony, Pennsylvania. That took him through to the end of Moroni's writings at the end of the book. Smith then returned that set of plates to a divine personage—presumably Moroni—who was the stranger whom Joseph and David Whitmer met on their way from Harmony to Fayette. The pack on the stranger's back contained the original plates Smith took from the stone box. Later in Fayette, Neville argues, Joseph Smith received the small plates that he translated there. For the witnesses to see the first set of plates, the angel had to bring them from Cumorah to Fayette.[10]

Neville's argument shows how complicated the picture becomes when the array of plates are examined closely, especially since Joseph Smith assigned a title meant to clarify the plates situation but which only muddied the waters. Smith referred to the source of Mormon's abridgment as the Plates of Lehi, trying to distinguish the large plates of Nephi from the small plates.[11] But the Book of Mormon itself shows that Mormon relied on the large plates of Nephi, not Lehi, for his abridgment.[12] Lehi kept a record that Nephi may have drawn upon, but Mormon did not use Lehi's record to compile his history. He used Nephi's large plates. As the title page explains, he took the Book of Mormon from the "Plates of Nephi."[13]

Looking at all this together, four accounts recorded the early history of the Nephites:

a. The record Lehi kept that Nephi drew on for his account.[14]

b. Nephi's large plates: the detailed record of government and military affairs referred to by Joseph Smith as the Plates of Lehi in the original Preface to the Book of Mormon but written by Nephi. These are the plates of Nephi referred to on the title page of the Book of Mormon.[15]

c. Nephi's small plates that Mormon added to the plates containing his record and that Joseph Smith translated to replace the lost 116 pages.[16]

d. Mormon's plates, his abridgment of Nephi's large plates that Joseph Smith recovered from the Hill Cumorah. The translation of the first part of Mormon's abridgment was written in the 116 pages that were lost.[17]

Going on from these plates, there was one more component of Joseph Smith's plates. Mormon's son Moroni added a lengthy and mysterious revelation that likely contained more leaves than the large and small plates together.[18] It is known as the sealed portion because in some fashion it was sealed up so as not to be read until the world was ready. Most commentators envision a physical band binding the sealed plates; the text itself also suggested that an untranslatable language was a kind of seal.[19] The sealed plates contain a massive vision granted to the Brother of Jared, a leader of the Jaredites, a party of migrants who fled from the Tower of Babel and made their way to the New World centuries before the Nephites. A man of great faith, the Brother of Jared had been granted a vision of Jesus and then of "all the inhabitants of the earth which had been, and also all that would be; and he withheld them not from his sight, even unto the ends of the earth." He was told to "write these things and seal them up; and I will show them in mine own due time unto the children of men." With the vision, the Lord gave two stones to the Brother of Jared that would "magnify to the eyes of men these things which ye shall write," enabling them to translate.[20] The stones were called interpreters (later Urim and Thummim). They descended through Jaredite history and then mysteriously came into the possession of King Mosiah. From then on, they accompanied the Nephite records and ultimately went into the stone box with Mormon's plates. These very stones were the ones Joseph Smith used to translate the Book of Mormon.[21]

The Jaredite records and the two stones entered Nephite history near its midpoint.[22] The records were found during the reign of King Mosiah, when a colony of Nephites who had moved from Zarahemla back to the original Nephite homeland attempted to find Zarahemla again. Their king, a man named Limhi, sent out a party of explorers to locate Zarahemla, though the route was unknown. While wandering in the wilderness, they stumbled on the ruins of another civilization. Fishing about, they came across a precious find: twenty-four gold plates engraved with characters in a language none of the Nephites understood. Intensely curious about the contents, King Limhi was delighted to learn that King Mosiah in Zarahemla could translate the records by means of two stones called interpreters. When he finally connected with Zarahemla, Limhi turned the Jaredite plates over to Mosiah for translation, and thus the plates and the interpreters joined the collection of sacred items passed from prophet to prophet, eventually coming to Moroni.[23] During his long, lonely years after his father Mormon died, Moroni abridged the record of the Jaredites and engraved the visions of the Brother of Jared on his plates. "I have written upon these plates the very things which the brother of Jared saw."[24] Moroni sealed up these writings along with the "interpreters" given to the Brother of Jared and both became part of the assemblage Joseph Smith received, either in its entirety at Cumorah, as has traditionally been believed, or in two batches as Jonathan Neville argues.

The sealed portion was an object of great curiosity among early Latter-day Saints. The scriptures informed them that the translation would come only when the people had prepared themselves. One Mormon leader speculated that the sealed portion would not be translated until the millennium.[25] And so they remain an obscure object in Mormon lore—except for a few bold interpreters who feel compelled to look further. In 2020 you could buy the second edition of *The Sealed Portion: The Final Testament of Jesus Christ* by Christopher Marc Nemelka in paperback for $26.97. Nemelka claimed to be the reincarnation of Hyrum Smith, Joseph Smith's brother, and to have been visited by Joseph himself.[26] Another Amazon ad offered *The Sealed Portion of the Brother of Jared* by The Brotherhood of Christ Church. The ad claimed that the ancient sage the Brother of Jared "has explained in remarkable detail the events surrounding the closing centuries of our world. His perspectives offer perhaps the ultimate solution to modern religious and ecological dilemmas. It is entirely possible that these writings contain nothing less than the essential religious world view that will dominate the closing centuries of the experience of humankind."[27] None of these attempts have the approval of the Church of Jesus Christ of Latter-day Saints or have much circulation among Latter-day Saints. But like the gold plates themselves, the sealed portion offers a means for aspiring prophets to stake a claim to divine guidance.

All of this speculation and analysis goes on within the world created by the Book of Mormon and its associated stories. In Mormon minds, it was a real world where evidence could be gathered and analyzed. In it, plates abound, record-keeping is an obsession, and modern researchers need to get it straight. The details had little to do with the religious import of the text, but they had a lot to do with giving the plates and Nephite history a palpable reality.

The Translation Debates

The word "translation" ill fits the process Joseph Smith went through to produce the Book of Mormon from the gold plates. Translation implies a person fluent in two languages transforming a text from one language to the other. Joseph Smith did not claim to know the reformed Egyptian of the gold plates or the original languages of any of the texts he translated: the Book of Mormon, the Bible, or the Book of Abraham. Yet he insisted on using "translation" to name what he did "by the gift and power of God." He even called his revisions of the English Bible a translation.[1]

It is no surprise, then, that the translation of the gold plates has always been wrapped in controversy. Recently, even his followers have differed in what he meant by the term.[2] Initially, the issue was quite straightforward: did Joseph Smith translate the plates, as Mormons thought, or did someone else make up the Book of Mormon? Beginning with James Bennett's 1831 newspaper report on Mormonism, nineteenth-century critics attributed the text to Sidney Rigdon, the Ohio preacher who surprised everyone by joining the Mormons in 1830.[3] Virtually every skeptic until around 1900 believed Rigdon had concocted the Book of Mormon by adding religious elements to Solomon Spaulding's story of Hebrews migrating to the Western Hemisphere. There was no discussion of translation itself because, in the critical view, there were no plates and thus no translation.

Translation figured in the critics' mind only as a way to show Joseph Smith's claims to miraculous powers were bogus. Henry Caswall tried to tempt the Prophet into translating a Greek Psalter. He hoped Joseph would try to translate the Greek and fail, proving he was a fake.[4] Likewise, the makers of the Kinderhook Plates apparently thought they could fool Smith into attempting a translation of characters that they burned into the metal.[5] Neither were interested in how translation worked. Their sole purpose was to demonstrate that Smith's claim to the gift of translation was a pretense.

Believers in Joseph Smith, of course, thought that God inspired their prophet to translate the book. They were curious about how he did it, but Smith never went beyond his brief statement in the Preface to the Book of Mormon that he translated by the gift and power of God. In an 1842 letter to a Chicago newspaper editor, he described "a curious instrument which the ancients called 'Urim and Thummim,' which consisted of two transparent stones set in the rim of a bow fastened to a breastplate. Through the medium of the Urim and Thummim I translated the record by the gift, and power of God."[6] Smith did not say how he used the instrument or what he saw.

Some people close to Smith during the translation period tried to elaborate on Smith's terse description. David Whitmer described the process in greater detail than anyone and underscored the use of a seer stone rather than the Urim and Thummim:

Joseph Smith would put the seer stone into a hat, and put his face in the hat, drawing it closely around his face to exclude the light; and in the darkness the spiritual light would shine. A piece of something resembling parchment would appear, and on that appeared the writing. One character at a time would appear, and under it was the interpretation in English. Brother Joseph would read off the English to Oliver

Cowdery, who was his principal scribe, and when it was written down and repeated to Brother Joseph to see if it was correct, then it would disappear, and another character with the interpretation would appear.[7]

Emma Smith confirmed the seer stone version of translation though in less detail. In 1879 she told her son in a formal interview that she wrote for her husband day after day, "he sitting with his face buried in his hat, with the stone in it and dictating hour after hour."[8]

Whitmer's and Emma Smith's accounts specified a different instrument—seer stone rather than Urim and Thummim—and a different process—reading text rather than translating it—than could readily be derived from Smith's own brief account. Which were Latter-day Saints to believe? Orson Hyde's summary in an 1842 history blended the two views:

Two transparent stones, clear as crystal, were found with the records. They were called "seers" and were used by the ancients. The manner in which they were used is as follows: These two stones, called Urim and Thummim, in diameter the size of an English crown (coin) but a little thicker, were placed where there was no light. Those using them then offered prayers unto the Lord and the answer appeared written with letters of light on the Urim and Thummim, but disappeared again soon after.[9]

Hyde followed Joseph's 1842 letter in using the name Urim and Thummim, but agreed with Whitmer in saying that Smith placed the stones out of the light and read letters that disappeared.

Perhaps because of the contradictions in early explanations, through the nineteenth-century descriptions became quite spare. John Jaques's *Catechism for Children*, which went through nine editions in English and ten more in German, Dutch, Danish, Swedish, and Hawaiian before the year 1900, said simply: "He translated them, by the power of God, through the Urim and Thummim, enduring much persecution at the time, from religious people, who said he was an impostor."[10] In his *Life of Joseph Smith, the Prophet*, George Q. Cannon summed up the process in a sentence: "Joseph dictated to Martin Harris from the plates of gold; as the characters thereon assumed through the Urim and Thummim the forms of equivalent modern words which were familiar to the understanding of the youthful Seer."[11] In the early twentieth century, some church publications said almost nothing about translation. In his *Essentials in Church History*, Joseph Fielding Smith said only that Joseph Smith translated a few characters for Martin Harris using the Urim and Thummim.[12]

In the years when translation was neglected in most accounts, a few Mormon scholars described the process in detail. John Henry Evans's *One Hundred Years of Mormonism* candidly observed that "the Prophet had a small stone, which he called a 'seerstone,' and which he and his brother Hyrum had found at the bottom of a well. This stone Joseph sometimes employed, instead of the urim and thummim, to translate the language on the plates."[13] B. H. Roberts, a General Authority of the Church, was far more expansive than either Joseph Fielding Smith or Evans. In the *Comprehensive History of the Church*, first published in installments between 1909 and 1915 in a non-Mormon periodical and then revised and reprinted in 1930, Roberts told the story pretty much as it is understood by most Church scholars today. Smith had a Urim and Thummim consisting of crystals set in bows like spectacles which he used to translate. Following David Whitmer, Roberts said that he "possessed a Seer Stone, by which he was enabled to translate as well as with the Urim and Thummim, and for convenience he sometimes used the Seer Stone." In the same passage, Roberts also quoted Whitmer's line about Joseph seeing something like parchment with the English interpretation underneath. Joseph would read it off to his scribe, and "when it was written down and repeated to brother Joseph to see if it was correct, then it would disappear." Roberts even speculated about the language of the translation. "There can be no doubt, either, that the interpretation thus obtained was expressed in such language as the Prophet could command, in such phraseology as he was master of and common to the time and locality where he lived." Smith read the words in the stones, but the language came from his own provincial American culture.[14]

Roberts's early account comes as a surprise to twenty-first-century readers because of the widespread belief that until recently, the Church had suppressed references to the seer stone. Only after the official Church adopted a policy of transparency in the past decade, it has been assumed, was the seer stone acknowledged. Actually, during the Roberts era, there were Latter-day Saint scholars who speculated rather freely about translation. In 1904 an instructor at Brigham Young University, Professor N. L. Nelson, in a short-lived periodical *Mormon Point of View*, attempted to deal with the rapid-fire translation of the Book of Mormon and its complexity. Nelson thought Moroni read the characters, which aroused thoughts which were then passed by the Spirit into the mind of Joseph who rendered them into English. "My idea, then, is that the translation of the Book of Mormon is the joint product of two men—Joseph Smith and most probably the Angel Moroni."[15]

In 1905, John Henry Evans in *One Hundred Years of Mormonism*, a book approved by the First Presidency for use in the Sunday Schools, also asked the question: "Did the English translation appear with the Nephite characters, or was Joseph enabled, by inspiration, to read the language of the plates, get the idea intended, and then express that idea in such language as he had at his command?" Evans worked through all the known facts about translation, including the presence of many grammatical errors, and concluded that "the Prophet Joseph obtained the idea through inspiration by means of the 'seer stone' on the urim and thummim, and expressed this in such language as he had at his command."[16]

Speculation about translation increased among secular scholars in the early twentieth century as the Spaulding –Rigdon hypothesis fell into disrepute. If Joseph Smith not Rigdon produced the manuscript, as I. Woodbridge Riley argued in 1903 in *The Founder of Mormonism*, the question of how Smith created the text became more pressing. Where did the words of the Book of Mormon come from? From Riley on, critics proposed sources for this element and that in the text: revivalist religion, conspiratorial secret societies, the great and abominable church, Hebrew origins of Native Americans, republican language.[17] Alexander Campbell, the reformed Baptist preacher, set the research agenda of this line of inquiry in 1831. The Book of Mormon, Campbell wrote, touched on "every error and almost every truth discussed in New York for the last ten years."[18]

Beyond the question of the book's contents, secular scholars have also had to confront the question of how Smith "translated." How at such a young age did he dictate this lengthy account in such a short space of time—no more than eighteen months, with most of the work compressed into ninety days? This line of inquiry has led to a search for parallels. Who else produced long complicated texts in a short period of time seemingly without the education required to explain the writing? J. E. Homans, a non-Mormon writing for the Church under the pseudonym Robert C. Webb, wrote in 1916 that "the latest, and, as considered in many quarters, the 'most scientific' theory of the origin of the Book of Mormon" was that it was "the product of 'automatic mental operations' of some kind."[19] The hypothesis survived, and in 2002, Scott C. Dunn, a technical writer with Mormon roots, compiled a list of texts produced by a process he termed "automaticity." He cited, for example, the writings of Pearl Curran, a St. Louis housewife who wrote a novel in the voice of Patience Worth, a seventeenth-century Englishwoman. Curran dictated poems and epigrams, novels, and plays of a quality far above her education or native talent. One was *The Sorry Tale*, a long historical novel on the life of Jesus Christ. Curran dictated a chapter of 5,000 words on the Crucifixion in a single evening. Dunn points out the parallels with Joseph Smith's dictation of the Book of Mormon: spoken in a steady stream without interruption, texts far beyond the speaker's education or known ability, evidence of familiarity with other times and forms of speech. Dunn's aim was to bring into question the inspiration behind the Book of Mormon. "There does not appear to be anything of a historical, theological, philosophical, or literary quality in the scriptural writings of Joseph Smith that has not been matched by those well outside the Mormon tradition."[20] Dunn, however, did not find parallels to Joseph Smith's gold plates. None of the automatic writers uncovered a mystical object on which their stories were written.

For a period in the late twentieth century, the means of translation became an open controversy among informed Latter-day Saints. Many believing scholars came to accept the accounts of David Whitmer and Emma Smith about Joseph using a seer stone and peering into a hat used to keep out the light, but in its official publications, the Church did not.[21] For some, seer stone versus Urim and Thummim became a test of honesty. Would the Church face up to the facts or not? Eventually it did. The Church History Department published all the sources and even released a picture of the seer stone in the Church's possession.[22] A "Gospel Topics" essay on the Church's website summed up what its historians had come to believe:

> Joseph Smith and his scribes wrote of two instruments used in translating the Book of Mormon. According to witnesses of the translation, when Joseph looked into the instruments, the words of scripture appeared in English. One instrument, called in the Book of Mormon the "interpreters," is better known to Latter-day Saints today as the "Urim and Thummim."
>
> The other instrument, which Joseph Smith discovered in the ground years before he retrieved the gold plates, was a small oval stone, or "seer stone." As a young man during the 1820s, Joseph Smith, like others in his day, used a seer stone to look for lost objects and buried treasure. As Joseph grew to understand his prophetic calling, he learned that he could use this stone for the higher purpose of translating scripture.[23]

In 2018, the Church's new official history, *Saints*, seamlessly folded the new scholarship into its account of the Book of Mormon translation. "Sometimes Joseph translated by looking through the interpreters and reading in English the characters," the history read, but "often he found a single seer stone to be more convenient. He would put the seer stone in his hat, place his face into the hat to block out the light, and peer at the stone. Light from the stone would shine in the darkness, revealing words that Joseph dictated as Oliver rapidly copied them down."[24] It seemed as if a new orthodoxy was emerging based on recognition of the evidence for use of the stone.

Recently, however, a challenge has been issued to the seemingly dominant seer stone explanation. There are those who believe that the repeated statements of nineteenth-century Church leaders about the key role of the Urim and Thummim must be taken seriously. They cannot be discredited out of hand in favor of the relatively few accounts of the seer stone. The seer stone stories, Jonathan Neville argues, originated in a performance for the Whitmer family to satisfy their curiosity and was not the actual means of translation. After Smith moved from his own house in Harmony to the Whitmers' in Fayette, he was aware of the burden he and his entourage imposed on the Whitmers. Smith felt an obligation to give the family an idea of what he was doing. He staged a gathering where the household and friends could view translation in action. To keep the Urim and Thummim concealed, he substituted a seer stone in a hat for the purpose of the demonstration. The presentation occurred in the Whitmers' living room, which could accommodate a gathering. This performance led to David Whitmer's confident claim about use of the seer stone. The actual translation, however, went on privately in an upstairs room where the Urim and Thummim could be safely brought out.[25] That meant that Smith's own references to the Urim and Thummim and the repeated references by Church leaders since his time represented the actual method of translation.

Since the questions raised by the seer stone came into focus in the late twentieth century, the debates over translation have both increased in number and changed in nature. For the past twenty years or so, the disagreements have occurred more among believing Mormons than between believers and critics. For these believing scholars, the question has not been Smith's inspiration; most parties to the debate agree God inspired him. The question has been: how was the inspiration delivered? So long as the Urim and Thummim was thought to be the instrument of translation, the process was intelligible: Smith looked in the crystals, saw or understood the words, and dictated the text. But in seer stone accounts, Smith did not even look at the plates.[26] Descriptions sometimes referred to the plates wrapped in a cloth on the table, not even in sight. If he was not reading from the plates, where did Joseph Smith find the words?

Royal Skousen, the meticulous editor of the original manuscripts written by Smith's scribes, has found tiny clues that Smith was tightly controlled in his use of words. Skousen concludes that Smith read the words in the stone or stones and was not given more words until after the scribe had read the words back to him. Smith dictated blocks of at least twenty to thirty words at a time, Skousen concluded, judging from occasional errors in the text where the scribe anticipated the dictation and wrote phrases prior to their actual place in the sentence. This kind of error occurs when the scribe is hearing dictation rather than when he is copying a text. Joseph Smith essentially read the text and the scribes heard and recorded the dictation.[27]

Other equally faithful scholars believe it was not so cut-and-dried. The problem for them is the language. The Book of Mormon contains vocabulary and phrasing not only from the King James Version of the Bible but from eighteenth- and nineteenth-century America. The book contains over 50,000 phrases of three or more words taken from the Bible.[28] A word search comparing the Book of Mormon text with a wide variety of writings from the century previous to its publication turned up an inordinate number of parallels from the writings of the eighteenth-century American theologian Jonathan Edwards.[29] How could that language appear on ancient plates engraved centuries before Edwards?

Jonathan Neville proposes that "the Lord prepared Joseph to act as translator by giving him the means, motives, and opportunity to read and listen to numerous Christian teachings. These terms, phrases, and arguments contributed to Joseph's mental language bank, upon which he drew to translate the plates after having studied the characters."[30] Brant Gardner likewise believes that Smith had to have been "an active participant in the process rather than a passive reader." What he read was influenced by what he thought and what he knew. Gardner argues that God imparted a pre-language impression of the text in Smith's mind that he then expressed in his own vocabulary. "I hypothesize that mentalese, or the prelanguage of the brain, holds the answer to how Joseph Smith translated the Book of Mormon." God or some divine influence "implanted the plate text in Joseph's brain in the brain's native prelanguage." Smith then translated these impressions into English, summoning the words accessible to him in his culture. Gardner suggests that another translator from another language culture would produce a different translation.[31]

Through the flurry of theories about Book of Mormon translation, Royal Skousen has not wavered in his original assertions. He still believes that Joseph Smith read the text that he dictated and that the language was not his own. Skousen has assembled a thousand pages of evidence to support the claim that the Book of Mormon employs archaic and early modern English, not nineteenth-century American diction. Neither does the book address nineteenth-century religious and political issues, Skousen thinks, but instead deals with questions more relevant to sixteenth- and seventeenth-century England: burning people at the stake for heresy, Trinitarianism, child and infant baptism, translation of the Bible, secret combinations, and confession and penance. Adding the doctrinal resonances to the evidence of early modern diction, Skousen argues, challenges the common belief that the Book of Mormon was heavily influenced by Joseph Smith's nineteenth-century culture.[32]

Samuel Brown goes to the opposite extreme from Skousen's reading theory of translation. He argues that it was an oral performance, not an act of reading words seen in the stone or responding to impressions from God. Brown points out that the Book of Mormon itself says nothing about the means of translation, so we should look instead for the means by which prophets received revelation in scriptural texts. He finds precedents in the panoramic visions of Nephi, the Brother of Jared, and of Moses, and suggests that Smith had similar visions which he then described in his own words. "In this model of a prophetic God's-eye-view of human history that creates scripture, the Book of Mormon text may illuminate at least part of its own production." Smith was not reading text or interpreting impressions, he was describing what he saw in a panoramic vision. It was an oral performance based on a visual experience. Brown identifies verbal false starts and missteps that would naturally occur if speaking the text but not if one was reading it.[33]

Ann Taves, who earlier had devised an explanation of how the gold plates came to seem so real to Smith, has peeled away less trustworthy accounts of translation in an effort to get down to translation as Joseph Smith experienced it. To sharpen that focus, she follows Scott Dunn in using an example of so-called automatic writing. Taves describes the work of Helen Schucman, a Columbia University psychologist who between the years 1965 and 1972 wrote out in shorthand *A Course in Miracles* as dictated to her by the "voice of Jesus." Schucman always carried a notebook to record the words whenever they flowed into her mind. She read the shorthand words to her colleague William Thetford, also a Columbia psychologist, who transcribed them. In its published form, *A Course in Miracles* came to 669 pages, an accompanying workbook was 448 pages, and a manual for teachers 92 pages.[34]

After sifting through the various accounts of Book of Mormon translation, Taves sees similarities between Smith's and Schucman's experience. Both "might have had a sense of meaning so immediate as to feel as if it were a word." Both were able to "shift from a 'flow of words' modality into a visual modality in which he was able to see words spelled out." In sum, she argued, "Smith had a highly focused awareness, a strong and immediate sense of meaning (experienced as a flow of words), a considerable degree of control over the experience, and even the ability (as needed) to shift into a visual modality in which he was able to see words spelled out."[35] Taves is not saying that Smith was inspired by God, but his description of translation as given by the "gift and power of God" truthfully described the experience. In his moments of high awareness, meaning was pressed upon him and shaped into words.

In an ingenious and provocative exploration, Jared Hickman displaces the usual meaning of translation with another meaning entirely, the translation of the body as recorded in the biblical stories of Enoch and Elijah moving from mortality to immortality without experiencing death. Unlike Skousen, Gardner, and Brown, Hickman believes Joseph Smith authored the Book of Mormon, but argues that the book is a magnificent creation when its meaning is pursued to the end. By loosening translation to imply metaphysical transitions, Hickman argues, the book's broad significance comes into view. Metaphysical translation could entail Joseph Smith "transposing all of sacred history to his America in the form of the Book of Mormon." In the American context, translation brought the reality of one era and people, the indigenous population, into juxtaposition with the Europeans who had wrested the land from the natives. "The quest with which Smith was entrusted was, as the historical sources repeatedly affirm, to 'bring forth' the subterranean voices of the American past onto the ground of the American present." For Hickman, the seer stone rather than the plates was the crucial technology for recovering this ancient world. "From the beginning, then, Smith was learning to translate himself into the ancient American world through the virtual reality technology of the seer stone and then translate that world back into his own through the virtual reality technology of oral storytelling." Translation brought together two historical realities. The ultimate object was to help European Christians understand a world inhabited by another and long unknown people—Native Americans. "This is where 'the translation of the Book of Mormon' begins: in practices of *metaphysical* translation that reconfigure space-time in consequential ways—specifically, altering the way Euro-Christian settlers inhabit the indigenous cosmos they find themselves in."[36]

Ingenious as speculations such as Hickman's are, the puzzle of translation has not been solved.[37] How the words came to flow from Joseph Smith's mouth into the ears of the scribes and then on to paper remains unresolved. We have plenty of hypotheses and no agreement. Among lay Latter-day Saints, the question is, Why the plates at all? So long as it was believed Joseph read from the plates through the Urim and Thummim, their purpose was clear. But if he read the text from a seer stone while the plates lay covered on the table, as many now believe, what part did they play? Why the effort to preserve them through the centuries, why the trouble to recover and protect them, why their presence? Sometimes it looks as if the plates were both essential to translation and useless. And so their story begins and ends in a puzzle.

Source Abbreviations

Book of Mormon, 1830 ed./*The Book of Mormon: An Account Written by the Hand of Mormon, upon Plates Taken from the Plates of Nephi.* Palmyra, NY: E. B. Grandin, 1830.

Doctrine and Covenants, 1835 ed./*Doctrine and Covenants of the Church of the Latter Day Saints: Carefully Selected from the Revelations of God.* Compiled by Joseph Smith, Oliver Cowdery, Sidney Rigdon, and Frederick G. Williams. Kirtland, OH: F. G. Williams, 1835.

EMD/Vogel, Dan, ed. *Early Mormon Documents.* 5 vols. Salt Lake City: Signature Books, 1996–2003.

JSP, D1/MacKay, Michael Hubbard, Gerrit J. Dirkmaat, Grant Underwood, Robert J. Woodford, and William G. Hartley, eds. *Documents, Volume 1: July 1828–June 1831.* Vol. 1 of the Documents series of *The Joseph Smith Papers,* edited by Dean C. Jessee, Ronald K. Esplin, Richard Lyman Bushman, and Matthew J. Grow. Salt Lake City: Church Historian's Press, 2013.

JSP, D2/Godfrey, Matthew C., Mark Ashurst-McGee, Grant Underwood, Robert J. Woodford, and William G. Hartley, eds. *Documents, Volume 2: July 1831–January 1833.* Vol. 2 of the Documents series of *The Joseph Smith Papers,* edited by Dean C. Jessee, Ronald K. Esplin, Richard Lyman Bushman, and Matthew J. Grow. Salt Lake City: Church Historian's Press, 2013.

JSP, D4/Godfrey, Matthew C., Brenden W. Rensink, Alex D. Smith, Max H. Parkin, and Alexander L. Baugh, eds. *Documents, Volume 4: April 1834–September 1835.* Vol. 4 of the Documents series of *The Joseph Smith Papers,* edited by Ronald K. Esplin, Matthew J. Grow, and Matthew C. Godfrey. Salt Lake City: Church Historian's Press, 2016.

JSP, D8/Rogers, Brent M., Mason K. Allred, Gerrit J. Dirkmaat, and Brett D. Dowdle, eds. *Documents, Volume 8: February–November 1841.* Vol. 8 of the Documents series of *The Joseph Smith Papers,* edited by Ronald K. Esplin, Matthew J. Grow, Matthew C. Godfrey, and R. Eric Smith. Salt Lake City: Church Historian's Press, 2019.

JSP, H1/Davidson, Karen Lynn, David J. Whittaker, Mark Ashurst-McGee, and Richard L. Jensen, eds. *Histories, Volume 1: Joseph Smith Histories, 1832–1844.* Vol. 1 of the Histories series of *The Joseph Smith Papers,* edited by Dean C. Jessee, Ronald K. Esplin, and Richard Lyman Bushman. Salt Lake City: Church Historian's Press, 2012.

JSP, R3, Part 1/Skousen, Royal, and Robin Scott Jensen, eds. *Revelations and Translations, Volume 3, Part 1: Printer's Manuscript of the Book of Mormon, 1 Nephi 1–Alma 35.* Facsimile edition. Part 1 of vol. 3 of the Revelations and Translations series of *The Joseph Smith Papers,* edited by Ronald K. Esplin and Matthew J. Grow. Salt Lake City: Church Historian's Press, 2015.

JSP, R4/Jensen, Robin Scott, and Brian M. Hauglid, eds. *Revelations and Translations, Volume 4: Book of Abraham and Related Manuscripts.* Facsimile edition. Vol. 4 of the Revelations and Translations series of *The Joseph Smith Papers,* edited by Ronald K. Esplin, Matthew J. Grow, Matthew C. Godfrey, and R. Eric Smith. Salt Lake City: Church Historian's Press, 2018.

JSP, R5/Jensen, Robin Scott, and Royal Skousen, eds. Revelations and Translations, Volume 5: Original Manuscript of the Book of Mormon. Facsimile edition. Vol. 5 of the Revelations and Translations series of The Joseph Smith Papers, edited by Matthew C. Godfrey, R. Eric Smith, Matthew J. Grow, and Ronald K. Esplin. Salt Lake City: Church Historian's Press, 2021.

Notes

Preface

1. Benjamin Knoll and Jana Riess, "'Infected with Doubt': An Empirical Overview of Belief and Non-Belief in Contemporary American Mormonism," *Dialogue* (Fall 2017): 19, https://doi.org/10.5406/dialjmormthou.50.3.0001. The figure of 77 percent is a recalculation of some of the figures in this article. My thanks to Benjamin Knoll and Jana Riess for supplying this data and to Theo Calderara for drawing my attention to it.
2. *Wayne Sentinel* (Palmyra, NY), June 26, 1829, in EMD 2:219. Donald Q. Cannon, "In the Press: Early Newspaper Reports on the Initial Publication of the Book of Mormon," *Journal of Book of Mormon Studies* 16, no. 2 (2007), 4–15, 92–93.
3. "Beware of Secret Associations," *Reflector* (Palmyra, NY), September 30, 1829; "Gold Bible, No. 2," *Reflector*, 18 January, 1831; in EMD, 2:227, 240.
4. Palmyra (NY) *Reflector*, January 18, February 14, February 28, 1831, *EMD*, 2:240–41, 244, 246. For an elaboration of this theme emphasizing magic, see Adam Jortner, "'Some Little Necromancy': Politics, Religion, and the Mormons, 1829–1838," in *Contingent Citizens: Shifting Perceptions of Latter-day Saints in American Political Culture*, ed. Spencer W. McBride, Brent M. Rogers, and Keith A. Erekson (Ithaca, NY: Cornell University Press, 2020), 17–28.
5. Mark Twain (Samuel Clemens), *Roughing It* (Hartford: American Publishing Company, 1875), 129.

Chapter 1

1. Early accounts of Joseph getting the plates are found in History, ca. Summer 1832, in *JSP*, H1:13–14; History, 1834–36, in *JSP*, H1:80–86; History Drafts, 1838–ca. 1841, in *JSP*, H1:218–26, 230-32 (Draft 2); "Church History," Mar. 1, 1842, in *JSP*, H1:494–95; "Latter Day Saints," 1844, in *JSP*, H1:524–30; see also Oliver Cowdery, "Letter VIII," *Latter Day Saints' Messenger and Advocate* (Kirtland, OH), October 1835, 196–200.
2. History, ca. Summer 1832, in *JSP*, H1:14–15; History Drafts, 1838–ca. 1841, in *JSP*, H1:236 (Draft 2); "Church History," March 1, 1842, in *JSP*, H1:495; "Latter Day Saints," 1844, in *JSP*, H1:530; Dean Jessee, "Joseph Knight's Recollection of Early Mormon History," *BYU Studies* 17, no. 1 (Autumn 1976): 31; Lucy Mack Smith, History, 1845, 105, Church History Library, Salt Lake City, available at josephsmithpapers.org.
3. Andrew H. Hedges, "'All My Endeavors to Preserve Them': Protecting the Plates in Palmyra, 22 September–December 1827," *Journal of Book of Mormon Studies*

8, no. 2 (1999): 21–23; Kyle R. Walker, "Katharine Smith Salisbury: Sister to the Prophet," *Mormon Historical Studies* 3, no. 2 (Fall 2002): 8.

4. In the Hebrew Bible, the Urim and Thummim apparently were small objects placed in the priest's breastplate and used to arrive at judgments. Cornelis Van Dam, *The Urim and Thummim: A Means of Revelation in Ancient Israel* (Winona Lake, IN: Eisenbrauns, 1997).

5. History, ca. Summer 1832, in *JSP*, H1:15; History Drafts, 1838–ca. 1841, in *JSP*, H1:222, 232, 236 (Draft 2); "Latter Day Saints," 1844, in *JSP*, H1:530–31; "Joseph Smith Documents Dating through June 1831," in *JSP*, D1:xxix–xxxii; see also Michael Hubbard MacKay and Gerrit J. Dirkmaat, *From Darkness unto Light: Joseph Smith's Translation and Publication of the Book of Mormon* (Provo, UT: Religious Studies Center, Brigham Young University; Salt Lake City: Deseret Book, 2015), ch. 4. For meditations on Joseph Smith as translator, see Samuel Morris Brown, *Joseph Smith's Translation: The Words and Worlds of Early Mormonism* (New York: Oxford University Press, 2020); and Richard Lyman Bushman, *Believing History: Latter-day Saint Essays*, ed. Reid L. Neilson and Jed Woodworth (New York: Columbia University Press, 2004), 233–47.

6. For surveys of the Smith family and treasure digging, see Richard Lyman Bushman, *Joseph Smith: Rough Stone Rolling* (New York: Alfred A. Knopf, 2005), 48–52; Richard S. Van Wagoner, *Natural Born Seer: Joseph Smith, American Prophet, 1805–1830* (Salt Lake City: Smith-Pettit Foundation, 2016), 168–80; Dan Vogel, *Joseph Smith: The Making of a Prophet* (Salt Lake City: Signature Books, 2004), 35–46; D. Michael Quinn, *Early Mormonism and the Magic World View*, rev. ed. (Salt Lake City: Signature Books, 1998), ch. 2; Eber D. Howe, *Mormonism Unvailed: Or, a Faithful Account of That Singular Imposition and Delusion, from Its Rise to the Present Time. With Sketches of the Characters of Its Propagators, and a Full Detail of the Manner in Which the Famous Golden Bible Was Brought before the World.* [. . .] (Painesville, OH: By the author, 1834), 238; and History Drafts, 1838–ca. 1841, in *JSP*, H1:234–36 (Draft 2).

7. History, ca. Summer 1832, in *JSP*, H1:15; History Drafts, 1838–ca. 1841, in *JSP*, H1:234–40 (Draft 2); "Church History," March 1, 1842, in *JSP*, H1:495; "Latter Day Saints," 1844, in *JSP*, H1:531, 538; John W. Welch, "The Miraculous Translation of the Book of Mormon," in *Opening the Heavens: Accounts of Divine Manifestations, 1820–1844*, ed. John W. Welch and Erick B. Carlson (Provo, UT: Brigham Young University Press; Salt Lake City: Deseret Book, 2005), 92, 98; Smith, History, 1845, 156–57.

8. News Item, *Wayne Sentinel* (Palmyra, NY), June 26, 1829, [3]; "Golden Bible," Palmyra (NY) *Freeman*, August 11, 1829, [2]; "Golden Bible," Rochester (NY) *Daily Advertiser and Telegraph*, August 31, 1829, [2]; "Golden Bible," *Gem, of Literature and Science* (Rochester, NY), September 5, 1829, 70.

9. Susan Easton Black and Larry C. Porter, *Martin Harris: Uncompromising Witness of the Book of Mormon* (Provo, UT: Brigham Young University Studies, 2018), ch. 7.

10. Orson Pratt, *A[n] Interesting Account of Several Remarkable Visions*, 1840, in *JSP*, H1:530. Later, Orson Pratt added a detail to the description. The characters inscribed on the plates were stained black. "Upon each side of the leaves of these plates there were fine engravings, which were stained with a black, hard stain, so as to make the

letters more legible and easier to be read." Orson Pratt, in *Journal of Discourses*, 26 vols. (Liverpool: F. D. Richards, 1855–86), 7:30–31.

11. News Item, *Wayne Sentinel* (Palmyra, NY), June 26, 1829, [3], italics in original.

12. Howe, *Mormonism Unvailed*, title page.

13. Traditionally, the president of the United States placed his hand on the Bible when he was sworn into office. An 1833 Baptist creed proclaimed that the Bible was "the supreme standard by which all human conduct, creeds, and opinions should be tried." In the half century after its founding in 1816, the American Bible Society distributed 21 million Bibles. Mark A. Noll, *America's God: From Jonathan Edwards to Abraham Lincoln* (New York: Oxford University Press, 2002), 37–71, 375; see also Paul C. Gutjahr, *An American Bible: A History of the Good Book in the United States, 1777–1880* (Stanford, CA: Stanford University Press, 1999), 30–34.

14. Exodus 25:10–14, 17–18, 23–31. A review of the uses and meaning of gold can be found in Peter L. Bernstein, *The Power of Gold: The History of an Obsession* (New York: John Wiley and Sons, 2000). For US currency, see An Act concerning the Gold Coins of the United States, and for Other Purposes [June 28, 1834], *The Public Statutes at Large of the United States of America* [. . .], ed. Richard Peters (Boston: Charles C. Little and James Brown, 1846), 23rd Cong., 1st Sess., vol. 4, ch. 95, p. 699, sec. 1.

15. Lucy Mack Smith, History, 1845, 115–16; Bushman, *Rough Stone Rolling*, 48, 61.

16. Valeen Tippetts Avery and Linda King Newell, "Lewis C. Bidamon, Stepchild of Mormondom," *BYU Studies* 19, no. 3 (1979): 2, 5–6; James M. McPherson, *Battle Cry of Freedom: The Civil War Era* (New York: Oxford University Press, 1988), 64; Adam Smith, *An Inquiry into the Nature and Causes of the Wealth of Nations* (London: W. Strahan and T. Cadell, 1776), 1:45.

17. History Drafts, 1838–ca. 1841, in *JSP*, H1:226, 230 (Draft 2); History, ca. Summer 1832, in *JSP*, H1:14; Book of Mormon, 1830 ed., 230–31, 444, 465–66, 518, 520–21, 583 [Alma 4:6–12; Helaman 13:28; 3 Nephi 6:10–15; 4 Nephi 1:46; Mormon 2:8–15; Moroni 8:27].

18. History Drafts, 1838–ca. 1841, in *JSP*, H1:220–22, 226 (Draft 2).

19. Lucy Mack Smith, History, 1845, 111–13.

20. Hedges, "Protecting the Plates in Palmyra," 21, 23; Lucy Mack Smith, History, 1845, 111, 116; Walker, "Katharine Smith Salisbury," 8.

21. Exodus 33:20; Anthony Metcalf, *Ten Years before the Mast. Shipwrecks and Adventures at Sea! Religious Customs of the People of India and Burmah's Empire. How I Became a Mormon and Why I Became an Infidel!* ([Malad City, ID], 1888), 71; John W. Barber and Henry Howe, *Historical Collections of the State of New York* [. . .] (New York: S. Tuttle, 1841), 581.

22. Book of Mormon, 1830 ed., [589]–[90]; P. Wilhelm Poulson, letter to the editor, *Deseret News* (Salt Lake City), August 21, 1878, 461; E. C. Briggs to Joseph Smith III, June 4, 1884, Chicago, in *Saints' Herald* (Lamoni, IA), June 21, 1884, 396; Edward Stevenson, Diary, February 9, 1886, in *David Whitmer Interviews: A Restoration Witness*, ed. Lyndon W. Cook (Provo, UT: Grandin Book, 1991), 181.

23. For an overview of skeptical tendencies in Smith's time, see Christopher Grasso, *Skepticism and American Faith: From the Revolution to the Civil War* (New York: Oxford University Press, 2018), 278, 324, 327–40.

24. David S. Reynolds, *Beneath the American Renaissance: The Subversive Imagination in the Age of Emerson and Melville* (New York: Oxford University Press, 1988), 39–40, 80; Branka Arsić, "Unqualified Pleasure: Poe on Forms of Life," in *The Oxford Handbook of Edgar Allan Poe*, ed. J. Gerald Kennedy and Scott Peeples (New York: Oxford University Press, 2019), 792–808.

25. Robert A. Davis, "Robert Owen and Religion," in *Robert Owen and His Legacy*, ed. Noel Thompson and Chris Williams (Cardiff: University of Wales Press, 2011), 91–111.

26. Andrew Delbanco, *Melville: His World and Work* (New York: Alfred A. Knopf, 2005), 13–14.

27. "Testimonies of Oliver Cowdery and Martin Harris," *Latter-day Saints' Millennial Star* (Liverpool, England), August 20, 1859, 545.

28. Richard Lyman Bushman, "The Visionary World of Joseph Smith," *BYU Studies* 37, no. 1 (1997–98): 183–90.

Chapter 2

1. History Drafts, 1838–ca. 1841, in *JSP*, H1:364 (Draft 2); Articles and Covenants, ca. Apr. 1830, in *JSP*, D1:120–21 [D&C 20:5–8]; History, ca. Summer 1832, in *JSP*, H1:10–13. On the First Vision, see Steven C. Harper, *Joseph Smith's First Vision: A Guide to the Historical Accounts* (Salt Lake City: Deseret Book, 2012) .

2. Charles G. Finney, *Lectures on Revivals of Religion*, 6th ed. (New York: Leavitt, Lord, 1835), 36, 45, 153.

3. Richard Lyman Bushman, "The Visionary World of Joseph Smith," *BYU Studies* 37, no. 1 (1997–98): 183–204.

4. History, ca. Summer 1832, in *JSP*, H1:15. Joseph Smith's contemporaries retranslated the Bible, but no one was claiming to translate new scripture. Richard Lyman Bushman, *Believing History: Latter-day Saint Essays*, ed. Reid L. Neilson and Jed Woodworth (New York: Columbia University Press, 2004), 233–38.

5. History Drafts, 1838–ca. 1841, in *JSP*, H1:244, 276 (Draft 2); "Original Manuscript of the Book of Mormon," in *JSP*, R5:xix–xxii; see also John W. Welch, "The Miraculous Translation of the Book of Mormon," in *Opening the Heavens: Accounts of Divine Manifestations, 1820–1844*, ed. John W. Welch and Erick B. Carlson (Provo, UT: Brigham Young University Press; Salt Lake City: Deseret Book, 2005), 83–98.

6. Book of Mormon, 1830 ed., [iii].

7. History, ca. Summer 1832, in *JSP*, H1:13–14.

8. "The Book of Mormon," *Evening and the Morning Star* (Independence, MO), January 1833, [2].

9. Sonia Hazard, "The Material Turn in the Study of Religion," *Religion and Society: Advances in Research* 4, no. 1 (2013): 64–69.

10. Dean Jessee, "Joseph Knight's Recollection of Early Mormon History," *BYU Studies* 17, no. 1 (Autumn 1976): 33.

11. History, ca. Summer 1832, in *JSP*, H1:13–14; History Drafts, 1838–ca. 1841, in *JSP*, H1:218–32 (Draft 2); Lucy Mack Smith, History, 1845, 79–84, Church History Library, Salt Lake City, available at josephsmithpapers.org.

12. History, ca. Summer 1832, in *JSP*, H1:14.

13. See Mark Ashurst-McGee, "Moroni as Angel and as Treasure Guardian," *Review of Books on the Book of Mormon 1989–2011* 18, no. 1 (2006): 40–43.

14. Eber D. Howe, *Mormonism Unvailed: Or, a Faithful Account of That Singular Imposition and Delusion, from Its Rise to the Present Time. With Sketches of the Characters of Its Propagators, and a Full Detail of the Manner in Which the Famous Golden Bible Was Brought before the World. [. . .]* (Painesville, OH: By the author, 1834), 238–39; "Mormonism—No. II," *Tiffany's Monthly* (New York City), August 1859, 164; Bainbridge (NY) Court Record, March 20, 1826, in *EMD*, 4:251–53.

15. For a summary of the treasure-seeking culture in the Smiths' environment, see Ashurst-McGee, "Moroni as Angel and as Treasure Guardian," 35–100; Mark Ashurst-McGee, "A Pathway to Prophethood: Joseph Smith Junior as Rodsman, Village Seer, and Judeo-Christian Prophet" (master's thesis, Utah State University, 2000), 11–26, 56–148; and Alan Taylor, "The Early Republic's Supernatural Economy: Treasure Seeking in the American Northeast, 1780–1830," *American Quarterly* 38, no. 1 (Spring 1986): 6–34.

16. Andrew H. Hedges, "The Refractory Abner Cole," in *Revelation, Reason, and Faith: Essays in Honor of Truman G. Madsen*, ed. Donald W. Parry, Daniel C. Peterson, and Stephen D. Ricks (Provo, UT: Foundation for Ancient Research and Mormon Studies, Brigham Young University, 2002), 447–75.

17. "Gold Bible," *Reflector* (Palmyra, NY), January 6, 1831, 76; "Gold Bible, No. 2," *Reflector*, January 18, 1831, 84; "Gold Bible, No. 3," *Reflector*, February 1, 1831, 92–93; "Gold Bible, No. 4," *Reflector*, February 14, 1831, 100–101; "Gold Bible, No. 5," *Reflector*, February 28, 1831, 109; "Gold Bible, No. 6," *Reflector*, March 19, 1831, 126–27; in *EMD* 2: 231–50.

18. Plain Truth, Letter to the Editor, *Reflector* (Palmyra, NY), January 6, 1831, 77, emphasis in original; "Gold Bible, No. 3," 92, italics in original, in *EMD* 2:23–32, 241–42.

19. "Gold Bible, No. 3," 92–93, italics in original, in *EMD* , 241–42.

20. "Gold Bible, No. 3," 92–93, in *EMD* 241–42.

21. "Gold Bible, No. 4," 101, in *EMD* 2:244–46.

22. "The Book of Pukei—Chap. 1," *Reflector* (Palmyra, NY), June 12, 1830, 37, in *EMD* 2:231–34, italics in original.

23. "Gold Bible, No. 4," 101, in *EMD* 2:244–46.

24. An article on the "Mormonites" in the *Evangelical Magazine and Gospel Advocate* published in Utica picked up on Cole's line of reasoning. The author, Abram W. Benton, was a South Bainbridge physician who in 1830 accused Smith of disturbing the peace. Benton knew of Smith's work for Josiah Stowell, who "spent large sums of money in digging for hidden money, which this Smith pretended he could see" and recounted Smith's trial in 1826 on charges of glass-looking. Benton's piece shows no signs of influence from Cole's essays, but Benton arrived at a similar conclusion. Smith, Benton thought, left South Bainbridge after the 1826 trial, returning

only now and then to hold "clandestine intercourse with his credulous dupes." But during this time "probably by the help of others more skilled in the ways of iniquity than himself, . . . he formed the blasphemous design of forging a new revelation . . . so that he might secure to himself the scandalous honor of being the founder of a new sect." The gold plates were the successor to the search for hidden money, with lots of carry-over. "The Book of Mormon was brought to light by the same magic power by which he pretended to tell fortunes, discover hidden treasures, &c." He translated with "two transparent stones, undoubtedly of the same properties, and the gift of the same spirit as the one in which he looked to find his neighbor's goods." "As for his book, it is only the counterpart of his money-digging plan. Fearing the penalty of the law, and wishing still to amuse his followers, he fled for safety to the sanctuary of pretended religion." Luman Walters did not figure in Benton's account; Benton conjectured that fear of the law, not Walters's influence, diverted Smith from glass-looking to translation in 1827. [Abram W. Benton], "Mormonites," *Evangelical Magazine and Gospel Advocate* (Utica, NY), April 9, 1831, 120, in *EMD*, 4:95–99; Introduction to *State of New York v. JS–B* and *State of New York v. JS–C*; Introduction to *State of New York v. JS–A*, available at josephsmithpapers.org; Gordon A. Madsen, "Joseph Smith's 1826 Trial: The Legal Setting," *BYU Studies* 30, no. 2 (1990): 91–92. Willard Chase's testimony to Philastus Hurlbut also blended the Smiths' treasure-seeking ventures with Joseph Jr.'s recovery of the plates to imply one emerged from the other, but without proposing an explicit explanation. Chase's statement aimed more at discrediting the Smiths' character. Howe, *Mormonism Unvailed*, 240–48. Pomeroy Tucker wrote a lengthy account of Smith's money-digging career, but attributed his abrupt change in 1827 to the coming of Sidney Rigdon. Pomeroy Tucker, *Origin, Rise, and Progress of Mormonism* [. . .] (New York: D. Appleton, 1867), 28, 46, 75–77.

25. "Gold Bible, No. 5," 109, in *EMD* 2:246–47.

26. Agreement of Josiah Stowell and Others, November 1, 1825, in *JSP*, D1:345–52.

27. Howe, *Mormonism Unvailed*, 251.

28. Lyndon W. Cook, ed., *David Whitmer Interviews: A Restoration Witness* (n.p.: Grandin Book, 1993), 26. In another interview published in 1881, Whitmer was reported to have stated, "I had conversations with several young men who said that Joseph Smith had certainly golden plates, and that before he attained them he had promised to share with them, but had not done so, and they were very much incensed with him. Said I, 'How do you know that Joe Smith has the plates?' They replied: 'we saw the plates in the hill that he took them out of just as he described it to us before he obtained them.' These parties were so positive in their statements that I began to believe there must be some foundation for the stories then in circulation all over that part of the country." Cook, *David Whitmer Interviews*, 60–61.

29. Lorenzo Saunders Interview, September 17, 1884, in *EMD*, 2:132; Jessee, "Joseph Knight's Recollection of Early Mormon History," 32–33; Howe, *Mormonism Unvailed*, 243.

30. Jessee, "Joseph Knight's Recollection of Early Mormon History," 32–33.

31. "Mormonism—No. II," 167.

32. Lucy Mack Smith, History, 1845, 108, 115; see also Kyle R. Walker, "Katharine Smith Salisbury's Recollections of Joseph's Meetings with Moroni," *BYU Studies* 41, no. 3 (2002): 15–16.

33. History, ca. Summer 1832, in *JSP*, H1:14.

34. History, 1834–36, in *JSP*, H1:75, 82–84.

35. Brigham Young, Sermon, March 8, 1868, George D. Watt Papers, ca. 1846–1868, Church History Library, Salt Lake City, shorthand transcribed by LaJean Purcell Carruth. For the insistence of Emma Smith's cousins, Joseph and Hiel Lewis, that Joseph spoke only of a treasure guardian at first, see Joseph and Hiel Lewis Statements, 1879, in *EMD*, 4:304; and Hiel Lewis to [James T. Cobb?], September 29, 1879, in *EMD*, 4:320. For Lucy Smith's version of the struggle to recover the plates, see Lucy Mack Smith, History, 1845, 85, 87–89.

36. For a similar view, see Brant A. Gardner, *The Gift and Power: Translating the Book of Mormon* (Salt Lake City: Greg Kofford Books, 2011), 95–96.

37. I am in accord with Mark Ashurst-McGee's view that "the possibility of a dual interpretation needs further emphasis, for treasure guardians and angels are not necessarily mutually exclusive beings." Ashurst-McGee further says that "although Joseph Smith may have understood Moroni to some extent as a treasure guardian, this was a secondary level of meaning for him." Mark Ashurst-McGee, "Moroni: Angel or Treasure Guardian?," *Mormon Historical Studies* 2, no. 2 (Fall 2001): 42, 47.

38. Introduction to *State of New York v. JS–A*; History Drafts, 1838–ca. 1841, in *JSP*, H1:234 (Draft 2); Agreement of Josiah Stowell and Others, November 1, 1825, in *JSP*, D1:345–52; Smith, History, 1845, 95–96; Bainbridge (NY) Court Record, March 20, 1826, in *EMD*, 4:248–49, 251. For the background of the incident, Richard L. Bushman, *Joseph Smith and the Beginnings of Mormonism* (Urbana: University of Illinois Press, 1984), 74–75.

39. W. D. Purple, "Joseph Smith, the Originator of Mormonism," *Chenango Union* (Norwich, NY), May 2 [3], 1877, [3].

40. Howe, *Mormonism Unvailed*, 242–43; Bushman, *Joseph Smith and the Beginnings of Mormonism*, 70. When dictating her history in 1844–1845, Lucy Mack Smith once had her amanuensis strike out the world "plates" and replace it with "record." See, for example, Lucy Mack Smith, History, 1844–45, bk. 4, p. [7], Church History Library, Salt Lake City, available at josephsmithpapers.org.

41. Howe, *Mormonism Unvailed*, 243.

42. Martha Lucretia Campbell to Joseph Smith, Elmira, NY, December 19, 1843, Joseph Smith Collection, 1827–1844, Church History Library, Salt Lake City.

43. Smith, History, 1845, 105; Jessee, "Joseph Knight's Recollection of Early Mormon History," 29–32; History Drafts, 1838–ca. 1841, in *JSP*, H1:236 (Draft 2).

44. Jessee, "Joseph Knight's Recollection of Early Mormon History," 32–33; Richard Lyman Bushman, *Joseph Smith: Rough Stone Rolling* (New York: Alfred A. Knopf, 2005), 59; Smith, History, 1845, 105–6.

45. Smith, History, 1845, 105–6; Jessee, "Joseph Knight's Recollection of Early Mormon History," 33.

46. In the 1838 account, Moroni also mentions the Urim and Thummim and translation. History Drafts, 1838–ca. 1841, in *JSP*, H1:232 (Draft 2); History, ca. Summer 1832, in *JSP*, H1:15.

47. History, 1834–36, in *JSP*, H1:82.

48. Howe, *Mormonism Unvailed*, 243.

49. Jessee, "Joseph Knight's Recollection of Early Mormon History," 33.

50. Book of Mormon, 1830 ed., 172–73, 545–46 [Mosiah 8:13; Ether 3:22–24; 4:5].

51. Book of Mormon, 1830 ed., 538 [Mormon 9:32].

52. For a discussion of translation in the first few months after recovery of the plates, see Michael Hubbard MacKay, "Performing the Translation: Character Transcripts and Joseph Smith's Earliest Translating Practices," in *Producing Ancient Scripture: Joseph Smith's Translation Projects in the Development of Mormon Christianity*, ed. Michael Hubbard MacKay, Mark Ashurst-McGee, and Brian M. Hauglid (Salt Lake City: University of Utah Press, 2020), 81–104; and Michael Hubbard MacKay, "'Git Them Translated': Translating the Characters on the Gold Plates," in *Approaching Antiquity: Joseph Smith and the Ancient World*, ed. Lincoln H. Blumell, Matthew J. Grey, and Andrew H. Hedges (Provo, UT: Religious Studies Center, Brigham Young University; Salt Lake City: Deseret Book, 2015), 83–116.

53. History Drafts, 1838–ca. 1841, in *JSP*, H1:240 (Draft 2); History, ca. Summer 1832, in *JSP*, H1:15; Jessee, "Joseph Knight's Recollection of Early Mormon History," 34–35.

54. Howe, *Mormonism Unvailed*, 270–71, italics in original; Richard E. Bennett, "'Read This I Pray Thee': Martin Harris and the Three Wise Men of the East," *Journal of Mormon History* 36, no. 1 (Winter 2010): 190–210.

55. History Drafts, 1838–ca. 1841, in *JSP*, H1:238, 240 (Draft 2).

56. History Drafts, 1838–ca. 1841, in *JSP*, H1:240 (Draft 2).

57. Smith, History, 1844–45, bk. 6, p. [3].

58. Jessee, "Joseph Knight's Recollection of Early Mormon History," 34. The *Gem, of Literature and Science* reported in September 1829 that when Harris went to New York City, "he went in search of some one to interpret the hieroglyphics, but found that no one was intended to perform that all important task but Smith himself." "Golden Bible," *Gem, of Literature and Science* (Rochester, NY), September 5, 1829, 70; see also Martin Harris Interview with *Rochester* (NY) *Gem*, ca. June 1829, in *EMD*, 2:273.

59. History Drafts, 1838–ca. 1841, in *JSP*, H1:222 (Draft 2); Bennett, "Martin Harris and the Three Wise Men of the East," 190–210; Michael Hubbard MacKay and Gerrit J. Dirkmaat, *From Darkness unto Light: Joseph Smith's Translation and Publication of the Book of Mormon* (Provo, UT: Religious Studies Center, Brigham Young University; Salt Lake City: Deseret Book, 2015), 44–50. Mitchill may have sent Harris on to Charles Anthon at Columbia because he was an avid collector of Indian rhetoric. Edmund Henry Barker to Charles Anthon, Thetford, England, July 9, 1827; Edmund Henry Barker to Charles Anthon, Thetford, England, December 11, 1828; Edmund Henry Barker Letters, 1827–31, Rare Book and Manuscript Library, Columbia University Library, New York City.

60. See Bushman, *Believing History*, 233–47.

61. History, ca. Summer 1832, in *JSP*, H1:15; History Drafts, 1838–ca. 1841, in *JSP*, H1:240, 244 (Draft 2).

62. History, ca. Summer 1832, in *JSP*, H1:15; Isaiah 29:11–12.

63. History, ca. Summer 1832, in *JSP*, H1:15. I am indebted to Craig Rossell for the line of reasoning in this paragraph.

64. History Drafts, 1838–ca. 1841, in *JSP*, H1:244 (Draft 2); Revelation, July 1828, in *JSP*, D1:8 [D&C 3:1–2]; Revelation, Mar. 1829, in *JSP*, D1:16 [D&C 5:2].

65. Elden Watson and John W. Welch have reconstructed the chronology of events from recovery of the plates to completion of the translation. Elden J. Watson, "Approximate Book of Mormon Translation Timeline," website, accessed June 7, 2021, http://www.eldenwatson.net/BoM.htm; Welch, "Miraculous Translation of the Book of Mormon," 77–117.

66. History, ca. Summer 1832, in *JSP*, H1:15–16; History Drafts, 1838–ca. 1841, in *JSP*, H1:244 (Draft 2); Edmund C. Briggs, "A Visit to Nauvoo in 1856," *Journal of History* 9, no. 4 (October 1916): 454; Jennifer Reeder, *First: The Life and Faith of Emma Smith* (Salt Lake City: Deseret Book, 2021), 82–85; Susan Easton Black and Larry C. Porter, *Martin Harris: Uncompromising Witness of the Book of Mormon* (Provo, UT: BYU Studies, 2018), 107–11; see also Emma Smith Bidamon Interview with Edmund C. Briggs, 1856, in *EMD*, 1:530–31. Emma Smith spoke of Joseph using the Urim and Thummim while translating with Martin Harris. John Clark after interviewing Martin Harris mentioned the blanket. Emma Smith Bidamon to Emma Pilgrim, Nauvoo, IL, Mar. 27, 1870, Emma Smith Papers, Community of Christ Library-Archives, Independence, MO; [John A. Clark], "Gleanings by the Way. No. VI," *Episcopal Recorder* (Philadelphia), September 5, 1840, 94; see also Emma Smith Bidamon to Emma Pilgrim, March 27, 1870, in *EMD*, 1:532.

67. History Drafts, 1838–ca. 1841, in *JSP*, H1:246–50, 252, 266 (Draft 2); see also Bushman, *Rough Stone Rolling*, 66–70; and Revelation, July 1828, in *JSP*, D1:8–9 [D&C 3:5–15]. William McLellin later said Joseph's "plates, his interpreters, and his gift were taken from him for some two months." William E. McLellin to Joseph Smith III, Independence, MO, July 1872, in *The William E. McLellin Papers, 1854–1880*, ed. Stan Larson and Samuel J. Passey (Salt Lake City: Signature Books, 2007), 484.

68. Smith, History, 1845, 135–38; History, ca. Summer 1832, in *JSP*, H1:16. He was translating in March 1829 when he received a revelation on showing the plates. "I say unto you Joseph when thou hast translated a few more pages & then shalt thou stop for a season." The next month Oliver Cowdery arrived in Harmony to assist. Revelation, March 1829, in *JSP*, D1:18 [D&C 5:30]; History Drafts, 1838–ca. 1841, in *JSP*, H1:276 (Draft 2).

69. History Drafts, 1838–ca. 1841, in *JSP*, H1:276 (Draft 2).

70. Bushman, *Rough Stone Rolling*, 76.

71. Title Page of Book of Mormon, ca. early June 1829, in *JSP*, D1:63–65; Nathaniel Hinckley Wadsworth, "Copyright Laws and the 1830 Book of Mormon," *BYU Studies* 45, no. 3 (2006): 83.

72. Emma Smith Bidamon Interview with Joseph Smith III, February 1879, in *EMD*, 1:539; Elizabeth Ann Whitmer Cowdery Affidavit, February 15, 1870, in *EMD*, 5:260; David Whitmer, *An Address to All Believers in Christ* (Richmond, MO: By the author, 1887), 12. Accounts of the translation process are reproduced in Welch, "Miraculous Translation of the Book of Mormon," 118–98.

73. Exodus 25:7; 28:15–21, 29–30; 35:9; 39:6–14; see also Cornelis Van Dam, *The Urim and Thummim: A Means of Revelation in Ancient Israel* (Winona Lake, IN: Eisenbrauns, 1997).

74. Book of Mormon, 1830 ed., 172–73 [Mosiah 8:13].

75. Jessee, "Joseph Knight's Recollection of Early Mormon History," 35; Howe, *Mormonism Unvailed*, 240–41.

76. History, 1834–36, in *JSP*, H1:26, 41, 59, 116. The term "Urim and Thummim" was in use among Latter-day Saints as early as 1832, when missionaries in Boston used the term in their preaching. "Questions Proposed to the Mormonite Preachers and Their Answers Obtained before the Whole Assembly at Julien Hall, Sunday Evening, August 5, 1832," *Boston Investigator*, August 10, 1832, [2].

77. Dale W. Adams, "Doctor Philastus Hurlbut: Originator of Derogatory Statements about Joseph Smith, Jr.," *John Whitmer Historical Association* 20 (2000): 79–85; see also Howe, *Mormonism Unvailed*, ch. 17. For an analysis of the affidavits, see Rodger I. Anderson, *Joseph Smith's New York Reputation Reexamined* (Salt Lake City: Signature Books, 1990), chs. 3–4. For witchcraft and the Smiths' reputation, see Manuel Padro, "Witchcraft Allegations in Early Mormon History," *Journal of Mormon History* 49, no. 1 (2023): 1–42

78. Smith, History, 1844–45, bk. 3, p. [10]; History Drafts, 1838–ca. 1841, in *JSP*, H1:234, 236 (Draft 2).

79. History, 1834–36, in *JSP*, H1:41–42.

80. History Drafts, 1838–ca. 1841, in *JSP*, H1:236 (Draft 2).

81. History Drafts, 1838–ca. 1841, in *JSP*, H1:240 (Draft 2); Revelation, Spring 1829, in *JSP*, D1:40 [D&C 10:1].

82. Doctrine and Covenants, 1835 ed., 163 [D&C 10:1].

83. Doctrine and Covenants 3 and 11.

Chapter 3

1. History Drafts, 1838–ca. 1841, in *JSP*, H1:222 (Draft 2); History, ca. Summer 1832, in *JSP*, H1:13–14.

2. D. Michael Quinn, *Early Mormonism and the Magic World View*, rev. ed. (Salt Lake City: Signature Books, 1998), ch. 4; Mark Ashurst-McGee, "Moroni: Angel or Treasure Guardian?," *Mormon Historical Studies* 2, no. 2 (Fall 2001): 39–75. For evidence Joseph Smith may have been exposed to Native American culture while writing the Book of Mormon, see Lori Elaine Taylor, "Joseph Smith in Iroquois Country: A Mormon Creation Story," in *Essays on American Indian and Mormon History*, ed.

P. Jane Hafen and Brenden W. Rensink (Salt Lake City: University of Utah Press, 2019), 41–60.

3. Eran Shalev, "An American Book of Chronicles: Pseudo-Biblicism and the Cultural Origins of *The Book of Mormon*," in *Americanist Approaches to "The Book of Mormon*," ed. Elizabeth Fenton and Jared Hickman (New York: Oxford University Press, 2019), 136–58.

4. On the contents of the Hebrew scriptures, see Grant Hardy, *Understanding the Book of Mormon: A Reader's Guide* (New York: Oxford University Press, 2010), 68–69, 89, 202, 228.

5. Book of Mormon, 1830 ed., title page.

6. Exodus 34:28.

7. Jeremiah 36:2; see also Jeremiah 36:14–32; Ezra 6:2; and Zechariah 5:1–2.

8. "Book," in John Brown, *A Dictionary of the Holy Bible [. . .]* (London: Thomas Tegg, 1824), 110; Nauvoo Library and Literary Institute Record, [20], January–June 1844, Church History Library, Salt Lake City; see also Kenneth W. Godfrey, "A Note on the Nauvoo Library and Literary Institute," *BYU Studies* 14, no. 3 (1974): 1–2. The list of books in the Nauvoo library gives only the title of the dictionary. The author may be James Wood, who wrote a book by the same name, but the descriptions of books were almost the same in both volumes. Other writers listed brass among the materials from which books were made in antiquity, but on a long list: leaves of trees, bark of trees, a table of wood, linen, papyrus, parchment, tables of lead, tables of brass, stones or rocks, tiles, and sand. Johann Jahn, a German scholar whose works on biblical culture were translated into English and published in many editions, judged that books, "which are described as well known as early as the time of Job, . . . were first written on skins, linen, cotton cloth, or the papyrus; and subsequently on parchment." He did, however, leave room for harder materials: "Such books as were engraved on tablets of wood, lead, brass, or ivory, were connected together by rings at the back, through which a rod was passed, and served as a handle to carry them by." James Wood, *A Dictionary of the Holy Bible [. . .]*, 2 vols. (New York: Griffin and Rudd, 1813); Michael G. Reed, "The Notion of Metal Records in Joseph Smith's Day" (paper presented at Summer Seminar on Mormon Culture, Brigham Young University, Provo, UT, August 18, 2011); Johann Jahn, *Archaeologia Biblica. A Manual of Biblical Antiquities*, trans. T. C. Upham, 3rd ed. (Oxford: D. A. Talboys, 1836), 86–89.

9. Book of Mormon, 1830 ed., [5], 7, 50, 73, 151 [1 Nephi 1:2, 17; 19:1–2; 2 Nephi 5:30–31; Omni 1:30].

10. John W. Welch and J. Gregory Welch, *Charting the Book of Mormon: Visual Aids for Personal Study and Teaching* (Provo, UT: Foundation for Ancient Research and Mormon Studies, 1999), charts 16 and 17.

11. Book of Mormon, 1830 ed., 326 [Alma 37:1].

12. Book of Mormon, 1830 ed., 585, 588 [Moroni 10:2, 34].

13. Book of Mormon, 1830 ed., 21, 73, 172–74, 464, 538 [1 Nephi 9:2; 2 Nephi 5:29–33; Mosiah 8:5, 8–9; 9:1–3; 3 Nephi 5:10–11; Ether 1:2]; Grant R. Hardy and Robert E. Parsons, "Book of Mormon Plates and Records," in *Encyclopedia of Mormonism*, ed. Daniel H. Ludlow (New York: Macmillan, 1992), 1:195–201.

14. Book of Mormon, 1830 ed., 151 [Words of Mormon 1:3].

15. Book of Mormon, 1830 ed., 21, 72, 124 [1 Nephi 10:1; 2 Nephi 5:18; Jacob 1:9, 15].

16. Book of Mormon, 1830 ed., 217, 220, 231–32, 366, 406, 410 [Mosiah 28:20; 29:42; Alma 4:15–18; 50:38; 63:11–13; Helaman 2:2].

17. Book of Mormon, 1830 ed., 526, 530 [Mormon 5:1; 6:12].

18. See Book of Mormon, 1830 ed., 143–53 [Enos 1; Jarom 1; Omni 1; Words of Mormon 1].

19. Book of Mormon, 1830 ed., 153–54 [Mosiah 1:3–4].

20. Book of Mormon, 1830 ed., 5 [1 Nephi 1:2].

21. Book of Mormon, 1830 ed., 153 [Mosiah 1:2].

22. Book of Mormon, 1830 ed., 538 [Mormon 9:32].

23. Book of Mormon, 1830 ed., 538 [Mormon 9:34].

24. Book of Mormon, 1830 ed., 463–64 [3 Nephi 5:7–10].

25. Book of Mormon, 1830 ed., 464 [3 Nephi 5: 12, 16].

26. For a provocative investigation of further complexities in the text, see Rosalynde Welch, "Lehi's Brass Ball: Astonishment and Inscription," *Journal of Book of Mormon Studies* 29 (2020): 20–49.

27. Johann Gottfried Eichhorn, *Introduction to the Study of the Old Testament*, trans. George Tilly Gollop (London: Spottiswoode, 1888), 74.

28. See Hardy, *Understanding the Book of Mormon*, 90–92, 102–14, 121–23, 144–51.

29. The Book of Mormon also bore on the lively interest in the history of native culture. The descriptions of Nephite cities associated Book of Mormon people with the mound-builders, a higher civilization thought to have been extinguished by the less civilized Indians that European settlers encountered in the New World. The gold plates bore specifically on the issue of a written language among Native Americans. No less a figure than George Washington claimed he had personally known Indians who could write in ways other Indians could understand. The gold plates would have confirmed Washington's views of a literate native people. George R. Milner, *The Moundbuilders: Ancient Peoples of Eastern North America* (London: Thames & Hudson, 2004); Douglas Hunter, *The Place of Stone: Dighton Rock and the Erasure of America's Indigenous Past* (Chapel Hill: University of North Carolina Press, 2017), 89–90.

30. David F. Holland, *Sacred Borders: Continuing Revelation and Canonical Restraint in Early America* (New York: Oxford University Press, 2011), ch. 5; Stephen J. Stein, "America's Bibles: Canon, Commentary, and Community," *Church History* 64, no. 2 (June 1995): 171–75; Gerald Bray, *Biblical Interpretation: Past and Present* (Leicester, England: Apollos, 1996), 225–29, 249–56; George T. Montague, *Understanding the Bible: A Basic Introduction to Biblical Interpretation*, rev. ed. (Mahwah, NJ: Paulist, 2007), 75–81; Mark Chapman, "Liberal Readings of the Bible and Their Conservative Responses," in *The New Cambridge History of the Bible*, ed. John Riches, vol. 4, *From 1750 to the Present* (New York: Cambridge University Press, 2015), 210–14; James Turner, *Philology: The Forgotten Origins of the Modern Humanities* (Princeton, NJ: Princeton University Press, 2014), ch. 8; John Rogerson, *Old Testament Criticism in the Nineteenth Century* (Minneapolis: Fortress, 1985), ch. 1.

31. Turner, *Philology*, 211, 220; Robert D. Richardson Jr., *Emerson: The Mind on Fire* (Berkeley: University of California Press, 1995), 50. The giant in the field was Friedrich August Wolf, who sought to establish the authorship, meaning, and authenticity of familiar classics. Caroline Winterer, *The Culture of Classicism: Ancient Greece and Rome in American Intellectual Life, 1780–1910* (Baltimore: Johns Hopkins University Press, 2002), 51.

32. Bray, *Biblical Interpretation*, 259–61, 264–68, 311–19; Rogerson, *Old Testament Criticism*, 28–35. By the same token, defense of Homer as a single author was invoked as a defense of the Old Testament's authors. Eichhorn was acutely aware of parallel searches in biblical and classical studies. Anyone who objects to biblical criticism, he admonished, must be unaware of similar inquiries among the classicists. Either the doubter is uninformed or "so entirely destitute of strength of mind as to be incapable of perceiving the serious consequence of omitting to apply a test of this nature." Only by adopting the critical method can an "otherwise invincible army of doubts" be "driven from their intrenchments." Eichhorn, *Old Testament*, 47, 50–51.

33. Eichhorn, *Old Testament*, ix.

34. Johann Gottfried Eichhorn, *An Account of the Life and Writings of Johann David Michaelis*, trans. Patton (Edinburgh, Scotland: Thomas Clark, 1835), 21–22; Bray, *Biblical Interpretation*, 245; Hans W. Frei, *The Eclipse of Biblical Narrative: A Study in Eighteenth and Nineteenth Century Hermeneutics* (New Haven, CT: Yale University Press, 1974), 159. For the history of vowel points, see Eichhorn, *Old Testament*, 125–37.

35. Bray, *Biblical Interpretation*, 248, 259–60.

36. Henning Graf Reventlow, "Towards the End of the 'Century of Enlightenment': Established Shift from *Sacra Scriptura* to Literary Documents and Religion of the People of Israel," in *Hebrew Bible/Old Testament: The History of Its Interpretation*, ed. Magne Sæbø, vol. 2, *From the Renaissance to the Enlightenment* (Göttingen: Vandenhoeck and Ruprecht, 2008), 1052; Eichhorn, *Old Testament*, 49.

37. Eichhorn, *Johann David Michaelis*, 6.

38. Jurgen Herbst, *The German Historical School in American Scholarship: A Study in the Transfer of Culture* (Ithaca, NY: Cornell University Press, 1965), 73–79; John H. Giltner, *Moses Stuart: The Father of Biblical Science in America*, Biblical Scholarship in North America (Atlanta: Scholars Press, 1988), 9–11; Richardson, *Emerson*, 13, 49–50; James Turner, *Without God, without Creed: The Origins of Unbelief in America* (Baltimore: Johns Hopkins University Press, 1985), 147–49. In Germany, the opposite was true. Eichhorn thought of himself as defending the value of the Hebrew scriptures against those who resented "the apparent improbability, incredibility, and in part the impossibility, of these representations, as to treat the Jewish Scriptures with mockery and contempt." Eichhorn wanted to restore respect for "these extremely important monuments of the human mind" by showing that the "greater part of the miracles and supernatural events are not contained in the books at all, but were introduced into them from mere misapprehension and ignorance." His ultimate goal was to demonstrate that "even amidst the imperfections of our present text, it becomes us nevertheless to reverence the exceeding wisdom of the Divine dispensation." Eichhorn, *Old Testament*, ix–x, 114.

39. Jerry Wayne Brown, *The Rise of Biblical Criticism in America, 1800–1870: The New England Scholars* (Middletown, CT: Wesleyan University Press, 1969), 5–6. Unitarians were drawn to German criticism because it also undermined traditional Calvinist orthodoxy. German critics gave more credence to the Gospels than to the later epistles where Calvinist theology was rooted. American Congregationalists inherited their views of biblical infallibility from the English Puritans. "Decisive was the view that Scripture is completely identical to the Word of God. As such, all of its various parts are equally authoritative. Therefore, Scripture was interpreted literally and construed as expressing a complete harmony. A presupposition was that, in terms of its content, the Bible was considered to be a book of law to instruct its readers in their obligations to God." Brown, *Rise of Biblical Criticism in America*, 31–32; Henning Graf Reventlow, *History of Biblical Interpretation*, trans. Leo G. Perdue, vol. 4, *From the Enlightenment to the Twentieth Century* (Atlanta: Society of Biblical Literature, 2010), 30.

40. Book of Mormon, 1830 ed., 31–32, 50, 122, 151–52, 464, 547–48, 587 [1 Nephi 13:35–40; 19:2; 2 Nephi 33:10–11, 15; Words of Mormon 1:4; 3 Nephi 5:18; Ether 5:1–4; Moroni 10:27–29]; Hardy, *Understanding the Book of Mormon*, 6–7, 10, 91.

41. Book of Mormon, 1830 ed., 151, 172 [Mosiah 8:5; Words of Mormon 1:3].

42. On errors, see Book of Mormon, 1830 ed., title page, 50, 532–33, 538, 564 [1 Nephi 19:6; Mormon 8:12, 16–17; 9:31; Ether 12:23–25]. On later corruption, see Book of Mormon, 1830 ed., 29–30 [1 Nephi 13:21–29]. The Book of Mormon did not adhere to all the findings of biblical criticism. Excerpts from both First and Second Isaiah, for example, appear in the Book of Mormon. Hardy, *Understanding the Book of Mormon*, 69–70. The resemblances came in a common understanding of scriptures emerging from a historical process of writing and compilation.

43. Book of Mormon, 1830 ed., title page.

44. Book of Mormon, 1830 ed., 5, 9–10, 15–16, 22, 48–50, 73 [1 Nephi 1:4; 3:4, 19; 5:10, 21; 10:4; 18:8, 23; 19:2–6; 2 Nephi 5:29].

45. Book of Mormon, 1830 ed., 5–7 [1 Nephi 1:1, 16].

46. Book of Mormon, 1830 ed., 532 [Mormon 8:3, 7].

47. Book of Mormon, 1830 ed., 7, 9, 15 [1 Nephi 2:1–4; 3:2–4; 5:10–16]; Hardy, *Understanding the Book of Mormon*, 16.

48. Book of Mormon, 1830 ed., 11, 13 [1 Nephi 3:24–26; 4:18].

49. Book of Mormon, 1830 ed., 12 [1 Nephi 4:10–16].

50. Book of Mormon, 1830 ed., 12 [1 Nephi 4:13]. John Welch has argued that the killing of Laban was justified by the Law of Moses, the law under which Nephi was then operating. John W. Welch, "Legal Perspectives on the Slaying of Laban," *Journal of Book of Mormon Studies* 1, no. 1 (1992): 119–41.

51. Book of Mormon, 1830 ed., 149–50, 207 [Omni 1:12–19; Mosiah 25:2].

52. Book of Mormon, 1830 ed., 153–54 [Mosiah 1:5].

53. Book of Mormon, 1830 ed., 109–12, 116–17 [2 Nephi 27; 29:10–13; 30:3–5].

54. Book of Mormon, 1830 ed., 30 [1 Nephi 13:24–25].

55. Book of Mormon, 1830 ed., 30 [1 Nephi 13:26–27].

56. Book of Mormon, 1830 ed., 30 [1 Nephi 13:29].

57. Book of Mormon, 1830 ed., 115 [2 Nephi 29:3, 6].

58. Book of Mormon, 1830 ed., 115–16 [2 Nephi 29:7, 11, 13, 14].

59. For an expansion of this theme, see Richard Lyman Bushman, *Believing History: Latter-day Saint Essays*, ed. Reid L. Neilson and Jed Woodworth (New York: Columbia University Press, 2004), 70–72.

60. Book of Mormon, 1830 ed., 50 [1 Nephi 19:4, 6].

61. Book of Mormon, 1830 ed., 52, 69, 78, 86, 126–27, 142, 148–49 [1 Nephi 19:22–23; 2 Nephi 4:15; 9:1, 4; 11:8; Jacob 2:23; 7:23; Omni 1:1–2, 9, 11]; see also Joseph M. Spencer, *The Vision of All: Twenty-Five Lectures on Isaiah in Nephi's Record* (Salt Lake City: Greg Kofford Books, 2016).

62. Book of Mormon, 1830 ed., 153–54, 276, 503 [Mosiah 1:2–3, 6, 7; Alma 18:38; 3 Nephi 23:14].

63. Book of Mormon, 1830 ed., 518 [4 Nephi 1:48].

64. Book of Mormon, 1830 ed., 50, 172, 216, 538 [1 Nephi 19:1; Mosiah 8:9; 28:11; Ether 1:2].

65. Book of Mormon, 1830 ed., 13 [1 Nephi 4:20].

66. Book of Mormon, 1830 ed., 148, 155, 329 [Omni 1:2; Mosiah 1:16; Alma 37:38].

67. Anthony Metcalf, *Ten Years before the Mast. Shipwrecks and Adventures at Sea! Religious Customs of the People of India and Burmah's Empire. How I Became a Mormon and Why I Became an Infidel!* ([Malad City, ID], 1888), 71; 2 Samuel 6:6–7; Exodus 33:20.

68. Emma Smith Bidamon Interview with Joseph Smith III, February 1879, in *EMD*, 1:538–42.

69. "Church History," March 1, 1842, in *JSP*, H1:500 [Articles of Faith 1:8].

Chapter 4

1. Robert A. Orsi, "Abundant History: Marian Apparitions as Alternative Modernity," *Historically Speaking* 9, no. 7 (September–October 2008): 14–15. For a critical analysis of Orsi's conception, see Stephen Taysom, "Abundant Events or Narrative Abundance: Robert Orsi and the Academic Study of Mormonism," *Dialogue: A Journal of Mormon Thought* 45, no. 4 (Winter 2012): 1–26.

2. The phrase "marvilous experience" was used by Smith to describe the series of early visions he had during "the rise of the church of Christ" as recorded in his 1832 History. History, ca. Summer 1832, in *JSP*, H1:10.

3. Orsi, "Abundant History," 14–15.

4. George A. Smith, "History of George Albert Smith" (ca. 1857–1875), 2, George A. Smith Papers, 1834–1877, Church History Library, Salt Lake City; see also George A. Smith Reminiscences, ca. 1846, 1857, and ca. 1858, in *EMD*, 1:567, 569.

5. Richard Lloyd Anderson, *Joseph Smith's New England Heritage: Influences of Grandfathers Solomon Mack and Asael Smith*, rev. ed. (Salt Lake City: Deseret Book; Provo, UT: Brigham Young University Press, 2003), 142–47; Richard Lyman Bushman, *The American Farmer in the Eighteenth Century: A Social and Cultural History* (New Haven, CT: Yale University Press, 2018), 17–22.

6. See Richard Lyman Bushman, "The Inner Joseph Smith," *Journal of Mormon History* 32, no. 1 (Spring 2006): 79–80.

7. Lucy Mack Smith, History, 1845, 173, Church History Library, Salt Lake City, available at josephsmithpapers.org.

8. Smith, "History of George Albert Smith," 2; see also George A. Smith Reminiscences, ca. 1846, 1857, and ca. 1858, in *EMD*, 1:569.

9. Jesse Smith to Hyrum Smith, Stockholm, NY, June 17, 1829, in Joseph Smith Letterbook 2, 1839–ca. summer 1843, 59–61, Joseph Smith Collection, 1827–1844, Church History Library, Salt Lake City, also available at josephsmithpapers.org.

10. Jesse Smith to Hyrum Smith, Stockholm, NY, June 17, 1829, 60.

11. Smith, History, 1845, 173.

12. Smith, History, 1845, 173.

13. Joseph Smith History, 1838–1856, vol. B-1, addenda, 5nR, in Historian's Office, History of the Church, 1838–ca. 1882, Church History Library, Salt Lake City, also available at josephsmithpapers.org.

14. Smith, History, 1845, 174–76; Anderson, *Joseph Smith's New England Heritage*, 149, 151.

15. Jesse Smith to Hyrum Smith, Stockholm, NY, June 17, 1829, 61.

16. Lavina Fielding Anderson, *Lucy's Book: A Critical Edition of Lucy Mack Smith's Family Memoir* (Salt Lake City: Signature Books, 2001), 609–11, 864, 869, 874.

17. History, ca. Summer 1832, in *JSP*, H1:10, underlining in original.

18. History, ca. Summer 1832, in *JSP*, H1:13–14.

19. History, ca. Summer 1832, in *JSP*, H1:12–14.

20. History, ca. Summer 1832, in *JSP*, H1:15–16.

21. History Drafts, 1838–ca. 1841, in *JSP*, H1:236 (Draft 2).

22. History Drafts, 1838–ca. 1841, in *JSP*, H1:238 (Draft 2).

23. Smith, History, 1845, 83–84.

24. William Clayton, Journal, July 12, 1844, William Clayton Journals, 1842–1846, Church History Library, Salt Lake City; Linda King Newell and Valeen Tippetts Avery, *Mormon Enigma: Emma Hale Smith; Prophet's Wife, "Elect Lady," Polygamy's Foe, 1804–1879* (Garden City, NY: Doubleday, 1984), ch. 14; Jennifer Reeder, *First: The Life and Faith of Emma Smith* (Salt Lake City: Deseret Book, 2021), 162–64; Irene M. Bates, "William Smith, 1811–93: Problematic Patriarch," *Dialogue: A Journal of Mormon Thought* 16, no. 2 (Summer 1983): 16–22.

25. Smith, History, 1845, 86–87. William remembered these meetings too. "I well remember the effect produced apon my father's family, when he told them he was to receive the plates; how they looked forward with joy.... We were all looking forward for the time to come, father, mother, brothers and sisters.... I remember how the family wept when they found Joseph could not get the plates at that time." C. E. Butterworth, "The Old Soldier's Testimony," *Saints' Herald* (Lamoni, IA), October 4, 1884, 643; see also William Smith Testimony, 1884, in *EMD*, 1:504–5.

26. William Smith remembered his father say, "What, Joseph, can we not see them?" Joseph said he was "forbidden to show them until they are translated, but you

can feel them." There were circles within circles. Butterworth, "Old Soldier's Testimony," 643–44.

27. Smith, History, 1844–1845, bk. 9, pp. [6]–[7]. Lavina Fielding Anderson renders this passage: "I did not receive a direct to my prayers for the space 20 years." Anderson, *Lucy's Book*, 56.

28. Smith, History, 1845, 105. Martin Harris later said that Emma knelt and prayed while Joseph dug. Harris also said that Smith hid the plates in a hollow "old black oak tree top." "Mormonism—No. II," *Tiffany's Monthly* (New York City), August 1859, 164–65.

29. Smith, History, 1845, 105–7; Smith, History, 1844–1845, bk. 5, p. [7].

30. Smith, History, 1845, 107–11.

31. Smith, History, 1845, 110.

32. Smith, History, 1845, 111–12.

33. Smith, History, 1845, 112. Willard Chase said Joseph asked him to make a chest for the plates. The chest never materialized, which may explain why Joseph was asking Hyrum for a chest after the plates were already taken from the hill. Eber D. Howe, *Mormonism Unvailed: Or, a Faithful Account of That Singular Imposition and Delusion, from Its Rise to the Present Time. With Sketches of the Characters of Its Propagators, and a Full Detail of the Manner in Which the Famous Golden Bible Was Brought before the World. [. . .]* (Painesville, OH: By the author, 1834), 245.

34. Smith, History, 1845, 112.

35. Richard Lyman Bushman, *Joseph Smith: Rough Stone Rolling* (New York: Alfred A. Knopf, 2005), 17–20, 27–34, 46–48.

36. Bushman, *Rough Stone Rolling*, 25–26, 36–37, 42, 47, 55, 262–63; Milton V. Backman Jr. and James B. Allen, "Membership of Certain of Joseph Smith's Family in the Western Presbyterian Church of Palmyra," *BYU Studies* 10, no. 4 (1970): 1–3; Smith, History, 1845, 52–53, 70–71.

37. Smith, History, 1845, 83–84, 89; Bainbridge (NY) Court Record, March 20, 1826, in *EMD*, 4:243, 260; W. D. Purple, "Joseph Smith, the Originator of Mormonism," *Chenango Union* (Norwich, NY), May 2 [3], 1877, [3]. For the background of the incident, Bushman, *Joseph Smith and the Beginnings of Mormonism*, 74–75.

38. Purple, "Joseph Smith, the Originator of Mormonism," [3], in *EMD*, 4:135.

39. Dean Jessee, "Joseph Knight's Recollection of Early Mormon History," *BYU Studies* 17, no. 1 (Autumn 1976): 37.

40. Bushman, "Inner Joseph Smith," 74–76.

41. Bushman, *Rough Stone Rolling*, 436–58, 472, 554.

42. See Kent P. Jackson, ed., *Manuscript Found: The Complete Original "Spaulding Manuscript"* (Provo, UT: Religious Studies Center, Brigham Young University, 1996).

43. Howe, *Mormonism Unvailed*, 288–90; Francis W. Kirkham, *A New Witness for Christ in America: The Book of Mormon; Attempts to Prove the Book of Mormon Man-Made Analyzed and Answered*, new ed. (Salt Lake City: Utah Printing, 1959), chs. 11–12. Others speculated that in 1823 Joseph Smith himself stole the Spaulding manuscript or copied it while working as a teamster for Onondaga Valley, New York, resident William H. Sabine. Years later, after Spaulding's manuscript was discovered and found

wanting as a source for the Book of Mormon, critics hypothesized that Spaulding had written a second, still-lost manuscript that provided material for the composition of the Book of Mormon. Kirkham, *New Witness for Christ*, chs. 13 and 17.

44. Emma Smith Bidamon Interview with Joseph Smith III, February 1879, in *EMD*, 1:538–42.

45. Emma Smith Bidamon Interview with Joseph Smith III, February 1879, in *EMD*, 1:538–39, 542.

46. Emma Smith Bidamon Interview with Joseph Smith III, February 1879, in *EMD*, 1:538–43.

47. Smith, History, 1845, 111. Willard Chase said much the same thing. Howe, *Mormonism Unvailed*, 246.

48. Howe, *Mormonism Unvailed*, 245.

49. "Mormonism—No. II," 166–68; Lorenzo Saunders Interview, November 12, 1884, in *EMD*, 2:158; George Collington, Smith Baker, Harriet Marsh, and Rebecca Nurse Interviews with Frederick G. Mather, July 1880, in *EMD*, 4:150, 158; Smith, History, 1845, 135.

50. "Mormonism," *Susquehanna Register, and Northern Pennsylvanian* (Montrose, PA), May 1, 1834, [1]; "Mormonism—No. II," 170; Smith, History, 1845, 121; Sally McKune, Mehetable Doolittle, Elizabeth Squires, Jacob I. Skinner, and Samuel Brush Interviews with Frederick G. Mather, July 1880, in *EMD*, 4:354.

51. Emma Smith Bidamon Interview with Joseph Smith III, February 1879, in *EMD*, 1:539; Nels Madson and Parley P. Pratt, "Visit to Mrs. Emma Smith Bidemon," 1877, Church History Library, Salt Lake City.

52. John W. Barber and Henry Howe, *Historical Collections of the State of New York [. . .]* (New York: S. Tuttle, 1841), 581.

53. Another possible reading of the plates can be derived from Jacques Lacan, "Seminar on 'The Purloined Letter,'" trans. Jeffrey Mehlman, in *The Purloined Poe: Lacan, Derrida, and Psychoanalytic Reading*, ed. John P. Muller and William J. Richardson (Baltimore: Johns Hopkins University Press, 1988), 28–54. As the letter passes from person to person, each one is reconfigured by its presence. As a commentator puts it: "The signifier applies its power over each character's unconscious, which causes notable changes in each character." Accessed August 9, 2013, http://culturemining .blogspot.com/2009/09/jacques-lacan-on-repetition-automatism.html.

54. "Mormonism—No. II," 167–69. Even after translation began, questions troubled Harris. While translating, Harris tested Smith by putting an ordinary stone in the translation hat in place of the seer stone. When Joseph asked why he did it, Martin said, "to stop the mouths of fools, who had told him that the Prophet had learned those sentences and was merely repeating them," a possibility he likely harbored in his own mind. Edward Stevenson, "One of the Three Witnesses," *Deseret Evening News* (Salt Lake City), December 13, 1881, [4].

55. Smith, History, 1845, 118–19, 123–24; see also Susan Easton Black and Larry C. Porter, *Martin Harris: Uncompromising Witness of the Book of Mormon* (Provo, UT: BYU Studies, 2018), 81–83.

56. Tzvetan Todorov, *The Fantastic: A Structural Approach to a Literary Genre*, trans. Richard Howard (Cleveland: Press of Case Western Reserve University, 1973), 25.

57. See David S. Reynolds, *Beneath the American Renaissance: The Subversive Imagination in the Age of Emerson and Melville* (New York: Oxford University Press, 1988), 41–47; Maurice S. Lee, *Uncertain Chances: Science, Skepticism, and Belief in Nineteenth-Century American Literature* (New York: Oxford University Press, 2012); and Christopher Grasso, "Skepticism and American Faith: Infidels, Converts, and Religious Doubt in the Early Nineteenth Century," *Journal of the Early Republic* 22, no. 3 (Autumn 2002): 465–508.

58. Smith, History, 1845, 132–34.

59. Black and Porter, *Martin Harris*, 100–103, 159–60, 162, 176–77, 180–81, 202, 207–12, 225–27. For more on Harris, see Ronald W. Walker, "Martin Harris: Mormonism's Early Convert," *Dialogue: A Journal of Mormon Thought* 19, no. 4 (Winter 1986): 29–43.

60. Beginning in 1841, the witness statements have been found in the front of the Book of Mormon.

61. See Leigh Eric Schmidt, *Hearing Things: Religion, Illusion, and the American Enlightenment* (Cambridge, MA: Harvard University Press, 2002), 16; and Constance Classen, ed., *A Cultural History of the Senses in the Age of Empire* (New York: Bloomsbury, 2014).

62. William Smith Interview with J. W. Peterson and W. S. Pender, 1890, in *EMD*, 1:508; "Mormonism—No. II," 166–67, 169; "Testimonies of Oliver Cowdery and Martin Harris," *Latter-day Saints' Millennial Star* (Liverpool, England), August 20, 1859, 545; J. W. Peterson, "Another Testimony," *Deseret Evening News* (Salt Lake City), January 20, 1894, 11; William Smith, *William Smith on Mormonism [. . .]* (Lamoni, IA: Herald Steam Book and Job Office, 1883), 12; Emma Smith Bidamon Interview with Joseph Smith III, February 1879, in *EMD*, 1:539, 541.

63. Revelation, March 1829, in *JSP*, D1:16–17 [D&C 5:1, 3, 7].

64. Revelation, March 1829, in *JSP*, D1:17 [D&C 5:11].

65. History Drafts, 1838–ca. 1841, in *JSP*, H1:316, 318, 320 (Draft 2).

66. Lyndon W. Cook, ed., *David Whitmer Interviews: A Restoration Witness* (n.p.: Grandin Book, 1993), 30; "Report of Elders Orson Pratt and Joseph F. Smith," *Deseret Evening News* (Salt Lake City), November 16, 1878, [1].

67. Book of Mormon, 1830 ed., [589].

68. Book of Mormon, 1830 ed., [589].

69. Book of Mormon, 1830 ed., [590]; History Drafts, 1838–ca. 1841, in *JSP*, H1:322 (Draft 2); Smith, History, 1845, 155–56, underlining in original; "Death of John Whitmer," *Deseret News* (Salt Lake City), August 14, 1878, 434. According to David Whitmer, his mother, Mary Whitmer, was also shown the plates in a private showing. Edward Stevenson, "The Thirteenth Witness to the Plates of the Book of Mormon," *Juvenile Instructor* 24, no. 1 (January 1, 1889): 22–23.

70. Book of Mormon, 1830 ed., [590]. After having established copyright, Joseph changed "the Author and Proprietor of this work" to "the translator of this work" in the second edition of the Book of Mormon. Book of Mormon, 1837 ed., [621].

71. Book of Mormon, 1830 ed., [590].

72. "Death of John Whitmer," 434.

73. Cornelius C. Blatchly, "The New Bible," *Gospel Luminary* (New York City), December 10, 1829, 194; see also Erin Jennings, "1829 Mormon Discovery," *Juvenile Instructor* (blog), August 21, 2012, https://juvenileinstructor.org/1829-mormon-discovery-brought-to-you-by-guest-erin-jennings/.

74. Royal Skousen, "Another Account of Mary Whitmer's Viewing of the Golden Plates," *Interpreter: A Journal of Latter-day Saint Faith and Scholarship* 10 (2014): 35–44; "Report of Elders Orson Pratt and Joseph F. Smith," [1]; "Whitmer, Mary Musselman," in Andrew Jenson, *Latter-day Saint Biographical Encyclopedia [. . .]* (Salt Lake City: Andrew Jenson History Company, 1901), 1:283.

Chapter 5

1. See Christopher Grasso, *Skepticism and American Faith: From the Revolution to the Civil War* (New York: Oxford University Press, 2018); Erik R. Seeman, *Speaking with the Dead in Early America* (Philadelphia: University of Pennsylvania Press, 2019), ch. 4; and Jonathan Israel, *Democratic Enlightenment: Philosophy, Revolution, and Human Rights, 1750–1790* (New York: Oxford University Press, 2011), 465–70.

2. See David Hume, *An Enquiry concerning Human Understanding; a Letter from a Gentleman to His Friend in Edinburgh; an Abstract of a Treatise of Human Nature*, ed. Eric Steinberg, 2nd ed. (Indianapolis: Hackett, 1993).

3. See J. C. D. Clark, *Thomas Paine: Britain, America, and France in the Age of Enlightenment and Revolution* (Oxford: Oxford University Press, 2018), 271–72, 331–49; Craig Nelson, *Thomas Paine: Enlightenment, Revolution, and the Birth of Modern Nations* (New York: Viking, 2006), 260–72, 335; and Harvey J. Kaye, *Thomas Paine: And the Promise of America* (New York: Hill & Wang, 2005), 82–84, 108–11.

4. Lucy Mack Smith, History, 1844–1845, [Miscellany], [10], Church History Library, Salt Lake City, available at josephsmithpapers.org. Paine's radicalism had lost some of its luster by the early 1800s. When Paine died in 1809, not many attended his funeral, "and few Americans mourned the passing of a Revolutionary hero who had strayed off the proper course toward atheism and Jacobinism." Seth Cotlar, *Tom Paine's America: The Rise and Fall of Transatlantic Radicalism in the Early Republic* (Charlottesville: University of Virginia Press, 2011), 214.

5. See Eric R. Schlereth, *An Age of Infidels: The Politics of Religious Controversy in the Early United States*, Early American Studies (Philadelphia: University of Pennsylvania Press, 2013), 5–17, 29–30; Kerry Walters, *Revolutionary Deists: Early America's Rational Infidels* (New York: Prometheus Books, 2011), ch. 1; and E. Brooks Holifield, *Theology in America: Christian Thought from the Age of the Puritans to the Civil War* (New Haven, CT: Yale University Press, 2003), ch. 7.

6. Orsamus Turner, *History of the Pioneer Settlement of Phelps and Gorham's Purchase, and Morris' Reserve [. . .]* (Rochester, NY: William Alling, 1851), 214; History, 1834–1836, in *JSP*, H1:56; Oliver Cowdery, "Letter IV," *Latter Day Saints' Messenger and Advocate* (Kirtland, OH), February 1835, 78.

7. History, ca. Summer 1832, in *JSP*, H1:12. The argument from design also appeared in the Book of Mormon. See Book of Mormon, 1830 ed., 308 [Alma 30:44]. On Joseph Smith's encounter with skepticism, see Richard Lyman Bushman, "Joseph Smith and Modernism," *BYU Studies Quarterly*, 59 (2) (2020), 121–34.

8. George A. Smith, "History of George Albert Smith" (ca. 1857–1875), June 1, 1834, 19, George A. Smith Papers, 1834–1877; Heber C. Kimball, Autobiography (ca. 1842–1858), June 1, [1834], 25, Heber C. Kimball Papers, 1837–1866, Church History Library, Salt Lake City; Richard Lyman Bushman, "Joseph Smith and Skepticism," Richard Lyman Bushman, *Believing History: Latter-day Saint Essays* (New York: Columbia University Press, 2004), 145–60.

9. A summary and analysis of evidential Christianity can be found in Holifield, *Theology in America*, ch. 8.

10. Samuel Stanhope Smith, *Lectures on the Evidences of the Christian Religion [. . .]* (Philadelphia: Hopkins and Earle, 1809); William Beauchamp, *Essays on the Truth of the Christian Religion* (Marietta, OH: Joseph Israel, 1811).

11. Charles Thompson, *Evidences in Proof of the Book of Mormon, Being a Divinely Inspired Record [. . .]* (Batavia, NY: D. D. Waite, 1841). On Thompson's style, see Peter Crawley, *A Descriptive Bibliography of the Mormon Church*, vol. 1, *1830–1847* (Provo, UT: Religious Studies Center, Brigham Young University, 1997), 178–79.

12. John L. Stephens, *Incidents of Travel in Central America, Chiapas, and Yucatan*, 2 vols. (New York: Harper & Brothers, 1841); Letter from John E. Page, September 1, 1841, in *JSP*, D8:258; see also Wilford Woodruff, Journal, September 13, 1841, Wilford Woodruff Journals and Papers, 1828–1898, Church History Library, Salt Lake City. The *Times and Seasons* took note of *Incidents of Travel in Central America, Chiapas, and Yucatan* in the June 15, 1841, issue shortly after the book appeared, and a few months later, John Bernhisel mailed a copy to Joseph Smith. "American Antiquities— More Proofs of the Book of Mormon," *Times and Seasons* (Nauvoo, IL), June 15, 1841, 440–42; Letter from John M. Bernhisel, September 8, 1841, in *JSP*, D8:260–62; see also Letter to John M. Bernhisel, November 16, 1841, in *JSP*, D8:367.

13. Stephen Burnett to Lyman Johnson, Orange Township, OH, April 15, 1838, in Joseph Smith Letterbook, 1837–1843, Joseph Smith Collection, 1827–1844, Church History Library, Salt Lake City, also available at josephsmithpapers.org; Richard Lyman Bushman, *Joseph Smith: Rough Stone Rolling* (New York: Alfred A. Knopf, 2005), 328–49; Susan Easton Black and Larry C. Porter, *Martin Harris: Uncompromising Witness of the Book of Mormon* (Provo, UT: BYU Studies, 2018), 290–93. In the same letter, Burnett claims that "the eight witnesses never saw them [the plates] & hesitated to sign that instrument for that reason, but were persuaded to do it." The documentary record left by the eight witnesses, however, says nothing of hesitation or compulsion. Steven C. Harper, "The Eleven Witnesses," in *The Coming Forth of the Book of Mormon: A Marvelous Work and a Wonder; the 44th Annual Brigham Young University Sidney B. Sperry Symposium*, ed. Dennis L. Largey, Andrew H. Hedges, John Hilton III, and Kerry Hull (Provo, UT: Religious Studies Center, Brigham Young University; Salt Lake City: Deseret Book, 2015), 117–32.

14. Black and Porter, *Martin Harris*, 290–95; Stephen Burnett to Lyman Johnson, Orange Township, OH, April 15, 1838.

15. Pomeroy Tucker, *Origin, Rise, and Progress of Mormonism [. . .]* (New York: D. Appleton, 1867), 4, 71.

16. Anthony Metcalf, *Ten Years before the Mast. Shipwrecks and Adventures at Sea! Religious Customs of the People of India and Burmah's Empire. How I Became a Mormon and Why I Became an Infidel!* ([Malad City, ID], 1888), 71; "The Testimony Which Martin Harris Gave to William Pilkington," April 23, 1939, 2, typescript, Church History Library, Salt Lake City.

17. Genesis 16:13; 32:30; Exodus 33:11, 20; Numbers 12:8. On preparation for divine theophanies, see Jared C. Calaway, *The Christian Moses: Vision, Authority, and the Limits of Humanity in the New Testament and Early Christianity* (Montreal: McGill-Queen's University Press, 2019), 46, 48, 50.

18. "Mormonism—No. II," *Tiffany's Monthly* (New York City), August 1859, 166; Stephen Burnett to Lyman Johnson, Orange Township, OH, April 15, 1838; see also Elizabeth J. Mott, "The Forbidden Gaze: The Veiling of the Gold Plates and Joseph Smith's Redefinition of Sacred Space" (working paper, Neal A. Maxwell Institute, Summer Seminar on Mormon Culture, 2011).

19. John Corrill, *A Brief History of the Church of Christ of Latter Day Saints [. . .]* (St. Louis: By the author, 1839), 7, 9–15, 17, available at josephsmithpapers.org; see also Solomon Chamberlin, Autobiography, ca. 1858, 1–13, Church History Library, Salt Lake City. The witnesses were one of many aspects of interest to potential converts. After hearing two Mormon missionaries preach the Book of Mormon near Paris, Illinois, in the summer of 1831, William McLellin rode his horse hundreds of miles to Missouri in search of further information. At Independence, McLellin and Hyrum Smith conversed for four hours. "I inquired into the particulars of the coming forth of the record, of the rise of the church and of its progress and upon the testimonies given to him &c.," McLellin wrote. William E. McLellin, Journal, July 18 and 30, 1831, 1–2; August 18–19, 1831, 5–6, William E. McLellin Papers, 1831–1878, Church History Library, Salt Lake City; William E. McLellin to Samuel McLellin, Independence, MO, August 4, 1832, photocopy, Church History Library, Salt Lake City; see also *The Journals of William E. McLellin, 1831–1836*, ed. Jan Shipps and John W. Welch (Provo, UT: BYU Studies; Urbana: University of Illinois Press, 1994), 29–30, 33, 79–80.

20. Lucy Mack Smith to Solomon Mack, Waterloo, NY, January 6, 1831, Church History Library, Salt Lake City; Book of Mormon, 1830 ed., 115, [590] [2 Nephi 29:7]; see also Janiece Johnson, "'Give Up All and Follow Your Lord': Testimony and Exhortation in Early Mormon Women's Letters, 1831–1839," *BYU Studies* 41, no. 1 (2002): 86. The testimony of witnesses did attract some converts. At the first Mormon meeting Eliza R. Snow attended in Ohio, in 1831, she heard two of the three witnesses of the Book of Mormon preach. "To hear men testify that they had seen a holy angel," she said, "thrilled my inmost soul." Yet Snow waited four years for baptism, wanting to "see whether the work was going to 'flash in the pan' and go out." Edward W. Tullidge, *The Women of Mormondom* (New York, 1877), 63–64.

21. Parley P. Pratt, *A Voice of Warning and Instruction to All People [. . .]* (New York: W. Sandford, 1837), 131–36; Parley P. Pratt, *The Autobiography of Parley Parker Pratt [. . .]*, ed. Parley P. Pratt Jr. (New York: Russell Brothers, 1874), 38, 43.

22. Parley P. Pratt, *A Voice of Warning, and Instruction to All People [. . .]*, 8th ed. (Liverpool: F. D. Richards, 1854), 115–23. In searching for archeological support for their scriptures, Mormons were in step with other Christians of this period. In 1805 William Richard Hamilton had formed the Syrian Society (later the Palestine Association) to shed additional light on biblical history. It petered out after four years, but interest revived in the late 1830s when Edward Robinson took up the search. When Nauvoo Mormons were reading Stephens and Catherwood about Native American ruins in Central America, Christians were learning about extant biblical cities in Palestine from Robinson and Smith. Ruth Kark and Haim Goren, "Pioneering British Exploration and Scriptural Geography: The Syrian Society/The Palestine Association," *Geographical Journal* 177, no. 3 (September 2011): 264–74; Neil Asher Silberman, *Digging for God and Country: Exploration, Archeology, and the Secret Struggle for the Holy Land, 1799–1917* (New York: Alfred A. Knopf, 1982), ch. 5.

23. When challenged by a judge in Hawaii to explain his belief in the Book of Mormon, George Q. Cannon referred to the witnesses. "He then pressed me for my proofs in favor of the Book of Mormon; I told him that in the first place we had the testimony of eleven living eye-witnesses, who solemnly declare and testify before the Lord, men and angels that they have seen and handled the plates upon which the Book was written, that three of them declare that these things were shown unto them and the Book declared to be true by an holy angel from heaven." George Q. Cannon, Journal, March 30, 1854, George Q. Cannon Journals, 1849–1854, Church History Library, Salt Lake City, also available at The Journal of George Q. Cannon, Church Historian's Press, accessed November 16, 2021, https://churchhistorianspress.org/george-q-cannon.

24. See *EMD*, 2:294–393.

25. Black and Porter, *Martin Harris*, 415–36, 456–68, 477–83, 491–508.

26. "Three Men Swear to Hearing Testimony of Martin Harris," *Deseret News* (Salt Lake City), July 15, 1933, Church section, 3; Martin Harris Interview with Ole A. Jensen, July 1875, in *EMD*, 2:375; "A Witness to the Book of Mormon," *Daily Iowa State Register* (Des Moines), August 28, 1870, [4]. The language of the tellings stressed Harris's conviction as much as his sensory experiences. In many accounts, it was not the fact that his witness proved the plates existed that impressed listeners but his unyielding, emphatic faith. Pilkington said that as he testified "his whole being became Electrified and it seemed that a changed man stood before me." When old and frail, Harris asked William Pilkington to help raise his arm to the square as he spoke. Edward Stevenson, "The Three Witnesses to the Book of Mormon," *Latter-day Saints' Millennial Star* (Liverpool, England), June 21, 1886, 390; Martin Harris Interviews with William Pilkington, 1874–1875, in *EMD*, 2:355; William Pilkington to Vern Poulter, Smithfield, UT, February 28, 1930, Church History Library, Salt Lake City; "Martin Harris' Dying Testimony Reported by Man at His Side," *Deseret News* (Salt Lake City), April 9, 1930, 6.

27. James H. Hart, "Interview with David Whitmer," *Deseret Evening News* (Salt Lake City), September 4, 1883, [2].

28. In 2022, the Interpreter Foundation released *Undaunted: Witnesses of the Book of Mormon* as a scholarly companion to the movie *Witnesses* that showed in Utah and elsewhere in 2021. *Undaunted* stressed that "none of whom [the witnesses] ever denied their claims." "Undaunted: Witnesses of the Book of Mormon," The Interpreter Foundation, accessed August 16, 2022, https://witnessesundaunted .com/. Richard L. Anderson examined the character of the witnesses to demonstrate that their statements were credible. Richard L. Anderson, *Investigating the Book of Mormon Witnesses* (Salt Lake City: Deseret Book, 1981). See also Steven C. Harper, "Evaluating the Book of Mormon Witnesses," *Religious Educator* 11, no. 2 (2010), 37–49.

29. Nathaniel W. Howell and Others to Ancil Beach, January 1832, in *EMD*, 3:11, 14.

30. Dale W. Adams, "Doctor Philastus Hurlbut: Originator of Derogatory Statements about Joseph Smith, Jr.," *John Whitmer Historical Association* 20 (2000): 82; Nathaniel W. Howell and Others to Ancil Beach, January 1832, in *EMD*, 3:11–12, 15–16.

31. Nathaniel W. Howell and Others to Ancil Beach, January 1832, in *EMD*, 3:14.

32. Nathaniel W. Howell and Others to Ancil Beach, January 1832, in *EMD*, 3:14, 16.

33. Adam Jortner, "'Some Little Necromancy': Politics, Religion, and the Mormons, 1829–1838," in *Contingent Citizens: Shifting Perceptions of Latter-day Saints in American Political Culture*, ed. Spencer W. McBride, Brent M. Rogers, and Keith A. Erekson (Ithaca, NY: Cornell University Press, 2020), 20–26.

34. Eber D. Howe, *Autobiography and Recollections of a Pioneer Printer: Together with Sketches of the War of 1812 on the Niagara Frontier* ([Painesville, OH]: Telegraph Steam, [1878?]), 45.

35. News Item, *Wayne Sentinel* (Palmyra, NY), June 26, 1829, [3], in *EMD* 2:219; Noah Webster, *An American Dictionary of the English Language [. . .]*, vol. 1 (New York: S. Converse, 1828), s.v. "Imposition"; Nathaniel W. Howell and Others to Ancil Beach, January 1832, in *EMD*, 3:16.

36. [Abram W. Benton], "Mormonites," *Evangelical Magazine and Gospel Advocate* (Utica, NY), April 9, 1831, 120, in *EMD*, 4:497.

37. Letter to the Editor, *Telegraph* (Painesville, OH), March 22, 1831, [2], in *EMD*, 9.

38. "Gold Bible, No. 2," *Reflector* (Palmyra, NY), January 18, 1831, 84, emphasis in original, in *EMD*, 2:240.

39. "Gold Bible, No. 2," 84, italics in original; "Gold Bible, No. 4," *Reflector*, February 14, 1831, 100–101; "Gold Bible, No. 5," *Reflector*, February 28, 1831, 109, in *EMD* 2:244, 246. For an elaboration of this theme emphasizing magic, see Jortner, "Politics, Religion, and the Mormons, 1829–1838," 17–28.

40. "Mormonites," *Working Man's Advocate* (New York City), May 14, 1831, [2]. William Owen made the same argument in "Mormon Bible," *Free Enquirer* (New York City), September 3, 1831, 364.

41. Alexander Campbell referred to the author of the Book of Mormon as "this Atheist Smith." Campbell drew on all of his rhetorical powers to distinguish the Bible from the Book of Mormon. "I would as soon compare a bat to the American eagle, a mouse to a mammoth, or the deformities of a spectre to the beauty of Him whom John saw in Patmos, as to contrast it with a single chapter in all the writings of the Jewish or

Christian prophets." "Delusions," *Millennial Harbinger* (Bethany, VA), February 7, 1831, 95–96.

42. Eber D. Howe, *Mormonism Unvailed: Or, a Faithful Account of That Singular Imposition and Delusion, from Its Rise to the Present Time. With Sketches of the Characters of Its Propagators, and a Full Detail of the Manner in Which the Famous Golden Bible Was Brought before the World. [. . .]* (Painesville, OH: By the author, 1834), 19.

43. Howe, *Autobiography*, 54–55.

44. Howe, *Mormonism Unvailed*, iii.

45. Howe, *Mormonism Unvailed*, v, ix. For an extended discussion of the preoccupation with impostors, see J. Spencer Fluhman, *"A Peculiar People": Anti-Mormonism and the Making of Religion in Nineteenth-Century America* (Chapel Hill: University of North Carolina Press, 2012), 21–48.

46. See Howe, *Mormonism Unvailed*, v–ix.

47. Henry Caswall, *The City of the Mormons; or, Three Days at Nauvoo, in 1842* (London: J. G. F. and J. Rivington, 1842), preface.

48. Craig L. Foster, "Henry Caswall: Anti-Mormon Extraordinaire," *BYU Studies* 35, no. 4 (1995–1996), 146–49.

49. Henry Caswall, *America, and the American Church* (London: J. G. and F. Rivington, 1839), 310, 322, 344–57.

50. Caswall, *City of the Mormons*, 3–5.

51. Caswall, *City of the Mormons*, 5, 7–10, 12.

52. "Book of Abraham and Related Manuscripts," in *JSP*, R4:xvi–xxii; "A Fac-Simile from the Book of Abraham. No. I," and "A Translation," *Times and Seasons* (Nauvoo, IL), March 1, 1842, 703–6; "The Book of Abraham," *Times and Seasons*, March 15, 1842, 719–22.

53. Caswall, *City of the Mormons*, 20–24, 29, 72–73.

54. Caswall, *City of the Mormons*, 35–36. For a summary of Joseph's busy life in the spring of 1842, see Bushman, *Rough Stone Rolling*, chs. 24 and 25.

55. Caswall, *City of the Mormons*, 35–37; Henry Caswall, *The Prophet of the Nineteenth Century; or, the Rise, Progress, and Present State of the Mormons, or Latter-day Saints [. . .]* (London: J. G. F. and J. Rivington, 1843), 223; Grammar and Alphabet of the Egyptian Language, ca. July–ca. November 1835, in *JSP*, R4:111–90.

56. Caswall, *City of the Mormons*, 43.

57. Don Bradley and Mark Ashurst-McGee argue that the conspirators only hoped to "startle the natives," not entrap Joseph Smith. Don Bradley and Mark Ashurst-McGee, "'President Joseph Has Translated a Portion': Joseph Smith and the Mistranslation of the Kinderhook Plates," in *Producing Ancient Scripture: Joseph Smith's Translation Projects in the Development of Mormon Christianity*, ed. Michael Hubbard Mackay, Mark Ashurst-McGee, and Brian M. Hauglid (Salt Lake City: University of Utah Press, 2020), 458.

58. Jason Frederick Peters, "The Kinderhook Plates: Examining a Nineteenth-Century Hoax," *Journal of the Illinois State Historical Society* 96, no. 2 (Summer 2003): 130–36.

59. "Ancient Records," *Times and Seasons* (Nauvoo, IL), May 1, 1843, 186.

60. "Singular Discovery—Material for Another Mormon Book," *Quincy* (IL) *Whig*, May 3, 1843, [2]; see also "Singular Discovery—Material for Another Mormon Book," *Times and Seasons* (Nauvoo, IL), May 1, 1843, 187.

61. Kenneth W. Godfrey, "The Zelph Story," *BYU Studies* 29, no. 2 (Spring 1989): 31, 35, 38–39, 41, 43–44; Letter to Emma Smith, June 4, 1834, in *JSP*, D4:57n266; Peters, "Kinderhook Plates," 133.

62. Parley P. Pratt to John Van Cott, Nauvoo, IL, May 7, 1843, Church History Library, Salt Lake City.

63. James B. Allen, *Trials of Discipleship: The Story of William Clayton, a Mormon* (Urbana: University of Illinois Press, 1987), 117.

64. Don Bradley, "'President Joseph Has Translated a Portion': Solving the Mystery of the Kinderhook Plates" (presentation, FAIR Conference, Sandy, UT, August 5, 2011); see also Bradley and Ashurst-McGee, "Joseph Smith and the Mistranslation of the Kinderhook Plates," 507–11.

65. The full meaning of the character, according to the Egyptian Alphabet book, is "honor by birth, kingly power by the line of Pharoah. possession by birth one who riegns [reigns] upon his throne universally—possessor of heaven and earth, and of the blessings of the earth." Bradley and Ashurst-McGee, "Joseph Smith and the Mistranslation of the Kinderhook Plates," 508. Don Bradley and Mark Ashurst-McGee argue that Smith did not attempt an inspired translation comparable to the Book of Abraham or Book of Mormon. "Smith attempted to translate the plates by ordinary methods of traditional translation—not by revelation." The Kinderhook plates were not a test of his revelatory gifts. Bradley and Ashurst-McGee, "Joseph Smith and the Mistranslation of the Kinderhook Plates," 453.

66. Peters, "Kinderhook Plates," 134–35; Bradley and Ashurst-McGee, "Joseph Smith and the Mistranslation of the Kinderhook Plates," 456.

67. Peters, "Kinderhook Plates," 140–42.

68. An 1830 revelation assigned the calling of translator permanently. His lasting title was to be "a seer & Translater & Prop[h]et an Apostle of Jesus Christ an Elder of the Church." Revelation, April 6, 1830, in *JSP*, D1:129 [D&C 21:1].

69. Revelation, April 1829-A, in *JSP*, D1:36 [D&C 6:26]; Account of John, April 1829-C, in *JSP*, D1:48 [D&C 7].

70. Michael Hubbard MacKay, "'Git Them Translated': Translating the Characters on the Gold Plates," in *Approaching Antiquity: Joseph Smith and the Ancient World*, ed. Lincoln H. Blumell, Matthew J. Grey, and Andrew H. Hedges (Provo, UT: Religious Studies Center, Brigham Young University; Salt Lake City: Deseret Book, 2015), 83–116.

71. Bushman, *Rough Stone Rolling*, 130–43; "The Book of Mormon," *Wayne Sentinel* (Palmyra, NY), March 26, 1830, [3]; Scott H. Faulring, Kent P. Jackson, and Robert J. Matthews, eds., *Joseph Smith's New Translation of the Bible: Original Manuscripts* (Provo, UT: Religious Studies Center, Brigham Young University, 2004).

72. "Book of Abraham and Related Manuscripts," in *JSP*, R4:xvii–xx, xxv–xxviii; Bushman, *Rough Stone Rolling*, 286; Terryl Givens, *The Pearl of Greatest Price: Mormonism's Most Controversial Scripture*, with Brian M. Hauglid (New York: Oxford University Press,

2019), 153–59; John A. Wilson, "The Joseph Smith Egyptian Papyri: Translations and Interpretations," *Dialogue: A Journal of Mormon Thought* 3, no. 2 (Summer 1968): 67–85; Klaus Baer, "The Breathing Permit of Hôr: A Translation of the Apparent Source of the Book of Abraham," *Dialogue: A Journal of Mormon Thought* 3, no. 3 (Autumn 1968): 109–34.

73. For a sophisticated comment on the relationship of holy objects to prophetic revelations, see Rosalynde Welch, "Lehi's Brass Ball: Astonishment and Inscription," *Journal of Book of Mormon Studies* 29 (2020): 20–49.

74. Aaron Smith et al., Statement, *Voree Herald* (Wisconsin Territory), January 1846, [4]; Roger Van Noord, *King of Beaver Island: The Life and Assassination of James Jesse Strang* (Urbana: University of Illinois Press, 1988), 4–11; "Revelation Given to James J. Strang, Sept. 1, 1845," *Voree Herald*, January 1846, [3]–[4].

75. News Item, *Voree Herald* (Wisconsin Territory), January 1846, [4]; "Revelation Given to James J. Strang, Sept. 1, 1845," [3]–[4]; Book of Mormon, 1830 ed., 531–32 [Mormon 8:1–4]; Noord, *King of Beaver Island*, 35; Letter of Appointment for James J. Strang, June 18, 1844, James Jesse Strang Collection, 1832–1947, Beinecke Rare Book and Manuscript Library, Yale University, New Haven, CT. The three small brass plates did not quite measure up to the promise in the September 1, 1845, revelation which spoke of "the record which was sealed from my servant Joseph. Unto thee it is reserved." The word "sealed" implied the sealed portion of the plates of the Book of Mormon, supposedly a grand revelation of the earth from beginning to end received by the Brother of Jared. Book of Mormon, 1830 ed., 545–46 [Ether 3:25–27; 4:4–7].

76. Aaron Smith et al., Statement, [4].

77. Milo M. Quaife, *The Kingdom of Saint James: A Narrative of the Mormons* (New Haven, CT: Yale University Press, 1930), 17.

78. "Revelation Given to James J. Strang, Sept. 1, 1845," [3].

79. "Extract from the Records of the Church," *Voree Herald* (Wisconsin Territory), August 1846, [1]–[2].

80. Lawrence Foster, "James J. Strang: The Prophet Who Failed," *Church History* 50, no. 2 (June 1981): 186. For samplings of Strang's prophetic writings, see *The Diamond: Being the Law of Prophetic Succession and a Defense of the Calling of James J. Strang as Successor to Joseph Smith [. . .]* (Voree, WI: Church of Latter Day Saints at Voree, Wisconsin, 1848); and William Shepard, Donna Falk, and Thelma Lewis, comps. and eds., *James J. Strang: Teaching of a Mormon Prophet* (Burlington, WI: Church of Jesus Christ of Latter Day Saints, Strangite, 1977).

81. William Smith to James Strang, Nauvoo, IL, March 1, 1846, in *Voree Herald* (Wisconsin Territory), July 1846, [3]; Noord, *King of Beaver Island*, 66–75; Foster, "James J. Strang," 182.

82. "Revelation," *Voree Herald* (Wisconsin Territory), July 1846, [2].

83. Noord, *King of Beaver Island*, 97; *The Book of the Law of the Lord, Consisting of an Inspired Translation of Some of the Most Important Parts of the Law Given to Moses, and a Very Few Additional Commandments, with Brief Notes and References* (St. James, MI: Royal Press, [1851]), [ii]; Alex D. Smith, "The Book of the Law of the Lord," *Journal of Mormon History* 38, no. 4 (Fall 2012): 131–63.

84. Don Faber, *James Jesse Strang: The Rise and Fall of Michigan's Mormon King* (Ann Arbor: University of Michigan Press, 2016), 92–93; *The Book of the Law of the Lord, Being a Translation from the Egyptian of the Law Given to Moses in Sinai, with Numerous and Valuable Notes* (St. James, MI: Royal Press, [1856]), viii–x.

85. Robin Scott Jensen, "Witness to the Plates: Aaron Smith, Strangism, and the Search for His Religion," *John Whitmer Historical Association Journal* 25 (2005): 123, 129.

86. Quaife, *Kingdom of Saint James*, 162–72; Noord, *King of Beaver Island*, 67, 125–32, 171–73, 179–80, 196, 199–200, 204, 233–37, 248–49; Faber, *James Jesse Strang*, 121–22, 127–28, 134–43.

Chapter 6

1. Lapham, "II.—The Mormons," Historical Magazine, May 1870, 305–6, in EMD, 1: was a uncertain about the exact date but it was likely 1830 or later, in *EMD*, 1:456–66.

2. E. G. Lee, *The Mormons, or, Knavery Exposed. Giving an Account of the Discovery of the Golden Plates [. . .]* (Frankford, PA: By the author, 1841), 3. For a survey of anti-Mormonism during Joseph Smith's lifetime, see J. Spencer Fluhman, *"A Peculiar People": Anti-Mormonism and the Making of Religion in Nineteenth-Century America* (Chapel Hill: University of North Carolina Press, 2012).

3. "Gold Bible," *Reflector* (Palmyra, NY), Jan. 6, 1831, 76, italics in original; "Gold Bible, No. 3," *Reflector*, Feb. 1, 1831, 92; "Gold Bible, No. 2," *Reflector*, Jan. 18, 1831, 84.

4. Eber D. Howe, *Mormonism Unvailed: Or, A Faithful Account of That Singular Imposition and Delusion, from Its Rise to the Present Time* (Painesville, Ohio: By the Author, 1834), v, ix.

5. Lapham, "II.—The Mormons," 306–7, 309 in EMD 1:456–66.

6. Richard H. Brodhead, "The American Literary Field, 1860–1890," in *The Cambridge History of American Literature*, ed. Sacvan Bercovitch, vol. 3, *Prose Writing, 1860–1920* (New York: Cambridge University Press, 2005), 14–15; Fluhman, *Peculiar People*, ch. 4; Ronald W. Walker, David J. Whittaker, and James B. Allen, *Mormon History* (Urbana: University of Illinois Press, 2001), 9–11. Moral indignation survived in the postbellum South and sometimes descended into anti-Mormon violence. Patrick Q. Mason, *The Mormon Menace: Violence and Anti-Mormonism in the Postbellum South* (New York: Oxford University Press, 2011), 10–15.

7. Nancy Bentley, "Museum Realism," in *The Cambridge History of American Literature*, ed. Sacvan Bercovitch, vol. 3, *Prose Writing, 1860–1920*, in EMD 4:129–37. (New York: Cambridge University Press, 2005), 65.

8. Lapham, "II.—The Mormons," 306–7, in EMD 1:456–66.

9. Richard Lyman Bushman, *Joseph Smith: Rough Stone Rolling* (New York: Alfred A. Knopf, 2005), 48–52; W. D. Purple, "Joseph Smith, the Originator of Mormonism," *Chenango Union* (Norwich, NY), May 2 [3], 1877, [3]. "Pitcher," "Columbus," and "Smyrna Lecture Course," *Chenango Union* (Norwich, NY), May 2 [3], 1877, [3].

10. W. D. Purple, "Joseph Smith, the Originator of Mormonism".

11. Brodhead, "American Literary Field," 23; Albert Johannsen, *The House of Beadle and Adams and Its Dime and Nickel Novels: The Story of a Vanished Literature*, 3 vols. (Norman: University of Oklahoma Press, 1950–1962); Terryl L. Givens, *The Viper on the Hearth: Mormons, Myths, and the Construction of Heresy* (New York: Oxford University Press, 1997), 103–20.

12. Purple, "Joseph Smith, the Originator of Mormonism," [3]; "The Dying Words of Capt. Robert Kidd: A Noted Pirate, Who Was Hanged at Execution Dock, in England," American Song Sheets, Rare Books and Special Collections, Library of Congress, Washington DC, https://www.loc.gov/resource/amss.as101910.0/. Purple misquoted slightly. The second line was actually "And dollars manifold."

13. Purple, "Joseph Smith, the Originator of Mormonism," [3].

14. Purple, "Joseph Smith, the Originator of Mormonism," [3], italics in original.

15. Purple, "Joseph Smith, the Originator of Mormonism," [3].

16. Bainbridge (NY) Court Record, March 20, 1826, in *EMD*, 4:248–56.

17. John Quidor, *The Money Diggers*, 1832, oil on canvas, $15\frac{15}{16}'' \times 20\frac{15}{16}''$ (40.5 cm × 53.2 cm), Brooklyn Museum, Brooklyn, NY, https://www.brooklynmuseum.org/opencollection/objects/971.

18. Purple, "Joseph Smith, the Originator of Mormonism," [3].

19. Purple, "Joseph Smith, the Originator of Mormonism," [3].

20. Purple, "Joseph Smith, the Originator of Mormonism," [3]; Bainbridge (NY) Court Record, March 20, 1826, in *EMD*, 4:254.

21. Bainbridge (NY) Court Record, March 20, 1826, in *EMD*, 4:254; Purple, "Joseph Smith, the Originator of Mormonism," [3].

22. T. S. Eliot pointed out a similar fascination with another world. The popularity of Donne, Herbert, and Dostoevsky in 1924, Eliot postulated, "represents a nostalgia for spiritual life amongst peoples deadened by centuries of more and more liberal protestantism. But what is this spiritual sensuality, as found in the seventeenth century? It is in fact a symptom of Dissolution of Christianity in protestant Europe, of the relaxing of the Christian system of the various needs of man." T. S. Eliot, "A Neglected Aspect of Chapman," *New York Review of Books*, November 7, 2013, 62–64, https://www.nybooks.com/articles/2013/11/07/neglected-aspect-chapman/?lp_txn_id=1343701.

23. William Horne Dame, "Journal of the Southern Exploring Company, 1854–1858, Iron County, UT," January 14, 1855, Dame-McBride Family Papers, 1825–1978, Special Collections, J. Willard Marriott Library, University of Utah, Salt Lake City. I am indebted to Craig Rossell for this citation and others relating to Mormon cave lore. For reproduction of the cave accounts, see Cameron J. Packer, "Cumorah's Cave," *Journal of Book of Mormon Studies* 13, no. 1 (2004): 50–57, 170–71.

24. Heber C. Kimball, in *Journal of Discourses*, 26 vols. (Liverpool: F. D. Richards, 1855–1886), 4:105. Quotation altered for readability; the first sentence in the original ends in a question mark.

25. Pomeroy Tucker, *Origin, Rise, and Progress of Mormonism [. . .]* (New York: D. Appleton, 1867), 48–49.

26. Pomeroy Tucker Reminiscence, 1858, in *EMD*, 3:62–67.

27. Hamilton Child, comp., *Gazetteer and Business Directory of Wayne County, N.Y., for 1867-8* (Syracuse, NY: Journal Office, 1867), 52–53; see also, e.g., "Early Mormon Haunts," *New-York Evangelist*, July 13, 1882, 2. A variation on the story was that Joseph Smith went to the cave to pray. "Mormons and Mormonism," *Christian Advocate* (New York City), October 12, 1905, 1616.

28. *EMD*, 2:81–164, 185–214.

29. "Mormon Leaders at Their Mecca," *New York Herald*, June 25, 1893, 12; Thomas L. Cook, *Palmyra and Vicinity* (Palmyra, NY: Palmyra Courier-Journal, 1930), 1, 10, 238. On Miner's Hill, see Dan Vogel, "The Locations of Joseph Smith's Early Treasure Quests," *Dialogue: A Journal of Mormon Thought* 27, no. 3 (Fall 1994): 200, 204–11.

30. Brigham Young, in *Journal of Discourses*, 19:38; Jesse Nathaniel Smith, *The Journal of Jesse Nathaniel Smith: Six Decades in the Early West; Diaries and Papers of a Mormon Pioneer, 1834–1906*, ed. Oliver R. Smith, 3rd ed. (Provo, UT: Jesse N. Smith Family Association, 1970), 217.

31. Elizabeth Kane, *A Gentile Account of Life in Utah's Dixie, 1872–73: Elizabeth Kane's St. George Journal* (Salt Lake City: Tanner Trust Fund, University of Utah Library, 1995), xxix, 75–76.

32. Brigham Young, in *Journal of Discourses*, 19:38.

33. Lily Dougall, *The Mormon Prophet* (Toronto: W. J. Gage, 1899); Lorraine McMullen, "Dougall, Lily," in *Dictionary of Canadian Biography*, vol. 15, accessed July 23, 2022, http://www.biographi.ca/en/bio/dougall_lily_15E.html; "A Mormon Prophet," *Arena*, September 1899, 421. For more on Dougall's life, see Joanna Dean, *Religious Experience and the New Woman: The Life of Lily Dougall* (Bloomington: Indiana University Press, 2007); and Lorraine McMullen, "Lily Dougall: The Religious Vision of a Canadian Novelist," *Studies in Religion* 16, no. 1 (1987): 79–90.

34. Ethan R. Yorgason, *Transformation of the Mormon Culture Region* (Urbana: University of Illinois Press, 2003), ch. 4; Gustive O. Larson, *The "Americanization" of Utah for Statehood* (San Marino, CA: Huntington Library, 1971).

35. Davis Bitton, *The Ritualization of Mormon History and Other Essays* (Urbana: University of Illinois Press, 1994), ch. 8.

36. "Mormon Prophet," 421.

37. William Alexander Linn, *The Story of the Mormons: From the Date of Their Origin to the Year 1901* (New York: Macmillan, 1902); Katharine E. Dopp, review of *The Story of the Mormons, from the Date of Their Origin to the Year 1901*, by William Alexander Linn, *American Journal of Sociology* 8, no. 5 (Mar. 1903): 708–9; Henry P. Wright, comp., *History of the Class of 1868: Yale College, 1864–1914* (New Haven, CT: Tuttle, Morehouse and Taylor, 1914), 180–85; I. Woodbridge Riley, *The Founder of Mormonism: A Psychological Study of Joseph Smith, Jr.* (New York: Dodd, Mead, 1903), v–vii, ix.

38. Alexander Campbell, *An Analysis of the Book of Mormon; with an Examination of Its Internal and External Evidences, and a Refutation of Its Pretences to Divine Authority* (Boston: Benjamin H. Greene, 1832).

39. Linn, *Story of the Mormons*, 28, 50–73.

40. Riley, *Founder of Mormonism*, 369–95, esp. 394; Dougall, *Mormon Prophet*, viii.

41. For another example of psychological analysis of Smith about this time, see Walter Franklin Prince, "Psychological Tests for the Authorship of the Book of Mormon," *American Journal of Psychology* 28, no. 3 (July 1917): 373–89.

42. Riley, *Founder of Mormonism*, 73–75, 345–66; McMullen, "Dougall, Lily," in *Dictionary of Canadian Biography*, vol. 15.

43. Dean, *Religious Experience and the New Woman*, chs. 1 and 7; McMullen, "Dougall, Lily," in *Dictionary of Canadian Biography*, vol. 15.

44. Dougall, *Mormon Prophet*, v, vii.

45. Dougall, *Mormon Prophet*, 2–6, 15–30, 63–67.

46. Dougall, *Mormon Prophet*, 28–29, 44–49.

47. Dougall, *Mormon Prophet*, 47.

48. Dougall, *Mormon Prophet*, 46–49.

49. Dougall, *Mormon Prophet*, 91, 136–38.

50. Dougall, *Mormon Prophet*, 95–108, 240–53, 353–62, 407–14.

51. Dougall, *Mormon Prophet*, vi–vii.

52. Ann Taves, *Fits, Trances, and Visions: Experiencing Religion and Explaining Experience from Wesley to James* (Princeton, NJ: Princeton University Press, 1999), 261–91.

53. Jeannette Stirling, *Representing Epilepsy: Myth and Matter* (Liverpool, England: Liverpool University Press, 2010), ch. 4; Matthew Woods, *Was the Apostle Paul an Epileptic?* (New York: Cosmopolitan, 1913). Occasional articles continue to connect Paul and epilepsy. See D. Landsborough, "St Paul and Temporal Lobe Epilepsy," *Journal of Neurology, Neurosurgery, and Psychiatry* 50, no. 6 (1987): 659–64.

54. Dougall, *Mormon Prophet*, 126–27.

55. Vardis Fisher, *Children of God: An American Epic* (New York: Harper & Brothers, 1939), dust jacket; see also Joseph M. Flora, "Vardis Fisher and the Mormons," *Dialogue: A Journal of Mormon Thought* 4, no. 3 (Autumn 1969): 48–55; and Terryl L. Givens, *People of Paradox: A History of Mormon Culture* (New York: Oxford University Press, 2007), 287–88.

56. Fisher, *Children of God*, 8, 15–17.

57. Fisher, *Children of God*, 17–19, italics in original.

58. Dougall, *Mormon Prophet*, 309. The story of Joseph Smith passing off the plates as a brick was a stock image in anti-Mormon accounts. Tucker, *Origin, Rise, and Progress of Mormonism*, 32; Linn, *Story of the Mormons*, 27; Bruce Kinney, *Mormonism: The Islam of America* (New York: Fleming H. Revell, 1912), 49; James H. Snowden, *The Truth about Mormonism* (Philadelphia: Westminster, 1926), 60.

59. For other nineteenth-century fictions where Mormons figure, see Sarah Barringer Gordon, *The Mormon Question: Polygamy and Constitutional Conflict in Nineteenth-Century America* (Chapel Hill: University of North Carolina Press, 2002), 29–54; Givens, *Viper on the Hearth*, chs. 6–7; and Leonard J. Arrington, "Mormonism: Views from Without and Within," *BYU Studies* 14, no. 2 (April 1974): 140–53.

Chapter 7

1. [W. W. Phelps], "New Hymns," *The Evening and the Morning Star* (Independence, MO), February 1833, [8]; see also Louise Helps, "Look Once Again at Cumorah's Hill: The Poet's View," *Journal of Book of Mormon Studies* 13, no. 1 (2004): 118.

2. Richard Lyman Bushman, *Joseph Smith: Rough Stone Rolling* (New York: Alfred A. Knopf, 2005), 122–23, 164–68, 191–92.

3. [Phelps], "New Hymns," [8]; see also Helps, "Look Once Again at Cumorah's Hill," 118.

4. Gordon M. Sayre, "Prehistoric Diasporas: Colonial Theories of the Origins of Native American Peoples," in *Writing Race across the Atlantic World: Medieval to Modern*, ed. Philip D. Beidler and Gary Taylor, Signs of Race (New York: Palgrave Macmillan, 2005), 51–75; Abram C. Van Engen, *City on a Hill: A History of American Exceptionalism* (New Haven, CT: Yale University Press, 2020), ch. 6; Robert Silverberg, *Mound Builders of Ancient America: The Archaeology of a Myth* (Athens: Ohio University Press, 1968), 82–96.

5. Michael D. Green, "The Expansion of European Colonization to the Mississippi Valley, 1780–1880," in *The Cambridge History of the Native Peoples of the Americas*, vol. 1, *North America, Part 1*, ed. Bruce G. Trigger and Wilcomb E. Washburn (Cambridge: Cambridge University Press, 1996), 462–69, 474–75, 510–23; Ned Blackhawk, *Violence over the Land: Indians and Empires in the Early American West* (Cambridge, MA: Harvard University Press, 2006), 170–73.

6. Edward Whitley, "*Book of Mormon* Poetry," in *Americanist Approaches to "The Book of Mormon*," ed. Elizabeth Fenton and Jared Hickman (New York: Oxford University Press, 2019), 422, italics in original.

7. Gilbert H. Muller, *William Cullen Bryant: Author of America* (Albany: State University of New York Press, 2008), 110–11. On the myth of pre-Indian mound builders in early national America, see Andrew Galloway, "William Cullen Bryant's American Antiquities: Medievalism, Miscegenation, and Race in *The Prairies*," *American Literary History* 22, no. 4 (Winter 2010): 731–34.

8. Charles H. Brown, *William Cullen Bryant* (New York: Charles Scribner's Sons, 1971), 217; William Cullen Bryant, *Poems* (Boston: Russell, Odiorne, and Metcalf, 1834), 39–43.

9. Whitley, "*Book of Mormon* Poetry," 423–27. Eliza Snow wrote "The Red Man of the West" in 1830 before she converted to Mormonism. Decades later, Snow revised the poem by incorporating Book of Mormon prophecy and retitled it "The Lamanite." Jill Mulvay Derr and Karen Lynn Davidson, eds., *Eliza R. Snow: The Complete Poetry* (Provo, UT: Brigham Young University Press; Salt Lake City: University of Utah Press, 2009), xxiv–xxv, 33–34, 691–95.

10. Derr and Davidson, *Eliza R. Snow*, 694.

11. Brigham Young, Parley P. Pratt, and John Taylor, eds., *A Collection of Sacred Hymns, for the Church of Jesus Christ of Latter-day Saints, in Europe* (Manchester, England: W. R. Thomas, 1840), 218–19; *Hymns of the Church of Jesus Christ of Latter-day Saints* (Salt Lake City: The Church of Jesus Christ of Latter-day Saints, 1985), 13–14. The official title

of the Manchester hymnal is *A Collection of Sacred Hymns, for the Church of Jesus Christ of Latter-day Saints, in Europe*, and it was compiled and edited by Pratt, John Taylor, and Brigham Young. According to Brett Nelson, as no authors were listed in Latter-day Saint hymnals until 1856, many hymns not actually composed by Parley Pratt have been attributed him. There is not enough evidence to definitively say whether or not "An Angel from on High" was written by Pratt. Brett Nelson, "A Question of Authorship: The Hymns of William W. Phelps and Parley P. Pratt," *Latter-day Saint Hymnology* (blog), December 30, 2018, https://ldshymnology.wordpress.com/2018/12/30/a-question-of-authorship-the-hymns-of-william-w-phelps-and-parley-p-pratt/.

12. Thomas Cole to Luman Reed, September 18, 1833, in *Mr. Luman Reed's Picture Gallery: A Pioneer Collection of American Art*, ed. Ella M. Foshay (New York: Harry N. Abrams, 1990), 130. For more on Cole's *The Course of Empire*, see Elizabeth Mankin Kornhauser and Tim Barringer, *Thomas Cole's Journey: Atlantic Crossings*, with Dorothy Mahon, Christopher Riopelle, and Shannon Vittoria (New York: Metropolitan Museum of Art, 2018), 204–17; and Tim Barringer et al., *Picturesque and Sublime: Thomas Cole's Trans-Atlantic Inheritance* (Catskill, NY: Thomas Cole National Historic Site, 2018), 39–42.

13. Parley P. Pratt, *The Millennium, and Other Poems: To Which Is Annexed, a Treatise on the Regeneration and Eternal Duration of Matter* (New York: W. Molineux, 1840), 47; see also Dean L. May, "The Millennial Hymns of Parley P. Pratt," *Dialogue: A Journal of Mormon Thought* 16, no. 1 (Spring 1983): 145–50.

14. Edward Stevenson, *Reminiscences of Joseph, the Prophet, and the Coming Forth of the Book of Mormon* (Salt Lake City: By the author, 1893), 11, 13–14.

15. Alfred Lambourne, *Hill Cumorah*, 1892, oil on canvas, 35″ × 74″, Church History Museum, Salt Lake City; Ronalee Macinnis, "Alfred Lambourne: Pioneer Painter, Pioneer Poet" (master's thesis, Brigham Young University, 1992).

16. Roger L. Miller, "'Hail, Cumorah! Silent Wonder': Music Inspired by the Hill Cumorah," *Journal of Book of Mormon Studies* 13, no. 1 (2004): 100.

17. Crawford Gates, "The Delights of Making Cumorah's Music," *Journal of Book of Mormon Studies* 13, no. 1 (2004): 71.

18. Theodore E. Curtis, "Cumorah," *Improvement Era*, March 1909, 373; J. M. White, "Cumorah Hill," *Liahona, the Elders' Journal*, February 16, 1915, 546; see also Helps, "Look Once Again at Cumorah's Hill," 118–19.

19. Whitley, "*Book of Mormon* Poetry," 432, italics in original.

20. Louisa L. Greene Richards, *Branches That Run over the Wall: A Book of Mormon Poem and Other Writings* (Salt Lake City: Magazine Printing Company, 1904); Michael R. Collings, *The Nephiad: An Epic Poem in Twelve Books, in the Manner of John Milton's "Paradise Lost" [. . .]* (Malibu, CA: Zarahemla Motets, 1996).

21. Clinton F. Larson, *Coriantumr and Moroni: Two Plays* (Provo, UT: Brigham Young University Press, 1961), 12–15, 18–19, 23, 29, 34.

22. Larson, *Coriantumr and Moroni*, 41, 44–45, 47, 51, 56, 61–64.

23. Larson, *Coriantumr and Moroni*, 50, 53, 62.

24. C. C. A. Christensen, *The Hill Cumorah*, ca. 1878, tempera on muslin, 204.5 cm × 294.6 cm, Brigham Young University Museum of Art, Provo, UT.

25. Stevenson, *Reminiscences of Joseph, the Prophet*, 21.

26. Kirkham projected as many as fifty titles, but contemporary newspapers reported only nineteen paintings in the exhibit. Donna L. Poulton, *Reuben Kirkham: Pioneer Artist*, ed. James L. Poulton (Springville, UT: CFI, 2011), 121–24, 203–4.

27. Linda Jones Gibbs, *Harvesting the Light: The Paris Art Mission and Beginnings of Utah Impressionism* (Salt Lake City: The Church of Jesus Christ of Latter-day Saints, 1987); Lewis A. Ramsey, *Moroni Delivering the Plates to Joseph Smith*, 1923, oil on canvas, 66″ × 42″, Church History Museum, Salt Lake City. I am indebted to Clayton Williams for drawing my attention to Ramsey's depiction.

28. Vern Swanson, "The Book of Mormon Art of Arnold Friberg: 'Painter of Scripture,'" *Journal of Book of Mormon Studies* 10, no. 1 (2001): 28–29, 31–32; Ted Schwarz, *Arnold Friberg: The Passion of a Modern Master* (Flagstaff, AZ: Northland, 1985), 11, 23, 26, 32, 51–53, 56–75, 88–97; Robert T. Barrett and Susan Easton Black, "Setting a Standard in LDS Art: Four Illustrators of the Mid-Twentieth Century," *BYU Studies* 44, no. 2 (2005): 29–31, 33, 35–36.

29. Barrett and Black, "Setting a Standard in LDS Art," 33.

30. Alex Ross, "How Wagner Shaped Hollywood," *New Yorker*, August 24, 2020, https://www.newyorker.com/magazine/2020/08/31/how-wagner-shaped-hollywood. "More than a thousand movies and TV shows feature the composer on their soundtracks."

31. Swanson, "The Book of Mormon Art of Arnold Friberg," 34.

32. "Illustrated Edition of Book of Mormon Published by Deseret Book," *Deseret News* (Salt Lake City), September 15, 1962, Church section, 13; Tom Lovell, *Mormon Burying the Gold Plates*, 1968, oil on canvas, 33″ × 23″, Book of Mormon Historic Press, Palmyra, NY.

33. Schwarz, *Arnold Friberg*, 108–13.

34. Barrett and Black, "Setting a Standard in LDS Art," 47, 49, 57, 60–61, 63; Tom Lovell, *Moroni Appearing to Joseph in His Bedroom*, 1970, oil on canvas, 84″ × 60″, Book of Mormon Historic Press, Palmyra, NY.

35. Avard T. Fairbanks, *Lehi-Nephi*, 1961, bas-relief stone, 128¼″ × 91½″; Avard T. Fairbanks, *Mormon-Moroni*, 1961, bas-relief stone, 128¼″ × 91½″, Harold B. Lee Library, Brigham Young University, Provo, UT; Eugene F. Fairbanks, *A Sculptor's Testimony in Bronze and Stone: The Sacred Sculpture of Avard T. Fairbanks*, rev. ed. ([Salt Lake City?]: By the author, 1994), 64–67.

36. David Croft, "Exhibit Tells Book of Mormon Story," *Church News* (Salt Lake City), September 15, 1973, 4.

37. John W. Welch and Doris R. Dant, *The Book of Mormon Paintings of Minerva Teichert* (Provo, UT: BYU Studies; Salt Lake City: Bookcraft, 1997), 28–29, 150–53; Minerva Teichert, *Moroni: The Last Nephite*, ca. 1949–1951, oil on masonite, 36″ × 48″; Minerva Teichert, *Last Battle between the Nephites and the Lamanites*, ca. 1949–1951, oil on masonite, 35$\frac{15}{16}$″ × 48″, Brigham Young University Museum of Art, Provo, UT. Teichert's *Destruction on the Western Continent* illustrates the disruptions accompanying the crucifixion of Christ rather than the destruction of the Nephites. Minerva Teichert, *Destruction on the Western Continent*, ca. 1949–1951, oil on masonite, 36″ × 48″, Brigham Young University Museum of Art, Provo, UT; Welch and Dant, *Book of Mormon Paintings of Minerva Teichert*, 142–43.

38. Bushman, *Rough Stone Rolling*, 109–10, 122–23, 407–9; James B. Allen and Glen M. Leonard, *The Story of the Latter-day Saints*, 2nd ed. (Salt Lake City: Deseret Book, 1992), 166, 288–89; *Deseret News 1989–90 Church Almanac* (Salt Lake City: Deseret News, 1988), 194.

39. Richard G. Oman, "Sacred Connections: LDS Pottery in the Native American Southwest," *BYU Studies* 35, no. 1 (1995): 109.

40. Oman, "LDS Pottery in the Native American Southwest," 107–28.

41. "Lucy Leuppe McKelvey, Diné-Navajo Nation Potter," Adobe Gallery, accessed July 8, 2022, https://www.adobegallery.com/artist/lucy-leuppe-mckelvey.

42. Oman, "LDS Pottery in the Native American Southwest," 112–14.

43. Hadi Pranato, *Joseph Smith Receives the Gold Plates*, ca. 1980, batik, 92 cm × 71.1 cm, Church History Museum, Salt Lake City; LaRene Gaunt, "Textile Testimonies: LDS Indonesian Batiks," *Ensign*, July 1991, 44, 46. I am indebted to Elisa Pulido for this citation and description.

44. Herman du Toit, "By Simple yet Propitious Means: The Art of Jorge Cocco Santangelo," *BYU Studies* 55, no. 2 (2016): 100; "LDS Art," Religious Art, Jorge Cocco Santángelo: Art for the Spiritual Intellect, accessed July 8, 2022, https://jorgecocco .com/category/religious-art/lds-art/.

45. du Toit, "Art of Jorge Cocco Santangelo," 100–102.

46. du Toit, "Art of Jorge Cocco Santangelo," 102–3.

47. "Angels Collection," in "LDS Art," Religious Art, Jorge Cocco Santángelo: Art for the Spiritual Intellect, accessed July 8, 2022, https://jorgecocco.com/2019/01/06/angels-collection/; Revelation 14:6.

48. The struggles of abstract artists can be seen in the career of George Dibble. Sarah Dibble, "George Dibble and the Struggle for Modern Art in Utah" (master's thesis, Brigham Young University, 2021).

49. Matt Stevens, "They Know Every Page of 'The Book of Mormon,'" *New York Times*, June 14, 2022, https://www.nytimes.com/2022/06/14/theater/the-book-of-mormon-actors.html; Lisa Schwarzbaum, "The Book of Mormon," *Entertainment Weekly*, March 24, 2011, https://ew.com/article/2011/03/24/book-mormon/.

50. Trey Parker, Robert Lopez, and Matt Stone, *The Book of Mormon: The Complete Book and Lyrics of the Broadway Musical* (New York: Newmarket, 2011), 35–40, 82–87.

51. Stephen Galloway, "Why South Park's Trey Parker and Matt Stone Now Say It's 'Wrong' to Offend," *Hollywood Reporter*, March 24, 2011, https://www.hollywood reporter.com/news/general-news/why-south-parks-trey-parker-171189/.

52. *South Park*, season 7, episode 12, "All about Mormons," directed by Trey Parker, written by Trey Parker, aired November 19, 2003, on Comedy Central.

53. Eric Samuelsen, "Mormon Drama," in *Mormons and Popular Culture: The Global Influence of an American Phenomenon*, vol. 1, *Cinema, Television, Theater, Music, and Fashion*, ed. J. Michael Hunter (Santa Barbara, CA: Praeger, 2013), 160.

54. Tony Kushner, *Angels in America: A Gay Fantasia on National Themes; Part Two: Perestroika* (New York: Theatre Communications Group, 1994). Cristine Hutchison-Jones argues that Kushner admires Mormon communitarianism and objects more to the conservative politics of contemporary Mormonism than he does its theology. Cristine Hutchison-Jones, "Center and Periphery: Mormons and American

Culture in Tony Kushner's *Angels in America*," in *Peculiar Portrayals: Mormons on the Page, Stage, and Screen*, ed. Mark T. Decker and Michael Austin (Logan: Utah State University Press, 2010), 11, 18.

55. James Rollins, *The Devil Colony: A Sigma Force Novel* (New York: William Morrow, 2011).

56. Orson Scott Card, *Prentice Alvin: The Tales of Alvin Maker III* (New York: TOR, 1989), 257–59, 298–302. Of the six volumes in the series, see Orson Scott Card, *Alvin Journeyman: The Tales of Alvin Maker IV* (New York: TOR, 1995); and Orson Scott Card, *Heartfire: The Tales of Alvin Maker V* (New York: TOR, 1998). Plates also figure in Latter-day Saint author Brandon Sanderson's *The Hero of the Ages* (New York: TOR, 2008) in ways reminiscent of the Book of Mormon. The plates are a means of preserving knowledge that can save civilization.

Chapter 8

1. Allen P. Gerritsen, "The Hill Cumorah Monument: An Inspired Creation of Torleif S. Knaphus," *Journal of Book of Mormon Studies* 13, no. 1 (2004): 126–27; William G. Hartley, "Torleif Knaphus, Sculptor Saint," *Ensign*, July 1980, 11–13; Torleif Knaphus, SS *Cymric* Manifest, February 1906, MA, U.S., Arriving Passenger and Crew Lists, 1820–1963, Ancestry database, available at ancestry.com; Merwin G. Fairbanks, "S. L. Artist Says Little, Does Much," *Deseret News* (Salt Lake City), October 4, 1947, magazine section, 3.

2. Gerritsen, "Hill Cumorah Monument," 127–28.

3. Kathleen Flake, *The Politics of American Religious Identity: The Seating of Senator Reed Smoot, Mormon Apostle* (Chapel Hill: University of North Carolina Press, 2004), ch. 5; Keith A. Erekson, "American Prophet, New England Town: The Memory of Joseph Smith in Vermont" (master's thesis, Brigham Young University, 2002), ch. 3.

4. Minutes of "Great Indignation Meeting," January 13, 1870, and Introduction to Part 4: 1880–1892, in Derr et al., *The First Fifty Years of Relief Society: Key Documents in Latter-day Saint Women's History* (Salt Lake City: Church Historian's Press, 2016), 311–32, 441–46; J. Spencer Fluhman, *"A Peculiar People": Anti-Mormonism and the Making of Religion in Nineteenth-Century America* (Chapel Hill: University of North Carolina Press, 2012), 117, 121–22; Matthew J. Grow, *"Liberty to the Downtrodden": Thomas L. Kane, Romantic Reformer* (New Haven, CT: Yale University Press, 2009), 264–66.

5. Thomas G. Alexander, *Mormonism in Transition: A History of the Latter-day Saints, 1890–1930* (Urbana: University of Illinois Press, 1986), ch. 12; Ethan R. Yorgason, *Transformation of the Mormon Culture Region* (Urbana: University of Illinois Press, 2003), 127–29, 133–48, 175–76; Armand L. Mauss, *The Angel and the Beehive: The Mormon Struggle with Assimilation* (Urbana: University of Illinois Press, 1994), 21–28; Kathryn M. Daynes, *More Wives Than One: Transformation of the Mormon Marriage System, 1840–1910* (Urbana: University of Illinois Press, 2001), 208–10; Kathleen Flake, "Re-placing Memory: Latter-day Saint Use of Historical Monuments and

Narrative in the Early Twentieth Century," *Religion and American Culture: A Journal of Interpretation* 13, no. 1 (Winter 2003): 80–81.

6. For the exposition and the new position of the Church in the 1890s, see Reid L. Neilson, *Exhibiting Mormonism: The Latter-day Saints and the 1893 Chicago World's Fair, Religion in America* (New York: Oxford University Press, 2011), 7–8, 63–74, 115, 135–75; and Konden R. Smith, "The Dawning of a New Era: Mormonism and the World's Columbian Exposition of 1893," in *Mormons and Popular Culture: The Global Influence of an American Phenomenon*, ed. J. Michael Hunter, vol. 2, *Literature, Art, Media, Tourism, and Sports* (Santa Barbara, CA: Praeger, 2013), 187–208.

7. Susa Young Gates, "Memorial Monument Dedication," *Improvement Era*, February 1906, 308–19.

8. Susa Young Gates, "Memorial Monument Dedication," *Improvement Era*, March 1906, 375–88.

9. David F. Boone, "'A Man Raised Up': The Role of Willard W. Bean in the Acquisition of the Hill Cumorah," *Journal of Book of Mormon Studies* 13, no. 1 (2004): 25–32.

10. Gerritsen, "Hill Cumorah Monument," 129, 132.

11. C. C. A. Christensen, *The Hill Cumorah*, ca. 1878, tempera on muslin, 204.5 cm × 294.6 cm, Brigham Young University Museum of Art, Provo, UT.

12. Glen M. Leonard, *Nauvoo: A Place of Peace, a People of Promise* (Salt Lake City: Deseret Book; Provo, UT: Brigham Young University Press, 2002), 253–54.

13. Cyrus Dallin made the same point in the gold-plated figure of Moroni for the pinnacle of the Salt Lake Temple. His Moroni put a trumpet to his lips, symbolically preaching the gospel to the world. Levi Edgar Young, "The Angel Moroni and Cyrus Dallin," *Improvement Era*, April 1953, 234–35.

14. John Henry Evans, *Joseph Smith: An American Prophet* (New York: Macmillan, 1933), v, vii–viii.

15. Evans, *Joseph Smith*, 36–41, 329–32, 427–28, emphasis in original.

16. John Henry Evans, *One Hundred Years of Mormonism: A History of the Church of Jesus Christ of Latter-day Saints from 1805 to 1905*, 3rd ed. (Salt Lake City: Deseret Sunday School Union, 1909), iii, 39–47, 49–50.

17. Evans, *Joseph Smith*, 427–28.

18. J. Michael Hunter, "The Monument to Brigham Young and the Pioneers: One Hundred Years of Controversy," *Utah Historical Quarterly* 68, no. 4 (Fall 2000): 332–35. I am indebted to Nathan Rees for permission to use material from an unpublished essay in my possession.

19. Hunter, "Monument to Brigham Young and the Pioneers," 332–33.

20. Ephraim Edward Ericksen, *The Psychological and Ethical Aspects of Mormon Group Life [. . .]* (Chicago: University of Chicago Press, 1922), 59. On the University of Chicago scholars, see Thomas W. Simpson, *American Universities and the Birth of Modern Mormonism, 1867–1940* (Chapel Hill: University of North Carolina Press, 2016), 86–87, 102–11; and Casey Paul Griffiths, "The Chicago Experiment: Finding the Voice and Charting the Course of Religious Education in the Church," *BYU Studies* 49, no. 4 (2010): 91–130. Not all Latter-day Saint scholars who received training at the University of Chicago sought to shape Mormonism in the liberal image. See,

e.g., T. Edgar Lyon Jr., *T. Edgar Lyon: A Teacher in Zion* (Provo, UT: Brigham Young University Press, 2002), 131–32, 136.

21. Ericksen, *Psychological and Ethical Aspects of Mormon Group Life*, 13–17.

22. For the crackdown on the Chicago intellectuals, see Simpson, *American Universities*, 92–125. Even so, the plates were not always considered ripe for public consumption. The same year *American Prophet* appeared, the Church downplayed supernatural elements of its past in an exhibit at the Century of Progress Exposition in Chicago. A bas-relief sculpture by Avard Fairbanks represented the Mormon canon—the Bible, the Book of Mormon, the Doctrine and Covenants, and the Pearl of Great Price— as books without saying anything of their origins. Nearby, a stained-glass depiction of the "First Vision" shows Joseph Smith kneeling as rays of light shoot down from the sky without any representation of the divine beings he claims to have seen. "The Church Century of Progress Display," *Improvement Era*, December 1933, 864–65; Marden E. Broadbent, "The Mormon Exhibit at the Century of Progress Exposition at Chicago," *Improvement Era*, October 1934, 579–81, 608–9.

23. LeGrand Richards, *A Marvelous Work and a Wonder* (Salt Lake City: Deseret Book, 1950), v.

24. Lucile C. Tate, *LeGrand Richards: Beloved Apostle* (Salt Lake City: Bookcraft, 1982), 236–37.

25. Richards, *Marvelous Work and a Wonder*, 1. Richards was off by one year. The monument was erected in 1935, not 1936.

26. Richards, *Marvelous Work and a Wonder*, 49–61; Ezekiel 37:15–20; Isaiah 29:11; John 10:16.

27. Richard Anderson, comp., "A Plan for Effective Missionary Work," 1949, 1, 3, 11–15, copy at Church History Library, Salt Lake City.

28. Jonathan A. Stapley, "Mormon Missiology," in *Mormonism: A Historical Encyclopedia*, ed. W. Paul Reeve and Ardis E. Parshall (Santa Barbara, CA: ABC-CLIO, 2010), 260–63; *A Systematic Program for Teaching the Gospel: Prepared for the Use of Missionaries of The Church of Jesus Christ of Latter-day Saints* ([Salt Lake City]: Corporation of the President of The Church of Jesus Christ of Latter-day Saints, 1952), 93–106; *A Uniform System for Teaching Investigators* ([Salt Lake City]: The Church of Jesus Christ of Latter-day Saints, 1961), 6, 29–38.

29. *The Plan of Our Heavenly Father: Discussion 1*, Uniform System for Teaching the Gospel (Salt Lake City: The Church of Jesus Christ of Latter-day Saints, 1986), 14, 22.

30. Bible prophecy scriptures from past missionary lessons—Ezekiel 37:15–19 and John 10:14–16—were relegated to a "Scriptural Resources" section that offered additional helps. Isaiah 29:11–12 was not included. *Plan of Our Heavenly Father*, 16.

31. *"Preach My Gospel": A Guide to Missionary Service* (Salt Lake City: The Church of Jesus Christ of Latter-day Saints, 2004), 106.

32. *Preach My Gospel* [2004], 38, 106.

33. *Preach My Gospel* [2004], 32–38.

34. *Preach My Gospel* [2004], 38. The 2018 edition of *Preach My Gospel* alters these words a little. *Preach My Gospel: A Guide to Missionary Service* (Salt Lake City: The Church of Jesus Christ of Latter-day Saints, 2018), 39. "In answer to our prayers, the Holy

Ghost will teach us truth through our feelings and thoughts. Feelings that come from the Holy Ghost are powerful, but they are also usually gentle and quiet. As we begin to feel that what we are learning is true, we will desire to know all that we can about the Restoration." *Preach My Gospel* [2004], 39.

35. *Preach My Gospel* [2004], 39.

36. *Preach My Gospel* [2004], 39. The passage goes on, "Knowing that the Book of Mormon is true leads to a knowledge that Joseph Smith was called as a prophet and that the gospel of Jesus Christ was restored through him."

37. Lowell L. Bennion, *The Religion of the Latter-day Saints: A College Course* (Salt Lake City: L.D.S. Department of Education, 1939), 130–31; Mary Lythgoe Bradford, *Lowell L. Bennion: Teacher, Counselor, Humanitarian* (Salt Lake City: Dialogue Foundation, 1995), 87–88, 101n10.

38. William Edwin Berrett, *The Restored Church: A Brief History of the Origin, Growth and Doctrines of The Church of Jesus Christ of Latter-day Saints* ([Salt Lake City]: Department of Education of The Church of Jesus Christ of Latter-day Saints, 1936), ix, 31.

39. Berrett, *Restored Church*, 28–75.

40. *Church History in the Fulness of Times: The History of The Church of Jesus Christ of Latter-day Saints* (Salt Lake City: The Church of Jesus Christ of Latter-day Saints, 1989), 37–47, 59–61.

41. For the static visuals on the Book of Mormon, see "Book of Mormon—All Gospel Art," Gospel Art, Media Library, The Church of Jesus Christ of Latter-day Saints, accessed June 5, 2022, https://www.churchofjesuschrist.org/media/collection/book-of-mormon-all-gospel-art-images?lang=eng. For the videos, see "Book of Mormon," Scriptures, Video Collections, Media Library, The Church of Jesus Christ of Latter-day Saints, accessed June 4, 2022, https://www.churchofjesuschrist.org/media/collection/scriptures-book-of-mormon?lang=eng.

42. "Video Collections," Media Library, The Church of Jesus Christ of Latter-day Saints, accessed June 4, 2022, https://www.churchofjesuschrist.org/media/collection/video.

43. BMC Team, "Incredible Video Explains the Story of the Plates of Mormon," Book of Mormon Central, October 23, 2019, https://bookofmormoncentral.org/blog/incredible-video-explains-the-story-of-the-plates-of-mormon.

44. "Moroni Invites All to Come unto Christ," video, 8:37, produced by The Church of Jesus Christ of Latter-day Saints, accessed June 4, 2022, https://www.churchofjesuschrist.org/media/video/2020-03-0800-moroni-invites-all-to-come-unto-christ-mormon-8-9-moroni-1-10-title-page?lang=eng&collectionId=b8df2040e24a4038a7969b166db8837d.

45. Katie Payne, *Moroni Greets a Dying Mormon after the Final Nephite Battles*, no date, in BMC Team, "Incredible Video Explains the Story of the Plates of Mormon," Book of Mormon Central, October 23, 2019, https://bookofmormoncentral.org/blog/incredible-video-explains-the-story-of-the-plates-of-mormon.

46. Clark Kelley Price, *Moroni Buries the Plates*, Religious Art, Clark Kelley Price, accessed Aug. 13, 2022, https://clarkkelleyprice.com/collections/religious-artwork/products/moroni-buries-the-plates.

47. See, e.g., Del Parson, *Joseph Smith Translating (Joseph Smith Translating the Gold Plates)*, Media Library, The Church of Jesus Christ of Latter-day Saints, accessed August 15, 2022, https://www.churchofjesuschrist.org/media/image/joseph-smith-translating-mormon-parson-25a0446?lang=eng.

48. Richard Van Wagoner and Steve Walker, "Joseph Smith: 'The Gift of Seeing,'" *Dialogue: A Journal of Mormon Thought* 15, no. 2 (Summer 1982): 48–68; Richard Lyman Bushman, *Joseph Smith: Rough Stone Rolling* (New York: Alfred A. Knopf, 2005), ch. 3; Brant A. Gardner, *The Gift and Power: Translating the Book of Mormon* (Salt Lake City: Greg Kofford Books, 2011), ch. 21; "Joseph Smith Documents Dating through June 1831," in *JSP*, D1:xxix–xxxii; John F., "Canonization of Kitsch," By Common Consent (blog), March 10, 2009, https://bycommonconsent.com/2009/03/10/canonization-of-kitsch/; "Book of Mormon Translation," Gospel Topics Essays, Church History, The Church of Jesus Christ of Latter-day Saints, accessed June 4, 2022, https://www.churchofjesuschrist.org/study/manual/gospel-topics-essays/book-of-mormon-translation?lang=eng.

49. Gary Ernest Smith, *Joseph with the Urim and Thummim*, no date, oil on linen, 20″ × 16″; Gary Ernest Smith, *Joseph Translating*, no date, oil, 36″ × 30″; Gary Ernest Smith, *Translation*, no date, oil, 18″ × 24″, FourSquare Art, https://foursquareart.com/artists/gary-ernest-smith-religious-paintings/; Anthony Sweat, *Repicturing the Restoration: New Art to Expand Our Understanding* (Provo, UT: Religious Studies Center, Brigham Young University; Salt Lake City: Deseret Book, 2020), 26–35.

50. Elspeth Young, *I Will Send Their Words Forth*, 2010, oil, 24″ × 36″, Al Young Studios, https://www.alyoung.com/art/work-jacob.html.

51. John W. Welch and Doris R. Dant, *The Book of Mormon Paintings of Minerva Teichert* (Provo, UT: BYU Studies; Salt Lake City: Bookcraft, 1997), 47, 150–51; Elaine Cannon and Shirley A. Teichert, *Minerva! The Story of an Artist with a Mission* (Salt Lake City: Bookcraft, 1997), 1, 6, 44, 53, 61, 73, 92, 117, 120, 127, 129; Minerva Teichert, *Last Battle between the Nephites and the Lamanites*, ca. 1949–1951, oil on masonite, $35\frac{15}{16}″ \times 48″$, Brigham Young University Museum of Art, Provo, UT.

52. Katie Payne, *Moroni Buries the Plates*, no date; Katie Payne, *Mormon and Moroni in the Records Cave Abridging the Plates*, no date, in BMC Team, "Incredible Video Explains the Story of the Plates of Mormon," Book of Mormon Central, October 23, 2019, https://bookofmormoncentral.org/blog/incredible-video-explains-the-story-of-the-plates-of-mormon.

53. For a survey of the early period, see Gary L. Bunker and Davis Bitton, *The Mormon Graphic Image, 1834–1914: Cartoons, Caricatures, and Illustrations* (Salt Lake City: University of Utah Press, 1983). For the later period, see Theric Jepson, "Mormons and American Comics," in *Mormons and Popular Culture: The Global Influence of an American Phenomenon*, vol. 2, *Literature, Art, Media, Tourism, and Sports*, ed. J. Michael Hunter (Santa Barbara, CA: Praeger, 2013), 81–94.

54. John W. Rich, comp., *The Book of Mormon on Trial: Based on the "Trial of the Stick of Joseph" by Jack West*, illustrated by Fritz O. Alseth (Sacramento, CA: Fritz 'n Rich, 1963).

55. Jepson, "Mormons and American Comics," 87–88; Andrew Knaupp, *The Golden Plates: Six Issue Collection*, illustrated by Michael Allred and Laura Allred (Utah: LDSComicBooks.com, 2017).

56. "Gold Plates Replica," Online Store, Book of Mormon Foundation, accessed June 4, 2022, https://www.bomf.org/online-store.html.

57. PioneerPlaysets, "3D Print Downloadable STL Files So You Can Make Your Own Full Scale 3D Printed Gold Plates Display Box Replica, Secret Compartment," Etsy, accessed Aug. 13, 2022, https://www.etsy.com/listing/1238991495/3d-print-downl oadable-stl-files-so-you; The Temple Store, "Gold Plates (Origins of the Book of Mormon) Scale Model (Made to Order)," Etsy, accessed June 4, 2022, https://www .etsy.com/listing/289742783/gold-plates-origins-of-the-book-of.

58. Cindy S. Pedersen, *Book of Mormon Family Night: Lessons That Teach with Treats* ([American Fork, UT]: Covenant Communications, 1994), 12–13; Stevie Kay, "Book of Mormon Krispies," *Spud Mamas* (blog), June 8, 2010, http://spudmamas.blogspot .com/2010/06/book-of-mormon-krispies.html.

59. Sondra, "Primary 3 Lesson 15," *Happy Clean Living* (blog), April 14, 2011, https:// murrayandmathews.blogspot.com/2011/04/primary-3-lesson-15.html.

60. Todd Huisken, *More Mormon Origami* (Springville, UT: Cedar Fort, 2014), 32–33.

61. Johnson Brothers Store, "Johnson Brothers LDS Book of Mormon Pin, Gold Plates Pin," Amazon, accessed August 10, 2022, https://www.amazon.com/Johnson-Brothers-Book-Mormon-Plates/dp/B07HR22MXQ; "Golden Plates Tie Clip," BuyLDSProducts .com, accessed August 10, 2022, https://www.buyldsproducts.com/golden-plates-tie-clip/; Loud Cufflinks, "Golden Plates Mormon Cufflinks," Amazon, accessed August 10, 2022, https://www.amazon.com/Loud-Cufflinks-Golden-Plates-Mormon/dp/B01 MSTKL7R.

62. PioneerPlaysets, "Large 3/4 Scale 3D Printed Gold Plates Display Box Replica, Secret Compartment, Made from Plastic, Golden Plates display, Gold Leafed Pages," Etsy, accessed August 10, 2022, https://www.etsy.com/listing/765823958/large-34-scale-3d-printed-gold-plates.

63. *The Book of Mormon for Young Readers* by Kelli Coughanour advertised itself as an attractive version: "Would you love for your children and grandchildren to get more out of reading the scriptures?" This book makes it easy "for children to understand and love the scriptures." Kelli Coughanour, comp., *The Book of Mormon for Young Readers* (Kennewick, WA: Point Publishing, 2015).

64. Brianne, "This Was Everything I Hoped For and More," April 1, 2020, comment on PioneerPlaysets, https://www.etsy.com/shop/PioneerPlaysets.

65. Shauna Gibby, *Heroic Stories from the Book of Mormon* (Salt Lake City: Deseret Book, 2017), available at https://deseretbook.com/p/heroic-stories-from-the-book-of-mor mon?variant_id=151038-hardcover.

Chapter 9

1. Monte S. Nyman, "Why Were the Book of Mormon Gold Plates Not Placed in a Museum So That People Might Know Joseph Smith Had Them?," *Ensign*, December 1986, 64–65.

2. Elliott Colla, *Conflicted Antiquities: Egyptology, Egyptomania, Egyptian Modernity* (Durham, NC: Duke University Press, 2007), 24, 67–68; *The Younger Memnon*, 19th Dynasty, granite statue, 266.80 cm × 203.30 cm, British Museum, London, https://www.britishmuseum.org/collection/object/Y_EA19; Kelvin Everest and Geoffrey Matthews, *The Poems of Shelley*, vol. 2, *1817–1819* (Harlow, England: Longman, 2000), 311.

3. Colla, *Conflicted Antiquities*, 17–18, 28–29.

4. John L. Brooke, *The Refiner's Fire: The Making of Mormon Cosmology, 1644–1844* (New York: Cambridge University Press, 1996).

5. Orson Pratt said "about two-thirds" of the plates were sealed. David Whitmer, who claims to have seen the plates, estimated that "half of the book was sealed." Orson Pratt, *Journal of Discourses*, 26 vols. (Liverpool: F. D. Richards, 1855–1886), 3:347; Lyndon W. Cook, ed., *David Whitmer Interviews: A Restoration Witness* ([Orem, UT]: Grandin Book, 1993), 21.

6. Bernt G. Lundgren, "Janne Mattson Sjodahl: Baptist Minister, Convert to Mormonism, Editor, Author and Missionary" (master's thesis, Brigham Young University, 1971), 6, 8–12, 15, 18, 26, 43–44, 58, 87, 95.

7. Janne M. Sjodahl, "The Book of Mormon Plates," *Improvement Era*, April 1923, 541, 544; see also Janne M. Sjodahl, "The Book of Mormon Plates," *Journal of Book of Mormon Studies* 10, no. 1 (2001): 22–23.

8. Janne M.Sjodahl, "The Book of Mormon Plates," 541–44.

9. John Gee, "Epigraphic Considerations on Janne Sjodahl's Experiment with Nephite Writing," *Journal of Book of Mormon Studies* 10, no. 1 (2001): 25, 79. Bruce Dale estimates that the Book of Mormon was engraved on about forty separate metal plates, covering a surface area of approximately 60 square feet. This is about 15 percent of the current surface area of the modern English translation of the book. Bruce E. Dale, "How Big a Book? Estimating the Total Surface Area of the Book of Mormon Plates," *Interpreter: A Journal of Latter-day Saint Faith and Scholarship* 25 (2017): 261–68.

10. Martin Harris said the plates weighed 40–50 pounds. William Smith said they weighed about 60 pounds. "Mormonism—No. II," *Tiffany's Monthly* (New York City), August 1859, 166; William Smith, *William Smith on Mormonism [. . .]* (Lamoni, IA: Herald Steam Book and Job Office, 1883), 12; C. E. Butterworth, "The Old Soldier's Testimony," *Saints' Herald* (Lamoni, IA), October 4, 1884, 644.

11. Read H. Putnam, "Were the Golden Plates Made of Tumbaga?," *Improvement Era*, September 1966, 789, 829–30; Janne M. Sjodahl, "The Book of Mormon Plates," *Improvement Era*, April 1923, 544–45. Putnam was not the first to suggest an alloy. Long before, William Smith had said that the plates were an alloy of gold and copper. C. E. Butterworth, "The Old Soldier's Testimony," *Saints' Herald* (Lamoni, IA), October 4, 1884, 644.

12. Putnam, "Were the Golden Plates Made of Tumbaga?," 829–31; see also John W. Welch, ed., *Reexploring the Book of Mormon: The F.A.R.M.S. Updates* (Salt Lake City: Deseret Book; Provo, UT: Foundation for Ancient Research and Mormon Studies, 1992), 275–77.

13. Jerry D. Grover Jr., *Ziff, Magic Goggles, and Golden Plates: The Etymology of Zyf and a Metallurgical Analysis of the Book of Mormon Plates* (Provo, UT: Grover Publishing,

2015); Jerry D. Grover Jr., *Geology of the Book of Mormon* (Provo, UT: By the author, 2017). For a similar investigation by a goldsmith, see "How Were the Book of Mormon Gold Plates Made? w/Brian Patch," https://www.youtube.com/watch?v=LsDfIJfEmUo. A contrary view is presented by "It's Me Jessie," "Joseph Smith and the Golden Plates—The Real Story!," https://www.youtube.com/watch?v=t3bgJ80-RP8.

14. Book of Mormon, 1830 ed., 178 [Mosiah 11:3, 8].

15. Robert K. Thomas, "A Literary Critic Looks at the Book of Mormon," in *A Believing People: Literature of the Latter-day Saints*, ed. Richard H. Cracroft and Neal E. Lambert (Salt Lake City: Bookcraft, 1979), 142–43; Grover, *Ziff, Magic Goggles, and Golden Plates*, 3, 37–42, 45–47, 67–95, 103.

16. Grover, *Ziff, Magic Goggles, and Golden Plates*, 87–90, 92–93; Emma Smith Bidamon Interview with Joseph Smith III, February 1879, in *EMD*, 1:539, 541.

17. Grover, *Ziff, Magic Goggles, and Golden Plates*, viii.

18. https://witnessesundaunted.com/.

19. The revelation authorizing Joseph Smith to show the plates to witnesses declared that unbelievers "would not believe you, my servant Joseph, if it were possible that you should show them all these things which I have committed unto you." Doctrine and Covenants 5:7.

20. J. Spencer Fluhman, *"A Peculiar People": Anti-Mormonism and the Making of Religion in Nineteenth-Century America* (Chapel Hill: University of North Carolina Press, 2012), chs. 1 and 4; Jan Shipps, *Sojourner in the Promised Land: Forty Years among the Mormons* (Urbana: University of Illinois Press, 2000), 62–66.

21. Fawn M. Brodie, *No Man Knows My History: The Life of Joseph Smith the Mormon Prophet* (New York: Alfred A. Knopf, 1945), 37, 41; Eber D. Howe, *Mormonism Unvailed: Or, a Faithful Account of That Singular Imposition and Delusion, from Its Rise to the Present Time. With Sketches of the Characters of Its Propagators, and a Full Detail of the Manner in Which the Famous Golden Bible Was Brought before the World.* [. . .] (Painesville, OH: By the author, 1834), 235–36.

22. Brodie, *No Man Knows My History*, 74, 76–78; Howe, *Mormonism Unvailed*, 13–14, 94–98; Thomas Ford, *A History of Illinois, from Its Commencement as a State in 1818 to 1847.* [. . .] (Chicago: S. C. Griggs, 1854), 257.

23. Ford, *History of Illinois*, 257; Brodie, *No Man Knows My History*, 79–80.

24. Dan Vogel, ed., *Early Mormon Documents*, 5 vols. (Salt Lake City: Signature Books, 1996–2003).

25. In 1857, John Hyde, a defector from Mormonism writing a virulent and strongly argued critique, likewise concluded that "every careful reader must be compelled to admit that Smith did have some plates of some kind." Hyde hypothesized that as an inveterate money-digger, Smith had come across plates hidden in the ground; he was one treasure-seeker who found treasure: "Smith's antecedents and subsequents, show that he did not have genius sufficient to originate the whole conception, without some palpable suggestion. The having chanced to have found some plates in a mound, as [Robert] Wiley [maker of the Kinderhook plates] found his, or as Chase discovered Smith's 'peepstone,' would be just such an event as would suggest every particular statement Smith made about his plates, at the same time account for what is known;

and, therefore, it is more than reasonable to conclude that Smith found his plates while digging gold." John Hyde Jr., *Mormonism: Its Leaders and Designs* (New York: W. P. Fetridge, 1857), 269.

26. Vogel, *Joseph Smith*, 98, 600n64, 600n66; Kirk B. Henrichsen, comp., "How Witnesses Described the 'Gold Plates,'" *Journal of Book of Mormon Studies* 10, no. 1 (2001): 18.

27. Vogel, *Joseph Smith*, 600nn64–66; Janne M. Sjodahl, "Notes on the Book of Mormon," *Improvement Era*, April 1927, 529–30.

28. Vogel, *Joseph Smith*, 3–4, 7, 31, 43–45; Joseph Smith, History Drafts, 1838–ca. 1841, in *JSP*, H1:208 (Draft 2); Milton V. Backman and James B. Allen, "Membership of Certain of Joseph Smith's Family in the Western Presbyterian Church of Palmyra," *BYU Studies* 10, no. 4 (Summer 1970): 482–84.

29. Vogel, *Joseph Smith*, 43–45, 47–48, 50.

30. Vogel, *Joseph Smith*, 56, 93.

31. Vogel, *Joseph Smith*, 45–47.

32. The best work on the idea of metal plates in Joseph Smith's environment has been done by Michael G. Reed, who points out (in collaboration with Michael Quinn) that John Hyde, writing in 1857, thought one defect of Joseph Smith's story was the claim to write on plates since the text of the Bible made clear the Jews did not use plates. "Now the Jews did not use plates of brass at that time. Their writing materials were 1. Tablets smeared with wax. 2. Linen rubbed with a kind of gum. 3. Tanned leather and vellum. 4. Parchment (invented by Attalus of Pergamos). 5. Papyrus. (M. Stuart, O. Test. Can.) All the writings of the Jews long anterior and subsequent to Zedekiah were in *rolls*. (Isa., xxxiv. 4; Jer., xxxvi. 25; Ezek., iii. 9, 10; Ps. xl. 7; Zech., v. 1, etc., etc.)." Michael G. Reed and D. Michael Quinn, "Metal Records and the Invention of Religious Tradition" (presentation, Sunstone, Jan. 2017), https://sunstone.org/metal-records-and-the-invention-of-religious-tradition/; Michael G. Reed, "The Notion of Metal Records in Joseph Smith's Day" (paper presented at Summer Seminar on Mormon Culture, Brigham Young University, Provo, UT, Aug. 18, 2011); Hyde, *Mormonism*, 217–18, italics in original.

33. Ann Taves, *Revelatory Events: Three Case Studies of the Emergence of New Spiritual Paths* (Princeton, NJ: Princeton University Press, 2016), 51.

34. Taves, *Revelatory Events*, 51–52, italics in original.

35. Taves, *Revelatory Events*, 59–62; Book of Mormon, 1830 ed., 539, 542–44, 548 [Ether 1:33; 2:16–25; 3:1–6; 6:2–3]; Genesis 11:1–9.

36. Taves, *Revelatory Events*, 62–63.

37. Brodie, *No Man Knows My History*, 16–17, 19.

38. John Henry Evans, for example, said Joseph "had the reputation of looking into peep-stones and hunting for treasures with a witch-hazel," without either confirming or denying the reputation. Some years later, the Mormon apologist and BYU professor of religion and history Hugh Nibley wrote that if solid evidence of the 1826 trial was ever brought forth, it would be "the most damning evidence in existence against Joseph Smith." John Henry Evans, *Joseph Smith: An American Prophet* (New York: Macmillan, 1933), 38, 377–82; Hugh Nibley, *The Myth Makers* (Salt Lake City: Bookcraft, 1961), 140–42.

39. Keith Thomas, *Religion and the Decline of Magic: Studies in Popular Beliefs in Sixteenth and Seventeenth Century England* (New York: Oxford University Press, 1971), 236–37. For America, see Herbert Leventhal, *In the Shadow of the Enlightenment: Occultism and Renaissance Science in Eighteenth-Century America* (New York: New York University Press, 1976), 107–19, 129–31, 262–67; and Jon Butler, "Magic, Astrology, and the Early American Religious Heritage, 1600–1760," *American Historical Review* 84, no. 2 (April 1979): 317–46.

40. "Book of Mormon Translation," Gospel Topics Essays, The Church of Jesus Christ of Latter-day Saints, accessed May 2, 2022, https://www.churchofjesuschrist.org/study/manual/gospel-topics-essays/book-of-mormon-translation?lang=eng. Prior to 2013, several Mormon apostles had acknowledged the use of a seer stone in translation. See Neal A. Maxwell, " 'By the Gift and Power of God,' " *Ensign*, January 1997, 39; and Russell M. Nelson, "A Treasured Testament," *Ensign*, July 1993, 62.

41. *Saints: The Story of the Church of Jesus Christ in the Latter Days*, vol. 1, *The Standard of Truth, 1815–1846* (Salt Lake City: The Church of Jesus Christ of Latter-day Saints, 2018), 21, 31, 33, 34.

42. L. Hannah Stoddard and James F. Stoddard III, *Seer Stone v. Urim and Thummim: Book of Mormon Translation on Trial* (Salem, UT: Joseph Smith Foundation, 2019), 1–8, 196, 208.

43. Jonathan Neville, *A Man That Can Translate: Joseph Smith and the Nephite Interpreters* (n.p.: Digital Legend, 2019–2021), 79–88.

44. D. Michael Quinn, *Early Mormonism and the Magic World View*, rev. ed. (Salt Lake City: Signature Books, 1998), 155, 201.

45. Book of Mormon, 1830 ed., iii, 21 [1 Nephi 9:2–4].

46. "Ancient Records," *Times and Seasons* (Nauvoo, IL), May 1, 1843, 186.

47. Janne M. Sjodahl, "Notes on the Book of Mormon," *Improvement Era*, April 1927, 530.

48. Gordon B. Hinckley, "Metal Plates in the British Museum," *Improvement Era*, March 1936, 154.

49. Franklin S. Harris, "Gold Plates in Persia," *Improvement Era*, December 1940, 714–15, 764; Ali Mousavi, *Persepolis: Discovery and Afterlife of a World Wonder* (Boston: De Gruyter, 2012), 177–78.

50. Franklin S. Harris Jr., "Others Kept Records on Metal Plates, Too," *Instructor*, October 1957, 318–21.

51. Letter from Mark E. Petersen to Paul R. Cheesman, June 27, 1974, in MSS 2049, box 1, fd. 6, Paul R. Cheesman (1921–1991) Papers, L. Tom Perry Special Collections, Harold B. Lee Library, Brigham Young University.

52. Mark E. Petersen, *Those Gold Plates!* (Salt Lake City: Bookcraft, 1979); Paul R. Cheesman, *Ancient Writing on Metal Plates: Archaeological Findings Support Mormon Claims* (Bountiful, UT: Horizon, 1985), 11, 32, 50–52, 81.

53. John L. Sorenson, *An Ancient American Setting for the Book of Mormon* (Salt Lake City: Deseret Book; Provo, UT: Foundation for Ancient Research and Mormon Studies, 1985), 278–88; John L. Sorenson, *Mormon's Codex: An Ancient American Book* (Provo, UT: Neal A. Maxwell Institute for Religious Scholarship; Salt Lake City: Deseret Book, 2013), 338–40. H. Curtis Wright dealt most directly with the

plates problem in H. Curtis Wright, "Ancient Burials of Metal Documents in Stone Boxes," in *By Study and Also by Faith: Essays in Honor of Hugh W. Nibley [. . .]*, ed. John M. Lundquist and Stephen D. Ricks, vol. 2 (Salt Lake City: Deseret Book; Provo, UT: Foundation for Ancient Research and Mormon Studies, 1990), 273–334; H. Curtis Wright, "Metallic Documents of Antiquity," *BYU Studies* 10, no. 4 (Summer 1970): 457–77.

54. Hamblin, "Sacred Writing on Metal Plates in the Ancient Mediterranean," 37–54.

55. Hamblin, "Sacred Writing on Metal Plates in the Ancient Mediterranean," 39, 42, 52–54.

56. Ryan Thomas, "The Gold Plates and Ancient Metal Epigraphy," *Dialogue: A Journal of Mormon Thought* 52, no. 2 (Summer 2019): 38–40, 46–48, 57. Thomas's examples of ancient metal writing can be found at https://www.dialoguejournal.com/articles/the-gold-plates-appendix/.

57. Reed, "Notion of Metal Records in Joseph Smith's Day," 1–16; see also Reed and Quinn, "Metal Records and the Invention of Religious Tradition," (presentation, Sunstone, January 2017).

58. Reed, "Notion of Metal Records in Joseph Smith's Day," 1, 3n9, 5n12, 6n13, 6n15, 8–9n17, 11–14.

59. Sonia Hazard, "The Material Turn in the Study of Religion," *Religion and Society: Advances in Research* 4 (2013): 58–59, 64–68.

60. Sonia Hazard, "How Joseph Smith Encountered Printing Plates and Founded Mormonism," *Religion and American Culture: A Journal of Interpretation* 31, no. 2 (2021): 138–48, 153–73.

61. Hazard, "How Joseph Smith Encountered Printing Plates," 181. Expanding on this thought, Hazard says: "Some might find the printing-plates hypothesis to be deflating or reductive. Viewed from another angle, the reverse is true. In a moment when dissatisfactions over the limitations of critical humanist approaches creep like a fog over much recent work in religious studies and the humanities, materiality itself may even offer its own form of enchantment, in the sense of directing scholarly attentions toward human-nonhuman arrangements in which experiences of wonder, and unusual episodes of cultural and religious creativity, occur in ways that cannot be reduced, in the last instance, to one or another operation of human thought."

62. Hazard, "How Joseph Smith Encountered Printing Plates," 171–78.

Chapter 10

1. Dorothy Ross, "Historical Consciousness in Nineteenth-Century America," *American Historical Review* 89, no. 4 (October 1984): 910.

2. Solomon Spaulding, *Manuscript Found: The Complete Original "Spaulding Manuscript,"* ed. Kent P. Jackson, Religious Studies Center Specialized Monograph Series 11 (Provo, UT: Religious Studies Center, Brigham Young University, 1996), viii, 1, 5; Lester E. Bush Jr., "The Spalding Theory Then and Now," *Dialogue: A Journal of Mormon Thought* 10, no. 4 (Autumn 1977): 40–69.

3. In 1809, Washington Irving published *A History of New York, from the Beginning of the World to the End of the Dutch Dynasty* by Diedrich Knickerbocker as ostensibly the work of an eccentric roomer in a hotel who had departed without packing his manuscript. Although Irving later confessed his subterfuge, he initially thought that the device of a found manuscript added to the appeal of his work. Jerome McGann, "Washington Irving, *A History of New York*, and American History," *Early American Literature* 47, no. 2 (2012): 349–76.

4. *Fragments of Ancient Poetry, Collected in the Highlands of Scotland, and Translated from the Galic or Erse Language* (Edinburgh, Scotland: G. Hamilton and J. Balfour, 1760); Paul J. Degategno, "'The Source of Daily and Exalted Pleasure': Jefferson Reads the Poems of Ossian," in *Ossian Revisited*, ed. Howard Gaskill (Edinburgh, Scotland: Edinburgh University Press, 1991), 98–99; Henry David Thoreau, *A Week on the Concord and Merrimack Rivers* (Boston: James Munroe, 1849), 362–63; Nicholas Delbanco, *Why Writing Matters* (New Haven, CT: Yale University Press, 2020), 105. On Johnson's dispute with Macpherson, see Thomas M. Curley, *Samuel Johnson, the Ossian Fraud, and the Celtic Revival in Great Britain and Ireland* (Cambridge: Cambridge University Press, 2009), ch. 4.

5. Horace Walpole [Onuphrio Muralto, pseud.], *The Castle of Otranto, a Story* (London: Tho. Lownds, 1765); Horace Walpole, *The Castle of Otranto*, ed. Michael Gamer (London: Penguin Books, 2001), vii–xxxv.

6. Anthony Grafton, *Forgers and Critics: Creativity and Duplicity in Western Scholarship* (Princeton, NJ: Princeton University Press, 1990), 9, 14–15.

7. James H. Charlesworth, ed., *The Old Testament Pseudepigrapha*, vol. 1, *Apocalyptic Literature and Testaments* (New York: Doubleday, 1983), xxi–xxix; Annette Yoshiko Reed, "The Modern Invention of 'Old Testament Pseudepigrapha,'" *Journal of Theological Studies* 60, no. 2 (October 2009), 403–6; James L. Kugel, *The God of Old: Inside the Lost World of the Bible* (New York: Free Press, 2003), 39–41.

8. Charlesworth, *Old Testament Pseudepigrapha*, 1:xxi–xxix; Richard Bauckham, James R. Davila, and Alexander Panayotov, *Old Testament Pseudepigrapha: More Noncanonical Scriptures* (Grand Rapids, MI: William B. Eerdmans, 2013), 1:vii–ix, xvii–xxiii; Reed, "Modern Invention of 'Old Testament Pseudepigrapha,'" 403–36. A century before the Book of Mormon was published Johann Albert Fabricius's *Codex pseudepigraphus Veteris Testamenti* cataloged the massive number of works associated with prophets and patriarchs from the Bible. Reed, "Modern Invention of 'Old Testament Pseudepigrapha,'" 406.

9. Michael A. Knibb, *The Ethiopic Book of Enoch: A New Edition in the Light of the Aramaic Dead Sea Fragments*, in consultation with Edward Ullendorff (Oxford: Clarendon Press, 1978), 1; Richard Laurence, *The Book of Enoch the Prophet: An Apocryphal Production [. . .]* (Oxford: University Press for the Author, 1821); Reed, "Modern Invention of 'Old Testament Pseudepigrapha,'" 414. Pseudepigrapha differ from the pseudo-biblical texts that appeared with great frequency in American newspapers in the late eighteenth and early nineteenth centuries. They offered commentary on current political events in a language borrowed from scripture but made no pretense of originating in antiquity. Eran Shalev, "An American Book of Chronicles: Pseudo-Biblicism and the Cultural Origins of the Book of Mormon," in *Americanist Approaches to "The Book of Mormon*," ed. Elizabeth Fenton and Jared Hickman (New York: Oxford University Press, 2019), 136–58.

10. John S. Strong, *Relics of the Buddha* (Princeton, NJ: Princeton University Press, 2004), 115–22, 124–48.

11. Christopher Dickenson, "Contested Bones: The Politics of Public Burial in Roman Greece (c. 200 BC–200 AD)," *Ancient Society* 46 (2016): 95–163; Charles Freeman, *Holy Bones, Holy Dust: How Relics Shaped the History of Medieval Europe* (New Haven, CT: Yale University Press, 2011), 7, 14, 33–35, 101; Robert Bartlett, *Why Can the Dead Do Such Great Things?: Saints and Worshippers from the Martyrs to the Reformation* (Princeton, NJ: Princeton University Press, 2013), 239–50, 255; Acts 19:11–12.

12. J. M. Hussey, *The Orthodox Church in the Byzantine Empire* (Oxford: Clarendon Press, 1986), 46–49; Bartlett, *Why Can the Dead Do Such Great Things?*, 279–80, 303–4, 309–10, 444–46; Freeman, *Holy Bones, Holy Dust*, 101, 119; "Relics," in *The Catholic Encyclopedia: An International Work of Reference on the Constitution, Doctrine, Discipline, and History of the Catholic Church*, ed. Charles G. Herbermann et al. (New York: Robert Appleton, 1911), 12:737; Drew Holtmann, "Blood and Bones: A Theology of Christian Relics," *Journal of Theta Alpha Kappa* 41, no. 2 (2017): 61–78.

13. Freeman, *Holy Bones, Holy Dust*, 254–56; "On the Worship of Reliques," *Catholic Layman* 2, no. 18 (June 1853): 65; "Relics," in *Catholic Encyclopedia*, 12:734.

14. Eamon Duffy, "Introduction to the 2012 Edition," in Jacobus de Voragine, *The Golden Legend: Readings on the Saints*, trans. William Granger Ryan (Princeton, NJ: Princeton University Press, 2012), xi–xx; Sherry L. Reames, *The Legenda aurea: A Reexamination of Its Paradoxical History* (Madison: University of Wisconsin Press, 1985), 3–8.

15. Charles Matson Odahl, *Constantine and the Christian Empire* (New York: Routledge, 2004), 153–59; "Relics," in *Catholic Encyclopedia*, 12:735.

16. Peter Brown, *The Cult of the Saints: Its Rise and Function in Latin Christianity*, The Haskell Lectures on History of Religions, New Series, no. 2 (Chicago: University of Chicago Press, 1981), 86–88; Cameron J. Packer, "A Study of the Hill Cumorah: A Significant Latter-day Saint Landmark in Western New York" (master's thesis, Brigham Young University, 2002), 36, 43–46, 63–66, 70–84, 104, 106, 128, 147.

17. The pageant went by various titles over the years. For a review, see Gerald S. Argetsinger, "The Hill Cumorah Pageant: A Historical Perspective," *Journal of Book of Mormon Studies* 13, nos. 1–2 (2004): 58–60, 69; and Packer, "Study of the Hill Cumorah," 133–39.

18. The basic difference between Protestants and Catholics can be seen in their respective approach to divine "presence." See, e.g., Robert A. Orsi, *History and Presence* (Cambridge, MA: Belknap Press of Harvard University Press, 2016), ch. 1.

19. On the Ten Commandments, see, e.g., Michael Coogan, *The Ten Commandments: A Short History of an Ancient Text* (New Haven, CT: Yale University Press, 2014); Henning Graf Reventlow and Yair Hoffman, eds., *The Decalogue in Jewish and Christian Tradition* (New York: T&T Clark, 2011); and Lesley Smith, *The Ten Commandments: Interpreting the Bible in the Medieval World*, Studies in the History of Christian Traditions (Boston: Brill, 2014).

20. For background on the stone tables, see "Ark of the Covenant" and "Decalogue," in *The Jewish Encyclopedia: A Descriptive Record of the History, Religion, Literature, and*

Customs of the Jewish People from the Earliest Times to the Present Day, ed. Isidore Singer et al., 12 vols. (New York: Funk and Wagnalls, 1901–1909), 2:103–7; 4:492–96.

21. "Decalogue," in *Jewish Encyclopedia*, 4:492–96. The relationship between the Ethical Decalogue (Exodus 20) and the Ritual Decalogue (Exodus 34) has been the subject of much biblical scholarship. Summarizing this scholarship, Michael Coogan argues that Exodus 20 appeared as a late redaction (sixth century BCE) of an early version of Exodus 34 (tenth/ninth century BCE). Coogan, *Ten Commandments*, 35–37; see also Raymond F. Collins, "Ten Commandments," in *The Anchor Bible Dictionary*, ed. David Noel Freedman (New York: Doubleday, 1992), 6:383–84.

22. For recent speculation about Lehi's history, see Don Bradley, *The Lost 116 Pages: Reconstructing the Book of Mormon's Missing Stories* (Salt Lake City: Greg Kofford Books, 2019).

23. "Decalogue" and "Decalogue, the, in Jewish Theology," in *Jewish Encyclopedia*, 4:494, 497.

24. Exodus 25:10–22; "Ark of the Covenant," in *Jewish Encyclopedia*, 2:103–4.

25. Joshua 3:15–17; 6:1–21; Numbers 10:35; 31:6; 1 Samuel 4:4–5; 14:18; 2 Samuel 6:6–7; 11:11; "Ark of the Covenant," in *Jewish Encyclopedia*, 2:103.

26. Genesis 32:30; Exodus 33:20; Deuteronomy 5:24.

27. 1 Nephi 3:24–25; 4:9, 18; 16:10; Alma 37:38. For a recent treatment of Enoch's plate, see R. John Williams, "The Ghost and the Machine: Plates and Paratext in the Book of Mormon," in *Americanist Approaches to "The Book of Mormon,"* ed. Elizabeth Fenton and Jared Hickman (New York: Oxford University Press, 2019), 62.

28. For a comparison of the Liahona to astrolabes, see Timothy Gervais and John L. Joyce, "'By Small Means': Rethinking the Liahona," *Interpreter: A Journal of Latter-day Saint Faith and Scholarship* 30 (2018): 207–32.

29. Mosiah 8:9; Ether 1:2. For an approach to these treasured objects, see "Why Did the Nephites Preserve Some Items as 'National Treasures?,'" KnoWhys, Book of Mormon Central, April 14, 2020, https://knowhy.bookofmormoncentral.org/knowhy/why-did-the-nephites-preserve-some-items-as-national-treasures.

30. Hebrews 9:3–4.

31. Donald S. Lopez Jr., *The Tibetan Book of the Dead: A Biography* (Princeton, NJ: Princeton University Press, 2011), 2, 52, 54–55, 135; Francesca Fremantle, *Luminous Emptiness: Understanding the "Tibetan Book of the Dead"* (Boston: Shambhala, 2001), 16–20, 49–50, 135; Grant Underwood, "Attempting to Situate Joseph Smith," *BYU Studies* 44, no. 4 (2005): 46.

32. Walter Evans-Wentz, *The Tibetan Book of the Dead or the After-Death Experiences on the Bardo Plane, According to Lāma Kazi Dawa-Samdup's English Rendering* (New York: Oxford University Press, 1927); Lopez, *Tibetan Book of the Dead*, 2, 3–4, 22–28, 74, 101–6, 128.

33. Lopez, *Tibetan Book of the Dead*, 61–65.

34. Lopez, *Tibetan Book of the Dead*, 1, 4, 11, 139, 147–48, italics in original.

35. Lopez, *Tibetan Book of the Dead*, 150–52.

36. Lopez, *Tibetan Book of the Dead*, 54–55; Fremantle, *Luminous Emptiness*, 17.

Appendix A

1. Words of Mormon 1:3–6.
2. Ether 4:4. On the structure of the Book of Mormon, see Grant Hardy, *Understanding the Book of Mormon: A Reader's Guide* (New York: Oxford University Press, 2010).
3. History Drafts, 1838–ca. 1841, in *JSP*, H1:244, 246 (Draft 2); History, ca. Summer 1832, in *JSP*, H1:15–16.
4. Revelation, Spring 1829, in *JSP*, D1:41–42 [D&C 10:30, 41].
5. Original Manuscript of the Book of Mormon, ca. April 12, 1828–ca. July 1, 1829, in *JSP*, R5:7; John W. Welch, "Timing the Translation of the Book of Mormon: 'Days [and Hours] Never to Be Forgotten,'" *BYU Studies* 57, no. 4 (2018): 22–23.
6. Revelation, Spring 1829, in *JSP*, D1:40–41 [D&C 10:14–33]; Book of Mormon, 1830 ed., [iii].
7. 2 Nephi 5:30–32.
8. Jack M. Lyon and Kent R. Minson, "When Pages Collide: Dissecting the Words of Mormon," *BYU Studies* 51, no. 4 (2012): 120–36.
9. Words of Mormon 1:6.
10. Jonathan Neville, *Whatever Happened to the Golden Plates?*, rev. ed. (n.p.: Digital Legend, 2022), 27–28, 72, 75–76, 166–67, 171–72, 180.
11. Book of Mormon, 1830 ed., [iii]–iv.
12. Words of Mormon 1:3, 5, 9; Mormon 6:6.
13. Book of Mormon, 1830 ed., title page.
14. 1 Nephi 1:16–17; 6:1; 19:1–2. Kent Brown argues that Lehi may have recorded his history on material other than metal plates. S. Kent Brown, *From Jerusalem to Zarahemla: Literary and Historical Studies of the Book of Mormon* (Provo, UT: Religious Studies Center, Brigham Young University, 1998), 30–32. For an imaginative reconstruction of Lehi's record, see Don Bradley, *The Lost 116 Pages: Reconstructing the Book of Mormon's Missing Stories* (Salt Lake City: Greg Kofford Books, 2019).
15. 1 Nephi 1:17; 9:2, 4; 19:1–4; Words of Mormon 1:9–10; Book of Mormon, 1830 ed., title page, [iii].
16. 2 Nephi 5:28–33; Omni 1:25; Words of Mormon 1:3–6, 10.
17. Words of Mormon 1:3; Mormon 8:1. The various sets of plates are described and graphically represented in Grant R. Hardy and Robert E. Parsons, "Book of Mormon Plates and Records," in *Encyclopedia of Mormonism*, ed. Daniel H. Ludlow (New York: Macmillan, 1992), 1:195–201.
18. Ether 3:21; 4:4–5. In an 1878 interview, David Whitmer said that about "half" of the plates were sealed. In another interview given three years later, he said "about one-third" of the plates were "loose" and "the other solid, but with perceptible marks where the plates seemed to be sealed." Orson Pratt said two-thirds of the plates were sealed. "Interview with David Whitmer," *Deseret Evening News* (Salt Lake City), August 16, 1878, [2]; Lyndon W. Cook, ed., *David Whitmer Interviews: A Restoration Witness* (Orem, UT: Grandin Book, 1991), 75; Orson Pratt, in *Journal of Discourses*, 26 vols. (Liverpool: F. D. Richards, 1855–1886), 3:347.
19. Ether 3:22, 24; "Church History," March 1, 1842, in *JSP*, H1:495. For the ancient practice of sealing valuable documents, see John W. Welch, "Doubled, Sealed, Witnessed

Documents: From the Ancient World to the Book of Mormon," in *Mormons, Scripture, and the Ancient World: Studies in Honor of John L. Sorenson*, ed. Davis Bitton (Provo, UT: Foundation for Ancient Research and Mormon Studies, 1998), 396–418. For the nature of the seal, see D. Michael Quinn, *Early Mormonism and the Magic World View*, rev. ed. (Salt Lake City: Signature Books, 1998), 195–96; and "An Analysis of Claims Made in the Wikipedia Article 'Golden Plates'—'Sealed' Portion," FAIR, accessed September 5, 2022, https://www.fairlatterdaysaints.org/answers/Mormonism_and_Wikipedia/Golden_plates/Sealed_portion.

20. Ether 3:6–16, 22–25, 27–28.

21. Revelation, June 1829-E, in *JSP*, D1:84 [D&C 17:1].

22. On the transmission of the sealed portion and the Brother of Jared's vision, see Valentin Arts, "A Third Jaredite Record: The Sealed Portion of the Gold Plates," *Journal of Book of Mormon Studies* 11, no. 1 (2002): 53–56.

23. Mosiah 8:7–19; 9:1–6; 21:27–28; 22:13–14; 28:11–19; Header of the Book of Ether.

24. Ether 1:1–2; 4:4; Mormon 8:3. For evidence that Moroni Christianized the Jaredite record, see Hardy, *Understanding the Book of Mormon*, 235–40.

25. Ether 4:4–7; Orson Pratt, in *Journal of Discourses*, 19:216–17; Bruce R. McConkie, "The Bible, a Sealed Book," in *Teaching Seminary: Preservice Readings* (Salt Lake City: The Church of Jesus Christ of Latter-day Saints, 2004), 124.

26. Christopher Marc Nemelka, *The Sealed Portion: The Final Testament of Jesus Christ*, 2nd ed. ([Salt Lake City]: Worldwide United, 2005); Bill McKeever, "Christopher Nemelka—The Reincarnated Hyrum Smith," Mormonism Research Ministry, accessed September 5, 2022, https://www.mrm.org/christopher-nemelka.

27. The Brotherhood of Christ Church, *The Sealed Portion of the Brother of Jared*, vol. 1 (Leawood, KS: Leathers, 2001).

Appendix B

1. Book of Mormon, 1830 ed., [iii]; History, ca. Summer 1832, in *JSP*, H1:16; Letter to Noah C. Saxton, January 4, 1833, in *JSP*, D2:354; History Drafts, 1838–ca. 1841, in *JSP*, H1:286 (Draft 2); "Church History," March 1, 1842, in *JSP*, H1:495; Joseph Smith History, 1838–1856, vol. A-1, 216, 240, 271, in Historian's Office, History of the Church, 1838–ca. 1882, Church History Library, Salt Lake City, also available at josephsmithpapers.org.

2. For the current state of the debate, see Grant Hardy, "The Book of Mormon Translation Process," *BYU Studies* 60, no. 3 (2021): 203–11.

3. James Gordon Bennett Account, 1831, in *EMD*, 3:282, 288–89.

4. Henry Caswall, *The City of the Mormons; or, Three Days at Nauvoo, in 1842* (London: J. G. F. and J. Rivington, 1842).

5. Jason Frederick Peters, "The Kinderhook Plates: Examining a Nineteenth-Century Hoax," *Journal of the Illinois State Historical Society* 96, no. 2 (Summer 2003): 130–45.

6. Book of Mormon, 1830 ed., [iii]; Revelation, Spring 1829, in *JSP*, D1:40 [D&C 10:1]; "Church History," March 1, 1842, in *JSP*, H1:495. The sources on translation from the

early period have been compiled in John W. Welch, "The Miraculous Translation of the Book of Mormon," in *Opening the Heavens: Accounts of Divine Manifestations, 1820–1844*, ed. John W. Welch and Erick B. Carlson (Provo, UT: Brigham Young University Press; Salt Lake City: Deseret Book, 2005), 118–98; and, more recently, in Jonathan Neville, *A Man That Can Translate: Joseph Smith and the Nephite Interpreters*, 2nd ed. (n.p.: Museum of the Book of Mormon, 2020), 242–99.

7. David Whitmer, *An Address to All Believers in Christ* (Richmond, MO: By the author, 1887), 12.

8. Emma Smith Bidamon Interview with Joseph Smith III, February 1879, in *EMD*, 1:539. For other descriptions of seer stone usage, see Richard Van Wagoner and Steve Walker, "Joseph Smith: 'The Gift of Seeing,'" *Dialogue: A Journal of Mormon Thought* 15, no. 2 (Summer 1982): 48–68.

9. Orson Hyde, *Ein Ruf aus der Wüste, eine Stimme aus dem Schoose der Erde [. . .]* (Frankfurt, Germany: Im Selbstverlage des Verfassers, 1842), 27. English translation of *Ein Ruf aus der Wüste* available at josephsmithpapers.org.

10. John Jaques, *Catechism for Children, Exhibiting the Prominent Doctrines of the Church of Jesus Christ of Latter-day Saints* (Liverpool: F. D. Richards, 1854), 78; Peter Crawley, *A Descriptive Bibliography of the Mormon Church*, vol. 3, *1853–1857* (Provo, UT: Religious Studies Center, Brigham Young University, 2012), 152.

11. George Q. Cannon, *The Life of Joseph Smith, the Prophet* (Salt Lake City: Juvenile Instructor Office, 1888), 56.

12. Joseph Fielding Smith, *Essentials in Church History: A History of the Church from the Birth of Joseph Smith to the Present Time (1922) [. . .]* (Salt Lake City: The Church of Jesus Christ of Latter-day Saints, 1922), 62.

13. John Henry Evans, *One Hundred Years of Mormonism: A History of the Church of Jesus Christ of Latter-day Saints from 1805 to 1905*, 3rd ed. (Salt Lake City: Deseret Sunday School Union, 1909), 58.

14. Davis Bitton, "B. H. Roberts as Historian," *Dialogue: A Journal of Mormon Thought* 3, no. 4 (Winter 1968): 26–27; B. H. Roberts, *A Comprehensive History of The Church of Jesus Christ of Latter-day Saints: Century I*, 6 vols. (Salt Lake City: The Church, 1930), 1:127–33. Roberts's explanation was picked up almost immediately by J. E. Homans, author of an apologetic work published under the pseudonym Robert C. Webb. Robert C. Webb [James E. Homans], *The Real Mormonism: A Candid Analysis of an Interesting but Much Misunderstood Subject in History Life and Thought* (New York: Sturgis and Walton, 1916), 30–31.

15. "Human Side of the Book of Mormon," *Mormon Point of View* 1, no. 2 (April 1, 1904): 127–28.

16. Evans, *One Hundred Years of Mormonism*, iii, 69–71.

17. Richard Lyman Bushman, *Joseph Smith: Rough Stone Rolling* (New York: Alfred A. Knopf, 2005), ch. 4; Terryl L. Givens, *By the Hand of Mormon: The American Scripture That Launched a New World Religion* (New York: Oxford University Press, 2002).

18. "Delusions," *Millennial Harbinger* (Bethany, VA), February 7, 1831, 93.

19. Webb, *Real Mormonism*, 33.

20. Scott C. Dunn, "Automaticity and the Dictation of the Book of Mormon," in *American Apocrypha: Essays on the Book of Mormon*, ed. Dan Vogel and Brent Lee Metcalfe (Salt Lake City: Signature Books, 2002), 26–30, 36.

21. Two Latter-day Saint apostles mentioned the seer stone in The Church's official magazine, but The Church's history curriculum for university students never mentioned the seer stone. Neal A. Maxwell, "'By the Gift and Power of God,'" *Ensign*, January 1997, 39; Russell M. Nelson, "A Treasured Testament," *Ensign*, July 1993, 62; *Church History in the Fulness of Times: The History of The Church of Jesus Christ of Latter-day Saints* (Salt Lake City: The Church of Jesus Christ of Latter-day Saints, 1989), chs. 4–5.

22. *JSP*, R3:xx–xxi.

23. "Book of Mormon Translation," Gospel Topics Essays, Church History, The Church of Jesus Christ of Latter-day Saints, accessed September 5, 2022, https://www.churchofjesuschrist.org/study/manual/gospel-topics-essays/book-of-mormon-translation?lang=eng.

24. *Saints: The Story of the Church of Jesus Christ in the Latter Days*, vol. 1, *The Standard of Truth, 1815–1846* (Salt Lake City: The Church of Jesus Christ of Latter-day Saints, 2018), 61.

25. Neville, *Man That Can Translate*, 79–80, 89–96.

26. On the seer stones, see Michael Hubbard MacKay and Nicholas J. Frederick, *Joseph Smith's Seer Stones* (Provo, UT: Religious Studies Center, Brigham Young University; Salt Lake City: Deseret Book, 2016).

27. Royal Skousen, *The History of the Text of the Book of Mormon*, part 3, *The Nature of the Original Language*, with the collaboration of Stanford Carmack (Provo, UT: Foundation for Ancient Research and Mormon Studies, Brigham Young University, 2018), 37–43; Royal Skousen, "How Joseph Smith Translated the Book of Mormon: Evidence from the Original Manuscript," *Journal of Book of Mormon Studies* 7, no. 1 (1998): 23–31; Royal Skousen, "Translating the Book of Mormon: Evidence from the Original Manuscript," in *Book of Mormon Authorship Revisited: The Evidence for Ancient Origins*, ed. Noel B. Reynolds (Provo, UT: Foundation for Ancient Research and Mormon Studies, 1997), 61–93. Stan Spencer questions the idea of reading the text from the crystals or the stones. The instruments were instead "aids to faith." They inspired Joseph Smith to see "imaginative visions" where he saw the text of the Book of Mormon. Stan Spencer, "Seers and Stones: The Translation of the Book of Mormon as Divine Visions of an Old-Time Seer," *Interpreter: A Journal of Latter-day Saint Faith and Scholarship* 24 (2017): 27–98.

28. Philip L. Barlow, "Before Mormonism: Joseph Smith's Use of the Bible, 1820–1829," *Journal of the American Academy of Religion* 57, no. 4 (Winter 1989): 756.

29. Jonathan Neville has found almost four hundred non-biblical phrases of three words or more common to Edwards's writings and the Book of Mormon. Jonathan Edward Neville, *Infinite Goodness: Joseph Smith, Jonathan Edwards, and the Book of Mormon* (n.p.: Museum of the Book of Mormon, 2021), 8–9, 239–81.

30. Neville, *Man That Can Translate*, 183–84, 222–31. Neville and fellow scholar James Lucas speculate in a forthcoming book that Joseph saw a literal translation in the Urim and Thummim crystals which he then couched in colloquial English, drawing on his nineteenth-century vocabulary. Personal communication, June 2022. For a

pathbreaking study of intertextuality, see Nicholas J. Frederick, *The Bible, Mormon Scripture, and the Rhetoric of Allusivity*, Fairleigh Dickinson University Press Mormon Studies Series (Madison, NJ: Fairleigh Dickinson University Press, 2016).

31. Brant A. Gardner, *The Gift and Power: Translating the Book of Mormon* (Salt Lake City: Greg Kofford Books, 2011), 251–57, 274–77, 279.

32. Royal Skousen with Stanford Carmack, *The History of the Text of the Book of Mormon: Part Three, The Nature of the Original Language* (Provo, Utah: Foundation for Ancient Research and Mormon Studies; Brigham Young University Studies, 2018), 11, 14, 37, 64, 64–89 passim.

33. Samuel Morris Brown, "Seeing the Voice of God: The Book of Mormon on Its Own Translation," in *Producing Ancient Scripture: Joseph Smith's Translation Projects in the Development of Mormon Christianity*, ed. Michael Hubbard MacKay, Mark Ashurst-McGee, and Brian M. Hauglid (Salt Lake City: University of Utah Press, 2020), 137–68.

34. Ann Taves, "Joseph Smith, Helen Schucman, and the Experience of Producing a Spiritual Text: Comparing the Translating of the Book of Mormon and the Scribing of *A Course in Miracles*," in *Producing Ancient Scripture: Joseph Smith's Translation Projects in the Development of Mormon Christianity*, ed. Michael Hubbard MacKay, Mark Ashurst-McGee, and Brian M. Hauglid (Salt Lake City: University of Utah Press, 2020), 169–86.

35. Taves, "Joseph Smith, Helen Schucman, and the Experience of Producing a Spiritual Text," 185–86.

36. Jared Hickman, "'Bringing Forth' the Book of Mormon: Translation as the Reconfiguration of Bodies in Space-Time," in *Producing Ancient Scripture: Joseph Smith's Translation Projects in the Development of Mormon Christianity*, ed. Michael Hubbard MacKay, Mark Ashurst-McGee, and Brian M. Hauglid (Salt Lake City: University of Utah Press, 2020), 73, 77–78, 80, italics in original.

37. Don Bradley speculates that the translation process drew on the symbolism of the Jewish temple: a veil like the one that concealed the Ark of the Covenant, a breastplate resembling the one worn by the Jewish high priest, and stones linked to the biblical Urim and Thummim. Don Bradley, *The Lost 116 Pages: Reconstructing the Book of Mormon's Missing Stories* (Salt Lake City: Greg Kofford Books, 2019), ch. 3.

Index

A Course in Miracles, 180
Abundant events, 39–40
Afton, New York, 84
Allred, Michael, 132
Alseth, Fritz O., 132
Ancient Writings on Metal Places, 152
Anderson, Harry, 108
Anderson, Richard Lloyd, 126, 134
Anthon, Charles, 20–2
Appearance of plates, 2
Ark of the Covenant, 163–4
Articles and Covenants, 8
Articles of Agreement, 13
Artifaction, 135–6
Ashurst–McGee, Mark, 73
Automatic writing, 177–8, 180

Batik, 112–13
Beach, Ancil, 64–5
Bean, Willard Bean, 121
Beman, Alvah, 11
Bennion, Lowell, 128
Benton, Abram, 65
Bernadette, 39
Berrett, William E., 128
Bible
    corrupted, 34–5
    as history, 31–3
    and other scriptures, 35–6
    prophesies the Book of Mormon, 125–6,
        134
    writing materials of, 28, 150–1
Bidamon, Lewis, 3
Blatchly, Cornelius, 56
Book of Abraham,
    and Greek Psalter, 68–71
    translation of, 74–5
Book of Mormon
    depictions of
        for children, 132–4

    in poetry, 97–104
    in Spokane Exposition, 108
    in videos, 129–132
Evans, John Henry, explains, 123–4
global reach, 110–1
higher criticism and, 32–3
history valued by, 33–6
plates comprising, 171–4
plates' role in, 28–9, 35–6, 150–1, 154
as record
    contents of, 27
    by elites, 29
    editorial process of, 30–1
    juxtaposes European and American
        histories, 181
    language of, Egyptian, 29–30
    modern language in, 179–9
as scripture 35–8
sealed portion, 174
Book of Mormon Central (now Scripture
    Central), 129
Book of Mormon Foundation, 132–3
The Book of Mormon (musical), 116–7
Book of Moses, 74
Bradley, Don, 73
British Museum, 135–6
Brodie, Fawn McKay
    on gold plates, 142–3
    on Joseph Smith as treasure–seeker, 148
    on witnesses, 143
Brown, Charles Brockden, 5
Brown, Samuel, 180
Brownson, Orestes, 5, 7
Bryant, William Cullen, 99–100
Burnett, Stephen, 60

Campbell, Alexander, 177
Campbell, Joseph, 169
Canandaigua, N.Y., 64
Cannon, George Q., 176

Card, Orson Scott, 117–8, 169
Caswall, Henry, 68–71, 175
Cave lore, 87–90
Chase, Willard, 13, 16–7
Cheesman, Paul, 152–3
Chicago World's Fair, 120, 124
Children, plates for, 132–4
Christensen, C.C.A., 104–5, 111
Christianity, doubts about, 66
Church, Frederic, 5, 6, 102
Church History in the Fulness of Times, 128
Cocco Santángelo, Jorge, 114–5
Cole, Abner, 81
    on Book of Mormon, 12
    on superstition, 66
    on treasure–seeking and gold plates,
        11–2, 137, 147–8
Cole, Thomas, 5, 6
    Course of Empire, 100
Colla, Elliott, 135–6
Collings, Michael R., 103
Containers for plates, 4, 50–1
Cook, Thomas L., 89
Coriantumr and Moroni, 103–4
Corrill, John, 61–2
Course of Empire, 100
Cowdery, Oliver
    account of Joseph Smith and Moroni,
        14–5
    on cave with plates, 89–90
    and Cornelius Blatchly, 56
    hypnotized by Joseph Smith, 143
    on Joseph Smith's skepticism, 59
    records translation, 23–4
    on Urim and Thummim, 24–5
    witnesses plates, 53–5
Cumorah, Hill
    Curtis, Theodore, poem about, 102
    Lambourne, Alfred, paints, 102
    Moroni monument on, 119–22
    as shrine, 161–2
    Stevenson, Edward, writes about, 101
Curtis, Theodore, 102

Dallin, Cyrus, 124
Dame, William Horne, 87
Darius, plates of, 151–2
DeMille, Cecil B., 106

Deseret Book, 134
Documentary hypothesis, 31–3
Dougall, Lily, 142
    on gold plates, 95–7
    on Joseph Smith, 90–7
    on Spaulding–Rigdon hypothesis,
        91–2
    theological position of, 92
Dunn, Scott C., 177–8

Edwards, Jonathan, 179
Egyptian, 21, 26
    Joseph Smith likens to Greek, 70
    language of Book of Mormon, 29–30
    language of Kinderhook plates, 73
Eichhorn, Johann Gottfried, 32–3
    1826 Trial, 16, 18
Emerson, Ralph Waldo, 7
Enoch
    book of, 160
    gold plate of, 164
Ericksen, E. E., 124–5
Ether, Book of, 173–4
Evans, John Henry, 123–5, 176, 177
Evidentiary Christianity, 60

Fairbanks, Avard, 108
Finney, Charles, 5, 7
First Vision, 8
Fisher, Vardis, 96–7
Friberg, Arnold, 106–7, 129
Fugate, Wilburn, 73

Gardner, Brant, 179
Gates, Susa Young, 120
Gee, John, 139
German biblical scholarship, 31–3
Gibbon, Edward, 100
Gold
    and Bible, 3
    California gold rush, 3
    greed, 3
    meaning in history, 2
    Nephite plates not, 36–7
Golden Legend, 161
Gospel Topics Essays, 149
    on translating instruments, 178
Grafton, Anthony, 159

Grover, Jerry D.,
    analyzes plates, 139–40
    Ziff, Magic Goggles, and Golden Plates, 139
Guadalupe, Our Lady of, 39, 40

Hamblin, William, 153
Harris, Lucy, 51–3
Harris, Franklin S., 151–2
Harris, Martin
    Charles Anthon visit, 8, 19–22
    loses 116 pages of manuscript, 22
    money–diggers and, 13
    plates and, 5, 37, 51–3, 164
    translation scribe, 24
    Utah life, 62–3
    witnesses plates, 53–5
    witness questioned, 60–1
Hawthorne, Nathaniel, 5
Hazard, Sonia, 9, 169
    origin of plates' idea, 155–6
Hebrews, Book of
    and holy objects, 165
Hickman, Jared, 181
Hinckley, Gordon B., 151
The Historical Magazine, 82–3
Historicism, 157
Homans, George (Robert C. Webb), 177
Howe, Eber D., 81, 142
    discredits Smiths, 24–5
    fears Mormonism, 67–8
    Golden Bible on title page of book, 2
Howells, Adele Cannon, 106
Hudson River School, 5
Hurlbut, Philastus
    affidavits, 64
    biased, 148
Hybrid nature of gold plates, 4–5
Hyde, Orson, 176

Imposture, 65–7
    fades as description of Mormonism,
        81–8
    implied in naturalistic interpretations,
        141–2
Improvement Era, 135, 138–9
Ingersoll, Peter, 142
Interpreter Foundation, 141
Interpreters, 9, 17, 18–9, 173

see also Urim and Thummim, spectacles

Jakeman, Wells, 153
Jaques, John, 176
Jared, Brother of, 146–7

Kane, Elizabeth, 89–90
Kelley, William H., 88
Kimball, Heber C., 87–8
Kinderhook Plates, 71–4
    linked to gold plates, 71–2, 151, 175
Kirkham, Reuben, 105
Knaphus, Torlief, 125, 128, 134
    sculpts Moroni, 119–22
Knight, Joseph
    Joseph Smith employed by, 13
    recovery of plates and, 17–8
    translation and, 20
    witnesses Joseph Smith Sr's baptism,
        48–9
Knight, Newel, 94
Kugel, James, 159
Kushner, Tony, 116–8, 169

Ladd, George, 91
Lambourne, Alfred, 102
Lapham, Fayette, 81–3
Larson, Clinton F., 103–4
Laurence, Richard, 160
Lawrence, Samuel, 11, 13
    visits Hill Cumorah, 18
Lee, Ann, 7
Lehi, 108
Liahona, 165
Lincoln, Abraham, 5
Linn, William Alexander, 91
Lopez, Robert, 116–7, 169
Lord of the Rings, 169
Lovell, Tom, 107–8

Marvels, 5, 170
Material religion, 9–10
McKelvey, Lucy, 110–2
Melville, Herman, 5, 6
Memnon statue, 135–6
Michaelis, Johann David, 32
Miller, William, 5
Missionary teaching plans, 125–8

Mitchill, Samuel, 20–1
Moby Dick, 5
Modernity, 5
Moral guardians, 64–5
Mormon, 108
  Catholic saints differ from, 161
  in Clinton F. Larson drama, 103–4
  describes writing and editing process,
    29–31
Moroni, 108
  in batik, 113–14
  in Clinton F. Larson drama, 103–4
  on Cumorah monument, 121–2
  Joseph Smith sees, 8, 10
  and Mormon, 106
  plates returned by, 23
  in Tom Lovell painting, 108
Moses's tablets, 162–5
  size and weight of, 163–4
Mulekites, 34

Native Americans,
  in Book of Mormon poetry, 99–100
  pottery, 110–1
Nauvoo weathervane, 121–2
Nelson, N.L., 177
Nemelka, Christopher Mark, 174
Nephi, 108
Neville, Jonathan, 149–50
  on Book of Mormon language, 179
  on small plates, 172–3
  on translation, 178–9
New materialism, 9, 155
Nibley, Reid, 102
Nicaea, Council of, 161
Northwestern States Mission Plan, 126
Nyman, Monte, 135

Oman, Richard, 110–1
Orsi, Robert, 39–40
Owen, Robert, 5
Ozymandias, 135

Page, John, 60
Painesville Telegraph, 65
Palmyra Reflector, 11
Paris missionaries, 105–6

Parker, Trey, 116–7, 169
Payne, Katie, 129–31
Petersen, Mark E., 152
Phelps, W. W
  and cave lore, 87
  poetry about gold plates, 98
Pioneer Playsets, 133
Plates (other than Gold Plates)
  ancient record–keeping on, 150–6
  in Latin America, 152–3
  medium for writing, 137
Plural marriage ended, 120
Poe, Edgar Allan, 5
Poetry about gold plates, 97–104
Polycarp, 161
Pranato, Hadi, 112–4
Pratt, Parley
  Book of Mormon poetry by, 97–101
  and witnesses, 62
Pratt, Orson, 2
Price, Clark Kelley, 129
Proper, George, 11
Pseudepigrapha, 158–60
  as forgeries, 159–60
Purple, W.D., 83–5
Putnam, Read H., 13

Quaife, Milo, 78
Quidor, John, 86
Quinn, Michael, 150

Ramsey, Lewis, 106
Rationalism
  among Latter–day Saints, 59–63
  and religion, 66–8
  scientific approaches, 135–56
  Strangite use of, 76–8
Reed, Michael, 154–5
Re–enchantment, 168–9
Relics, 160–2
*Revelatory Events: Three Case Studies of the
    Emergence of New Spiritual Paths*, 146
Richards, LeGrand
  Cumorah monument, 125
  biblical prophecies, 125–6, 134
Richards, Lula Greene, 103
Rigdon, Sidney

authorship of Book of Mormon
    disputed, 91–2
    with Solomon Spaulding author of
        Book of Mormon, 49, 175
Riley, I. Woodbridge,
    explains Joseph Smith psychologically,
        91–2
    refutes Spaulding-Rigdon hypothesis,
        91–2
Roberts, B. H
    on translation, 176–7
Rollins, James. 117–8, 169
Royal Arch Freemasonry, 164–5

Sacrocubism, 115
Saints: The Standard of Truth, 149
    on translation, 178
Schucman, Helen, 180
Seerstone
    depicted, 130
    translation instrument, 23–4, 149, 176,
        178
    and Urim and Thummim, 176, 178
Size of plates, 138–9
Sjodahl, Janne,
    on plates in Bible, 151
    on size and weight of plates, 138–9
Skepticism
    golden plates and, 136–7
    Joseph Smith and, 59–60
    religious leaders and, 5
Skousen, Royal, 179–80
Small plates, 172–3
Smith, Asael
    family of, 40–2
Smith, Emma Hale
    accompanies Joseph Smith to obtain
        plates, 1, 13, 17
    experience with plates, 49–50, 54, 140
    marries Joseph Smith, 17
    translates, 22, 24, 176
Smith, Hyrum, 40–1
Smith, Jesse, 40–2
Smith Jr., Joseph
    Caswall, Henry and, 70–2
    cave lore and, 88–9
    as charlatan, 6

Cumorah monument to, 120–1
    doubts vision, 10
    Evans, John Henry, tells story of, 123–5
    histories by differ, 42
    as hypnotist, 143
    plates
        constructs, 143–4
        Dougall, Lily depicts imagining, 93–6
        experience with, 1, 42–4, 136on
        imagines, 93–6, 146–7
        Kinderhook plates and, 71–4
        sees as treasure, 14–6
        seeks, 1, 10
        Vogel on decision to claim
            were real, 145
    Purple, W.D. tells story of, 84–7
    scepticism of, 59–60
    Smith family in St. Lawrence County,
        writes to 40–1
    Smith, Joseph Sr. and, 48–9, 145
    Strang, James, imitates, 78–9
    transition from farmer to translator,
        10–22, 25–6
    translation by, 8–9, 18–22
    treasure–seeking involvement in, 11
    Vogel, Dan, on decision to claim plates
        were real, 145–6
Smith, Joseph Sr
    baptism, 48–9
    and Fayette Lapham, 81–2
    and magic, 144–5
    and plates, 10, 16–8, 48–9
    religious views of, 144
    and Smith family in St. Lawrence
        County, 40–1
    and treasure–seeking, 11, 14–6
Smith, Joseph Fielding, 176
Smith, Lucy
    experience with plates, 44–7
    religious views, 144
    on translation of plates, 20
    and witnesses of plates, 62
Smith, Mary Duty, 41
Smith, William, 53–4
Sociology of knowledge, 65–6
Sorensen, John, 153
South Park, 116

Space
  for Book of Mormon on plates, 137–9
Spaulding, Solomon
  pretends to discover a lost manuscript,
    158
  manuscript of as basis for Book of
    Mormon, 49, 175
  role in composition of Book of Mormon
    disputed, 91–2, 177
Spectacles
  with plates, 1, 18, 21
  translation and, 23
  see also: Interpreters, Urim and
    Thummim
Spiritual eyes, 61
Spokane Exposition, 108
Stafford, William, 11
Stevenson, Edward
  describes Cumorah, 101–2
  engraves recovery of plates, 104–5
Stoddard, L. Hannah and James F., 149
Stone, Matt, 116–7, 169
Stowell, Josiah, 13, 16, 17, 148–9
Strang, James, 5, 75–80
  finds plates, 76–7, 79
  imitates Joseph Smith, 78–80
  translates Lehi's plates, 79
Stephens, John Lloyd, 60
Sublime, 5

Taves, Ann, 169
  explains plates, 146–7
  sees Eucharist as parallel to plates, 147
  on translation as automatic writing, 180–1
Tchaikovsky, Pyotr Illyich, 102
Teichert, Minerva, 108–9, 131
Ten Commandments, 162–3
Terma, 165–8
Thomas, Ryan, 154
Thompson, Jonathan, 86–7
Those Gold Plates, 152
Todorov, Tzvetan, 52–3
Toynbee, Arnold, 100
Translation, 1
  debates about, 175–81
  depicted, 129–30
  Joseph Smith undertakes, 8–9, 18–22
  by learned, 8

  methods, 22–26
  stimulus for, 74–5
Treasure–seeking
  and gold plates, 11–8
  Smiths involved in, 11, 148–9
Treasure–seekers
  believe in plates, 13–4
Trent, Council of, 161
Tucker, Pomeroy, 88
Tumbaga, 139, 140
Turner, Nat, 7

Undaunted: Witnesses of the Book of
    Mormon, 141
Urim and Thummim
  depicted, 129–30
  described, 1, 175
  interpreters labeled as, 24–5
  with plates, 17, 18–9
  Strang translates with, 76, 78
  translating instrument, 9, 23, 178–9
  See also: interpreters, seerstone,
    spectacles

Videos, 129–32
Vogel, Dan
  and manufacture of plates, 143–4
  and plates idea, 145–46
  and psychological explanation of plates,
    144–5
Voree, 76

Wagner, Richard, 102, 106
  Arnold Friberg admires, 106–7
Walters, Luman, 12
Wayne Sentinel, 2
Weber, Max, 168
Weight of plates, 139
White, J. M., 102–3
Whitley, Edward, 99, 103
Whitmer, David
  and Mary Whitmer's witness of plates,
    57–8
  testimony of plates, 63
  and translation, 175
  and treasure–seekers, 13
  witnesses plates, 53–4

Whitmer, John C., 57
Whitmer, Mary, 57–8
Whitton, Bridge, 73
Wiley, Robert, 73
Williams, Frederick G., 42
Witnesses
  bullied, 143
  doubted, 56, 60–1
  hypnotized, 143
  revival of interest in, 141
  testimony of, little used, 61–2
  three and eight differ, 4–5, 55–6
  in Utah, 62–3

view plates, 53–6
  of Whitmer family, 57–8
Woodruff, Wilford, 120
Wright, H. Curtis, 153

Young, Brigham
  cave lore and, 89–90
  colonizer, 124
  on Joseph Smith and treasure, 15–6
Young, Elspeth, 131

Zelph, 72–3
Ziff, Magic Goggles, and Golden Plates, 139